THE BLUE PARAKEET

Also by Scot McKnight

A Fellowship of Differents
The Jesus Creed
The King Jesus Gospel
One.Life

THE BLUE PARAKEET

Rethinking How You
Read the Bible

Second Edition

SCOT MCKNIGHT

ZONDERVAN®

ZONDERVAN

The Blue Parakeet
Copyright © 2008, 2016, 2018 by Scot McKnight

This title is also available as a Zondervan ebook.

Requests for information should be addressed to:
Zondervan, *3900 Sparks Dr. SE, Grand Rapids, Michigan 49546*

Library of Congress Cataloging-in-Publication Data

Names: McKnight, Scot, author.
Title: The blue parakeet : rethinking how you read the bible / Scot McKnight.
Description: Second edition. | Grand Rapids, MI : Zondervan, [2018] | Includes bibliographical references.
Identifiers: LCCN 2017057361 | ISBN 9780310538929 (softcover)
Subjects: LCSH: Bible—Hermeneutics. | Bible—Criticism, Narrative.
Classification: LCC BS476 .M3475 2018 | DDC 220.601—dc23 LC record available at https://lccn.loc.gov/2017057361

All Scripture quotations, unless otherwise indicated, are taken from The Holy Bible, New International Version®, NIV®. Copyright © 1973, 1978, 1984, 2011 by Biblica, Inc.® Used by permission of Zondervan. All rights reserved worldwide. www.Zondervan.com. The "NIV" and "New International Version" are trademarks registered in the United States Patent and Trademark Office by Biblica, Inc.®

Other Bible versions are listed on page 271.

Any Internet addresses (websites, blogs, etc.) and telephone numbers in this book are offered as a resource. They are not intended in any way to be or imply an endorsement by Zondervan, nor does Zondervan vouch for the content of these sites and numbers for the life of this book.

Published in association with the literary agency of Daniel Literary Group, LLC, 1701 Kingsbury Drive, Suite 100, Nashville, TN 37215.

Cover design: Rob Monacelli
Cover photo: iStockPhoto
Interior design: Kait Lamphere

Printed in the United States of America

HB 06.27.2024

For Cheryl Hatch

CONTENTS

PART 4

READING THE BIBLE AS STORY:
Three Examples

PART 5

Women in Church Ministries Today

Appendices

CHAPTER 1

THE BOOK AND I

How, Then, Are We to Live the Bible Today?

When I was in high school, I went to a Christian camp in Muscatine, Iowa, with Kris, my beautiful girlfriend (now my wife), to horse around for a week. But one morning, we were asked by our cabin leader to go spend a little time in prayer before breakfast. So I wandered out of our cabin, down a hill, alongside a basketball court, and through an open field, and then I walked over to the campfire area, climbed a short incline, and finally sat next to a tree, and prayed what my cabin leader told us to pray: "Lord, fill me with your Holy Spirit." I wasn't particularly open to spiritual things, but for some reason I said that prayer as our counselor advised. The Lord to whom I prayed that prayer caught me off guard. To quote the words of John Wesley, "My heart was strangely warmed." I don't remember what I expected to happen (probably nothing), but what happened was surprising. That prayer, or I should say the answer to that prayer, changed my life. I didn't speak in tongues, I didn't "see Jesus," and I didn't "hear God." My eyes didn't twitter, and I didn't become catatonic. When I prayed, something powerful happened, and I went to breakfast a new person. Within hours I knew what I wanted to do for the rest of my life.

On that hot summer day, I unexpectedly became a Bible student with a voracious appetite to read. Prior to that prayer I had very little interest in the Bible, and when it came to routine reading, I read only what my teachers assigned and *Sports Illustrated*. Within a week or two I began to read the Bible through from Genesis to Revelation, four chapters a day. I finished my reading the next spring, getting ahead of schedule because there were too many days when four chapters were not enough. My habit at the time was to arise early to read at least two chapters before going off to school, and then to read two chapters or so at night before I went to bed. I read the *Scofield King James Bible*, and Paul's letter to the Galatians became my favorite book. The Bible was full of surprises for me, and my eyes, mind, and heart were stuck on wide-open wonder. All because I asked God's Spirit to fill me.

Some of my former Sunday school teachers were as surprised as I was by what was happening. My youth pastor encouraged me to read serious books, and he also modeled a way to study the Bible by teaching Romans to our youth group. He also suggested I learn Greek, which, because he had a spare beginning Greek grammar book, I began. I had no idea what I was doing, but I liked languages, so I plugged away, never knowing quite what to expect. My father gave me some books to read, like John Bunyan's *Pilgrim's Progress*. I devoured books. My teachers observed that I read books for class, not because I had to, but to learn and to engage in conversation.

I had no idea what I was getting into when I asked God's Spirit to fill me. I had no idea that I would go to college in Grand Rapids and become a bookaholic, buying books with money I didn't have! I hung out at Eerdmans and Zondervan and Baker and Kregel looking for bargains. I knew the sales clerks by name and they knew mine. I had no idea that I would then go on to seminary and from there for doctoral studies in England (Nottingham). I had no idea how hard it might be to find a teaching position. But I have lived a privileged life, teaching at a seminary for a dozen years, undergraduates for seventeen years, and now teaching a wonderfully diverse body of seminary students at Northern Seminary. I had no idea that I would eventually get to travel to and speak in churches around the world, that I would get to write books about Jesus and Paul and Peter and the Bible, and that I would become friends with Bible scholars all around the world. I just had no idea that teaching the Bible meant these things when I asked God's Spirit to fill me. All I know is that from the time I was converted, I wanted to study the Bible. I'm sitting right now in my study, surrounded by books, books about the Bible, and I love what I do. I just had no idea.

The Discovery of a Question

Throughout this process of conversion and reading the Bible, I made discoveries that created a question that disturbed me and still does. Many of my fine Christian friends, pastors, and teachers routinely made the claim that they were Bible-believing Christians, and they were committed to the whole Bible and that—and this was one of the favorite lines—"God said it, I believe it, that settles it for me!" They were saying two things, and I add my response (which expresses my disturbance):

One:	We believe everything the Bible says, *therefore* ...
Two:	We *practice* whatever the Bible says.
Three:	Hogwash!

Why say "hogwash," a tasty, salty word I learned from my father? Because I was reading the same Bible they were reading, and I observed that, in fact—emphasize that word "fact"—whatever they were claiming was not in "fact" what they were doing. (Nor was I.) What I discovered is that we all pick and choose, and I use "pick and choose" guardedly because for some picking and choosing is a license to find what they want and ignore the rest. I must confess this discovery did not discourage me as much as it disturbed me, and then it made me intensely curious (and it is why I wrote this book). The discoveries and disturbances converged onto one big question:

How, Then, Are We to Live Out the Bible Today?

This question never has been and never will be adequately answered with: The Bible says it, and that settles it for me. Why? Because no one does everything the Bible says. Perhaps you expected this question: How, then, are we to *apply* the Bible today? That's a good question, but I think the word "apply" is a bit clinical and not as dynamic as the phrase "live out." But we will get to that later.

Here's an example of my discovery process as a young student of the Bible. When you and I read the letter of James, brother of Jesus, we hear these words:

> Those who consider themselves religious and yet do not keep a tight rein on their tongues deceive themselves, and their religion is worthless. Religion that God our Father accepts as pure and faultless is this: to look after orphans and widows in their distress and to keep oneself from being polluted by the world. (James 1:26–27)

James knew what he was talking about, and truth be told, there's nothing hard about understanding what James said. It's about as plain as the directions on a stop sign. The clarity of these words is the problem. For all kinds of reasons, and we'll get to those soon, what James said had almost nothing to do with the Christian groups I knew:

- We didn't like the word "religious."
- We didn't measure Christian maturity by control of the tongue (according to what I was hearing).
- Pure and faultless—and that's pretty high quality, you must admit—religion, according to James, isn't measured by church attendance, Bible reading, witnessing, going to seminary, or anything else I found in our discipleship and church membership manuals.

Nope. For James, a pure Christian, the kind God approves of, was one who showed compassion to orphans and widows and avoided being polluted by sin at all costs. Frankly, we emphasized the not being polluted by sin, but we defined "polluted" in ways that had nothing to do with compassion for the marginalized and suffering. For instance, we were dead set against movies, drinking wine, and sex before marriage. In our version of reality, these three were all related—if you drank with your girlfriend, you'd lose your senses and go to a movie and end up having sex. I'm not only making fun of my past, I'm emphasizing how distorted things got—a good, solid Christian was one who didn't do specific things that were against the rules. It also had to do with what we *did*—which was go to church weekly, read the Bible daily, and witness as often as we could. These aren't bad things; in fact, I learned to love the Bible because of this context. But the one thing we didn't do was follow everything James said!

As I kept looking around me, this began to disturb me. How in the world were we reading the same Bible? One thing was clear, and it was irony: we were all reading the Bible the same way and that meant we had somehow learned not to follow the plain words of James!

What I learned was an uncomfortable but incredibly intriguing truth: Every one of us adopts the Bible and (at the same time) adapts the Bible to our culture. In less appreciated terms, I'll put it this way: Everyone picks and chooses. I know this sounds out of the box and off the wall for many, but no matter how hard we try to convince ourselves otherwise, it's true. We pick and choose. (It's easier for us to hear "we adopt and adapt," but the two expressions amount to the same thing.)

I believe many of us want to know *why* we pick and choose. Even more importantly, many of us want to know *how to do this in a way that honors God and embraces the Bible as God's Word for all times.* We'll get to that. First, I offer some examples of picking and choosing or "adopting and adapting."

Picking and Choosing

Sabbath

The Bible I read both instituted and did not appear to back down from the *Sabbath*. Observing the Sabbath meant not working from Friday night to Saturday night (Exodus 20:9–10), and I found numerous references in the Acts of the Apostles to the Christian observance of Sabbath. But as I was learning how to read the Bible inside a bundle of serious-minded Christians, I knew no one who really practiced the Sabbath. I quickly learned that the Christian Sunday, which focuses on fellowship and worship, is not the same as the Jewish Sabbath, which focuses on rest from labor. (You can read about this in any good Bible dictionary or on Wikipedia.) The Sabbath was described in the Bible, and it wasn't a "that settles it for me!" for anyone I knew.

What really got me going was that nobody seemed interested in this question. Yes, I did hear that some thought a passage like Colossians 2:16 may—but only *may*—have given gentiles permission not to keep Sabbath, but the issue was not crystal clear. I was learning in my days of youth that we sometimes, rightly or wrongly, live out the Bible by *not doing* something in the Bible![1]

Tithing

The Bible I read taught *tithing*, but the Bible does not insist that all of the tithe must go to a local church. Truth be told, the New Testament doesn't even bring up the tithe. In the Bible the tithe is a combination of spiritual support (for the temple) and social service (for the poor). Moses says tithes are to be given not only to the Levites (roughly the temple servants) but also to the alien, to the fatherless, and to the widow (Deuteronomy 26:12). We are back to James's "orphans and widows." The churches I was attending had nothing to do with immigrants, did little to help orphans, and so far as I knew did little to strengthen widows.

What was more, the tithe we were hearing about was something we were to give to our local church for buildings, maintenance, pastoral salaries, missionaries, and the like. But the Bible said that I—as a tither—was to give some of my tithe to the Levite and also to those who were marginalized and suffering. This was something neither I nor anyone I knew was doing. I was learning that we sometimes live out the Bible, rightly or wrongly, by *morphing* one thing into another, that is, by taking a tithe for temple assistants and also for the poor and turning it into a tithe for the local church. It might be fine to read the Bible like this, but we should at least admit what we are doing: in a word, we are morphing.

Foot Washing

Another discovery I made was that Jesus explicitly commanded *foot washing* in John 13:14. Widows who received benefits from the church were known as those who had washed the feet of saints (1 Timothy 5:10). St. Augustine, three and a half centuries later, writes about Christians washing the feet of the freshly baptized, so I knew that the practice continued well beyond the New Testament days. But I was surrounded by Bible believers and had never seen this happen. I learned that some Christians still practice this, but no one I knew (except a high school friend's church) was doing it. We were either ignoring what the Bible taught or morphing it into a cultural parallel like hanging up one another's coats and offering our guests something to drink. A New Testament scholar, Bill Mounce, in his exhaustive study of 1 Timothy, draws this conclusion about what Paul says of widows: "Paul is not asking if the widow followed church ritual [i.e., whether she physically washed feet]; he is asking if she was the type of person who had done good deeds throughout her life."[2] In other words, Paul is not speaking of something literal—real washing of feet—but of an underlying principle—serving others. What I learned is that sometimes we *look behind the text to grasp a timeless principle, and the principle is more important than doing the actual words.*

Bill Mounce might be right, but my question as a college student was this one: "How did we know Paul's words were really only describing a symptom of a person of good deeds instead of a literal requirement?"

Some suggested to me to quit asking such pesky questions and just follow along, but inside I was learning to pursue what for me has been a lifelong, joyous ride of exploring how we live out the Bible.

Charismatic Gifts

The more I became aware of the rise of the charismatic movement, the more I discovered Jesus, Paul, and Peter had the power to work *miracles* (Matthew 4:23; 10:8; Acts 4:1–12; 16:16–18). In my first year of Bible reading I learned that Christians in Paul's churches *gave words of prophecy* (1 Corinthians 12–14). And I knew Jesus said that his followers would do even greater things than he did. No one that I knew was doing miracles or giving words of prophecy. What I learned from this experience is an expression that sums up the way many read the Bible: *"That was then, but this is now."*

In other words, I learned that God spoke in various ways in various times. And I was taught that God wasn't saying *those* things today. I was only beginning to wonder just how enormous a dragon that little expression—"that was then, but this is now"—was hiding. I learned that sometimes *the Bible expects things that were designed for that time but not for our time.* I wasn't sure how we knew that, but I was sure we were making decisions like that. This really sealed my question: How do we know how to live out the Bible? But there are a few more examples for us to consider.

Surrendering Possessions

There is nothing clearer than this statement by Jesus about *possessions*: "In the same way, those of you who do not give up everything you have [possessions] cannot be my disciples" (Luke 14:33). Two chapters earlier Jesus said, "Sell your possessions and give to the poor" (12:33). If there is anything that is straightforward, those two verses are. I knew enough about church history to know that St. Francis did exactly what Jesus ordered, or at least he got very close. I also knew that we weren't following Jesus's words at all. In fact, I knew that most Christians were not living below their means and were in fact living well beyond their means.

The most common explanations I heard were either "but that was then" or "there were special expectations for Jesus's personal disciples." Others suggested that what Jesus was getting at for us was that we should "cut back" on our spending so we can be more generous. However we read them, these are statements made by Jesus, seemingly without condition; we weren't doing them as Jesus said; and they evidently belonged to a different era and a different culture (this principle kept coming up). How did we decide such things? How do we know what to do and what not to do? (I can't tell you how much these two questions have energized my forty years of Bible study.)

Contentious Issues

On top of these discoveries, I was encountering *contentious issues* like evolution, Calvinism, Vietnam and war, abortion, and homosexuality. I must confess, I loved the thrill of these debates. These hotly disputed issues took some of these discoveries of mine and stood them up into questions—questions of practical and present significance, questions that started to mound up into my one big question:

Do we conform the Bible to science, science to the Bible, or ...?
Is Calvinism or Arminianism right? Are both right? Is neither right?
What kind of music should we play in church?
Are charismatic gifts relevant today? All of them? Even miracles?
Should we oppose the conflict in the Middle East?
Which view of the second coming is biblical?
Should women be ordained? Can they preach and teach? Bless the bread and the wine?
What do we do about abortion?
What do we do about capital punishment and nuclear war?
Is homosexual behavior a sin?

And they became the one big question for me: How, then, are we to live out the Bible today?

The Question Is "How?"

What made me so curious and what gave me a deep discontent was *how* we came to our answers. Some people went straight to the Bible and stayed there; some took one passage and used that passage to overwhelm other passages; yet others read the Bible, appealing to history and change and then to theologians, science, pastors, psychologists, and even to "that's the way we do things at my church." I began to see that Christians read the Bible differently, and I began to see that no one group seemed to get it all right. At that time in my life I was asking questions like these:

- Why is it that one group thinks the charismatic gifts are dead and gone while other groups vibrate with speaking in tongues and words of prophecy?
- Why is it that two of us can sit down with the same Bible with the same question—Should Christians participate in war?—and come away with two different answers? One can appeal to Joshua and Judges, and another can appeal to Jesus's statement to love your enemies and to turn the other cheek, and yet another to the cruciform shape of God in the New Testament that challenges the warrior God of some Old Testament passages, even if some of my friends say the New Testament God's got some warrior in him too.
- Why do some churches ordain women and let them preach, while other churches have folks who get up and walk out when a woman opens her Bible for some teaching in front of men? Why did this teaching on complementarianism become so important today but arise only in the wake of the Equal Rights Amendment, but get taught as the way the church has always said things?
- Why do some of my pastor and theologian friends say things about the Trinity that are challenged by both very knowledgeable theologians and church historians and are what many think are "sub" orthodox? And how can they do this with many followers and very few criticizing them?

- Why do some issues become so incredibly politicized—like same-sex relations—and others—like greed and materialism and military violence and torture—are nearly ignored?

As a faithful attendee of churches, as one fully committed to the faith, who reads his Bible daily, and who watched and listened to debates unroll and even unravel, I became convinced that it was not as easy to "apply" the Bible as I thought it was. In fact, when it came to contentious issues, how we read the Bible helps us to decide how we are to live. To be perfectly honest, I knew there was plenty of picking and choosing *on both sides of every question.* I pressed on for two more decades, and I have now come to the conclusion that this question—How, then, are we to live out the Bible today?—is a pressing question for our day. I believe we need to begin asking this question and start explaining ourselves. I believe there is an inner logic to our picking and choosing, but we need to become aware of what it is. (To get to the simple answer that will unfold in the pages that follow, we read the Bible through the lens of our theology, and that's the basic and undeniable fact.)

Until we do, we will be open to accusations of hypocrisy. It's that simple, and it's that lethal. If you tell me you believe the Bible and seek to live out every bit of it, and if I can find one spot that you don't—especially if that spot is sensitive or politically incorrect or offensive—then we've all got a problem. I taught college students the Bible, and I can assure you that they are fully aware of the "pick-and-choose" method. They are fully convinced, at least many are, that the pick-and-choose method is an exercise in hypocrisy or worse. (What they are not as fully aware of is that they are doing the same thing.)

What I've learned is this: *People are afraid of this question once they turn it on themselves and others.* Too many of us don't want to think about this. Too many of us don't want to admit that we are picking and choosing. Even if we prefer (as I do) to say "adopting and adapting," we are doing something similar. But I think we need to face this squarely and honestly. I've learned that it is time to think about why and how we pick what we pick and why and how we choose what we choose. What can we do to get ourselves to face this question honestly?

What Will It Take to Get Us to Ask This Question?

Sometimes it is a classroom setting that provokes this question. I once had a student ask me point-blank in class about this passage: "As you go, proclaim this message: 'The kingdom of heaven has come near.' Heal the sick, raise the dead, cleanse those who have leprosy, drive out demons."

"Yo, Scot." (I had learned that "Yo" meant "Dr.") "Yo, Scot, since you believe we should preach the kingdom of God today, as Jesus said in Matthew 10:7, why don't you also believe we should heal the sick as in Matthew 10:8?" What he was asking me, in his playfully snarky way, was why I pick one to do and choose not to do the other. I have done lots of verse 7 but have never done any of verse 8. He had me, but it was one of those moments when I got to ask my favorite question: How, then, are we to live out the Bible today?

There's a story here, as there so often is. Joel Martens, the student, at that time was an active member in a Vineyard Church where charismatic gifts are emphasized. I wasn't either Vineyard or charismatic (though I always say, "I'm open!"). Does that mean he's given to exaggerating or that I'm given to minimizing Matthew 10:8? You answer the question. When I talked to Kris about this classroom experience, she asked why I didn't ask him, "Do you raise the dead at your church?" You can answer that one too. (When I see Joel next, I'll ask him in a snarky way.) Anyway, Joel got our class thinking about this question, and his question hasn't gone away for me.

More often than not, it is a *person* who enters into our world that shakes up our thinking and gets us asking this question. Perhaps we encounter someone who speaks in tongues or someone who thinks they can heal others or a friend's daughter who is a lesbian and a Christian.

It's one thing to say we think homosexuality is sin, which is the uniform church tradition and the best explanation of the Bible in its context, but it's a completely different pastoral reality when we know a gay or a lesbian and that someone happens to ask us why we believe in Leviticus 20:13a but not in 20:13b—the first prohibits homosexuality, and the second insists on capital punishment for it. Or if we are asked why we think the instruction from *nature* in Romans 1 about homosexuality is permanent and applicable today, but the one in 1 Corinthians 11 is evidently disposable.

Here's what Paul says about "nature" in Romans 1:26: "Even their women exchanged *natural* sexual relations for *unnatural* ones." But those same persons don't think Paul's instructions about *nature* in 1 Corinthians 11:14–15 are permanent: "Does not the very *nature* of things teach you that if a man has long hair, it is a disgrace to him, but that if a woman has long hair, it is her glory?" (emphasis added in both passages). So a lesbian asks why some embrace the appeal to "nature" in Romans 1 while their wives have short hair and their sons have hair pulled back into a ponytail. What then does "natural" mean? Why do we think it's permanent in one case and temporary in another? That's the only reason for this example. Again, before you answer that question, it would be really good if, while having coffee with a few friends, you open your Bible to these passages and ask yourselves this question: How, then, are we to live out the Bible today?

By such personal encounters we are driven to think aloud about what we believe, we are driven to think more carefully about what we think, we are driven back to the Bible and how we read it, we are driven to ask how it is that we are living out the Bible, and we are sometimes driven to our knees to ask for wisdom about contentious issues. One such issue, which will be the focus of the last part of this book, is the giftedness of women for various ministries in the church, including teaching and preaching and pastoring.

Perhaps we need a visitor to come by, and maybe this book will be that visitor, who gets us to ask this question. I believe we need to ask the question and, together, begin to work it out.

CHAPTER 2

THE BIRDS AND I

Which Way Do You
Read the Bible?

Kris and I are both bird-watchers, something we absorbed from Kris's Grandma Norman and Kris's father, Ron Norman, so we have a few bird feeders in our backyard. Which means, whether we like it or not, we feed sparrows and chase or throw things at squirrels. You know you are a birder if you chase squirrels from your feeders by running through the yard yelling wildly and squirting them with the water pistol you bought for your grandson's birthday next month. You know you are even more of a birder if you decide to keep the water pistol you bought for your grandson's birthday and get him another gift because squirting squirrels is both effective and a whole lot of fun.[1]

Squirrels are a problem, but so are sparrows. If we could get rid of sparrows, we would, because we prefer the cardinals, goldfinches, and chickadees, and we'd love it if some cedar waxwings would visit us. But sparrows are omnipresent in our yard, sometimes as many as fifty fighting for places on our feeders and knocking good seed onto the ground while they look for the perfect little chunk. Because we've been watching birds for about forty years, we've become adept at recognizing them. It is unusual when we see a bird we don't recognize. At times we'll see a rare visitor, like a white-throated sparrow or a rose-breasted grosbeak or a migrating warbler, but not very often. I was in Kansas not long ago and spotted a bird I didn't recognize, but a professor at Tabor College did from my description: a scissor-tailed flycatcher!

Sitting on my back porch reading in the summer of 2007, I looked up and saw a flash of soft blue in the bushes next to our fencerow. I didn't see the whole bird. Only part of it was visible through the green leaves. I got to wondering, and my bird-watching skills kicked in. I said—any birder will tell you this is how it happens, so don't think there's anything special here—"Not a blue jay, too small; not an eastern bluebird, the blue is too soft; not an indigo bunting, it is too large and the colors too soft." I began to look for those distinguishing marks that separate one bird from another. "What kind of a blue bird is this? Could it be a stray mountain bluebird?" No, that's not possible. Mountain bluebirds don't wander from the Rockies into the Great Lakes regions during the summer.

Then the bluish bird moved a bit. I stretched my neck to look closer and caught a full view. I was disappointed. It was someone's pet blue parakeet. It had escaped its cage and was now a free bird. Tempted to ignore it—after all, it was nothing but a stray pet—I began to take note of its manners. Odd thing, this chance encounter. I wondered how it would behave, and that got me to comparing its behavior with other birds in our yard.

I immediately saw that our sparrows were—and no other word describes their response—terrorized by our visitor. When the blue parakeet moved even a little, the sparrows scattered like teenage pranksters when a cop car wanders into the neighborhood. When it flew, the sparrows were scared witless and scattered into hiding in bushes or found distance landing on telephone lines. When the parakeet let out its obnoxious sound, the sparrows flew away. Odd, I thought, for the sparrows to be so fearful of a pet bird. Even though they scattered, they eventually found their way back to their usual locations.

The inhospitality of our sparrows bothered me, so I got up from my comfortable seat, went inside, found my Franciscan brown habit, put it on, tied the rope around my waist, went back on the back porch, and I preached—à la St. Francis according to Giotto—to our sparrows about how to treat visitors. (I really didn't do this, but I grew up Baptist, and we permit making things up as long as it is "preacher's license.") Anyway, the sparrows were scared, and I was learning.

I was now hooked on backyard social ethics when an odd sort of social miracle occurred before my eyes. The sparrows gradually became accustomed to the blue parakeet. Instead of being shocked by the odd sounds and sudden flights of the parakeet, they became unfazed. In fact, they not only got used to the parakeet, they became best friends, what my daughter Laura calls "BFFs." When it flew to the feeder, they joined it—not because they were hungry, but because they wanted to be near the blue parakeet. When it flew to the neighbor's roof, they followed. One time I saw about thirty sparrows surrounding the blue parakeet on the neighbor's garage.

Within an hour, the sparrows had adjusted to the parakeet's strange ways. They didn't try to teach it to fly as they did, nor did they silence its funny sounds. They let the blue parakeet be a blue parakeet. Our visitor maintained that obnoxious squawk and flew with glorious speed and capacity, taking sharp turns and sudden dips unlike any the sparrows had ever seen. The sparrows may have seemed adjusted, but every now and then that blue parakeet—he stayed around for about a month—did something that frightened the sparrows. The blue parakeet, like Narnia's Aslan, was not tame, but it became a familiar stranger to our sparrows.

Chance encounters sometimes lead us deeper into thought. The passages I mentioned in the previous chapter as well as comments from students are for me "blue parakeet experiences." When we encounter blue parakeet passages in the Bible or in the questions of others, whether we think of something as simple as the Sabbath or foot washing or as complex and emotional as women in church ministries or the warrior God theme in the Bible, we have to stop and think, *Is this passage for today or not?* Sometimes we hope the blue parakeets will go away—as I hoped. After all, it was just a pet. Or perhaps we shoo them away. Or we try to catch them and return them to their cage. I tried to see if I could catch the bird, but he (or she) didn't even let me get close. It had been caged, got loose, and it wanted to keep its freedom.

How we respond to passages and questions will determine if we become aware of what is going on or not. When chance encounters with blue parakeet passages in the Bible happen to come our way, we are given the opportunity to observe and learn. In such cases, we really do open ourselves to the thrill of learning how to read the Bible. But like the sparrows, we have to get over our fears and learn to adjust to the squawks of the Bible's blue parakeets. We dare not try to tame them.

How do you read the Bible? What happens to you when you encounter blue parakeet passages in the Bible will reveal all you need to know about how you read the Bible. I want to suggest there are three ways to approach the Bible.

Three Ways

There are actually more than three ways, but getting every possible option on the table is not important right now. If you'd like to think more about this, Appendix 1 is a quiz that many say creates all kinds of thinking about how to read the Bible. I have chosen to keep the ways simple in order to see the alternatives more starkly. Most people combine these ways, but most people are also often not aware of the way they read the Bible.

1. Reading to Retrieve

Some of us have been taught to read the Bible in such a way that we *return to the times of the Bible in order to retrieve biblical ideas and practices for today.* There are two kinds of "return and retrieve" readers—some try to retrieve *all of it,* and some admit we can retrieve only *what can be salvaged.*

Consider those who seek to retrieve *all of it.* If Jesus taught table fellowship, such persons sometimes suggest that we should focus on table fellowship and gather in homes instead of big churches. If Paul said we should speak in tongues, we should speak in tongues. If Jesus said we should wash feet, we should wash feet. If Peter says women should not wear gold jewelry or fine clothing, our women should not wear gold jewelry or fine clothing. If Paul says women should be silent, our women should be silent. If Exodus says the death penalty is proper, then it is proper today too (even for adulterers). If Deuteronomy exhorts the Israelites to permit the poor to glean from the crops, then farmers and gardeners need to leave some unpicked corn and beans and wheat and we nonfarmers and non-gardeners should at least find a cultural equivalent. In other words, we are to live out the Bible today by *returning to the early church and retrieving all of its ideas no matter how uncomfortable, no matter how politically incorrect, no matter what it costs us.* The emphasis here is to practice *whatever* the Bible teaches—to absorb and live out *all of it.*

There are some problems here. If we sit down and think about it, it is *impossible* to live a first-century life in a twenty-first-century world. "That was then, but this is now" is not an empty slogan that came my way to dismiss my questions as a college student. "That was then, but this is now" is bedrock reality within the Bible's own Story. Furthermore, it is *undesirable and unbiblical* to retrieve it all. Paul didn't even do that. What about the words of the apostle Paul in 1 Corinthians 9:19–23, where Paul says his strategy is one of constant adaptation? Paul's strategy was to be Jewish with Jews and to be like a gentile with gentiles. If Paul was already adapting first-century Jewish ideas to first-century gentile situations, can we expect to do anything else? Can we imagine Paul wanting to back up in time to Moses's day? To quote Paul, "By no means!"

What we've got in the pages of the New Testament are first-century expressions of the gospel and church life, not permanent, timeless expressions. They are timely expressions; they are Spirit-inspired expressions; but they were and remain first-century expressions. We aren't called to live first-century lives in the twenty-first century, *but twenty-first-century lives as we walk in the light of the revelation God gave to us in the first century.*

For some, and you may be one of them, this principle sounds like we are giving away too much. Some believe we are to return to the Bible, but we can retrieve only *what we can salvage for our day and for our culture.* This, of course, means culture dictates what is of value in the Bible. This is a mistake. But, before we say anything else, I want to applaud anyone and everyone who tries to bring the Bible into our modern culture. This is the impulse of the apostle Paul—and we see it in all of the New Testament writers who adopted the Story and adapted it to their contexts. I can think of a list of creative Christian thinkers today who are exceptional at adopting and adapting, but I'll avoid listing names.

The danger in "retrieving the essence" is that there can be too little adoption or not enough faithfulness and consistency with the Bible itself. Take women in church ministries as an example. Some contend that the argument over women pastors is a *justice* issue, and by that they mean equality, rights, freedom, and centuries of oppression. While I have respect for the "justice" issue when it comes to women in church ministries today (a short chapter on justice can be found on pp. 193–203, and the last section of this book on women in ministry will make this clear), I'm not so sure we are to judge what goes on in the church by the principles of our culture: "equality" and "rights" and "freedom." In fact, I'm certain this is not the way we are called by God to "apply" the Bible to our world—there is more to it than letting culture shape what we do. Before we go any further, we need to insert a parenthetical observation about Bible reading.

Those Days, Those Ways

One of the themes we will encounter in this book can be summed up like this:

God spoke in Moses's days in Moses's ways, and
God spoke in Job's days in Job's ways, and
God spoke in David's days in David's ways, and
God spoke in Solomon's days in Solomon's ways, and

God spoke in Jeremiah's days in Jeremiah's ways, and
God spoke in Jesus's days in Jesus's ways, and
God spoke in Paul's days in Paul's ways, and
God spoke in Peter's days in Peter's ways, and
God spoke in John's days in John's ways,
*and we are called to discern how God is carrying on that pattern
in our world today.*

The gospel is capable and designed to strike home in every culture, in every age, and in every language. (Some speak here of divine *accommodation* to each culture throughout the Bible's own history.) Any idea of imposing a foreign culture, age, or language on another culture, age, and language quenches the dynamic power of the gospel and the Bible. We need not become Jews to live the gospel, nor need we become first- or fourth- or sixteenth- or eighteenth-century Christians. Let me push hard for a moment. Yes, I think the first Jewish Christians probably kept kosher. That's not for today. Yes, the vestments of the Eastern Orthodox Church are brilliant and the liturgical order of services profound—but they are from a bygone era, with a bygone dress code, and a bygone form of expression, and do precious little for most of us today. They are not for today (at least for most of us). Yes, I love the history they unveil. If I appreciate and respect that history, that does not mean I have to live in those days now. I also love European cathedrals—monuments to the piety of a former era. Those cathedrals, apart from tourists and the rare exception, are empty today. I also love Martin Luther, John Calvin, and Jonathan Edwards, and they were leaders for their days in their ways. But I have no desire to impose their culture on our days and our ways. Frankly, I'm more concerned with their attitudes.

What we most need is not a return to the first or fourth or sixteenth or eighteenth century but a fresh blowing of God's Spirit on our culture, in our day, and in our ways. We need twenty-first-century Christians living out the biblical gospel in twenty-first-century ways. Even more, if we read the Bible properly, we will see that God never asked one generation to step back in time and live the way it had done before. No, God spoke in each generation in that generation's ways.

Most of us know one of the major failures of missionary work was the unfortunate (if naive and good-intentioned) imposing of Western ways on African or Asian or Central American ways. We now know that the gospel has the power to generate expressions of the gospel in every language, in every culture, and in every ethnic group. If we know this about current missionary work, doesn't that warn us about the danger of returning in order to retrieve it all? Next to my desk is a commentary on the entire Bible called *Africa Bible Commentary*.[2] The aim here was to write a commentary on the Bible by Africans for Africans instead of a commentary for Africans by Americans. The apostle Paul would have been the first one to stand in applause of this effort. I can't resist. Next to that Bible commentary I have a book called *The IVP Women's Bible Commentary*—by women for women.[3] And, yes, I think Paul would applaud that too.

The way of returning to retrieve it all is not the biblical way. The biblical way is the ongoing but organic adoption of the past and adaptation to new conditions and to do this in a way that is *consistent with and faithful to the Bible*. I've been teaching this idea for a long time, and I have learned to anticipate the next question: Who decides on what to adopt and how to adapt? Will it be you alone, will it be you and your friends, will it be you and your pastor, will it be your pastor and the elders, or will it be your denominational leaders? Will it be the Pope or the Patriarch? Who decides? This just might be the million-dollar question that will determine how you will live out the Bible today, and it leads to a second way we are reading the Bible so we can live it out today.

2. Reading through Tradition

We need to do a little work before we get to the main point of this section, but our overall point is this: ordinary people need to learn to read the Bible *through* tradition, or they will misread the Bible and create schisms in the church.

The most alarming danger of the "return and retrieve" way of Bible reading is found throughout the Western world: it seems too often that *everybody reads the Bible for herself or for himself, and everybody does what's right in her or his own eyes.* We see this in three groups. *Pastors* have come up with their own pet theory for how to read the Bible that no one in the history of the church has ever seen. *Books and catalogs* cross my desk daily with new ideas, and often they are advertised as an idea that's fresh, insightful, never-been-seen-before-but-straight-from-the-Bible, yada yada yada. Engaging with Christian Bible readers over the years leads me to the third group: God bless 'em, but *some folks* see some of the goofiest things in the Bible, and I wish I could just blow Holy Spirit air on them and cure them of their silliness.

Before I say another word, though, I must confess: I believe we are called to read the Bible for ourselves (but not entirely on our own). The Reformation's best and *most dangerous, revolutionary idea* was putting the Bible in the hands of ordinary Christians. One of John Calvin's deepest desires in the Reformation was to provide the tools for ordinary Christians to read the Bible by themselves. So what did he do? For pastors, he wrote his famous *Institutes of the Christian Religion* and his extensive *commentaries on the Bible,* and for laypeople he designed a *catechism* and wrote more lay-level *expositions.* He did this so that ordinary Christians could both read and understand the Bible. In this way, he believed, rightly, that the fires of revival could be set loose. But what strikes me about Calvin's plan was that he didn't just plop Bibles into the laps of everyone and say, "Here, read this! Nothing to it! Tell me what you think!" No, he wanted them to learn the Bible right, and to do that they would have to learn some basic theology.

I believe everyone should read the Bible, but no one has ever said that everyone should interpret the Bible for themselves and whatever they come up with is as good as anyone else's views. I now appeal to the other great reformer, Martin Luther. No one wanted the Bible in the hands of ordinary Germans more than Martin Luther. But Luther knew that bad interpretations create schisms and problems. What did he do? He wouldn't let schoolchildren read the Bible until they had mastered his *Catechism*. Even if you think Luther himself was being too strong here (and I do), it should reveal that no matter how much the Reformers wanted to place a Bible on the dinner table of every Christian, they also wanted to provide the readers with a sound method and theology that would lead them to read the Bible accurately. Sadly, in our world today many have neglected this Reformation strategy.

The basic strategy works because no matter who we are, when we open the Bible we read it through what we already believe. Yes, what we believe can be challenged by the Bible and lead us to shifts. But we can't deny this important starting point: we start where we are, and where we are is what we already believe. In addition to this starting point, another consideration: we do need a good solid orientation to the Bible—the Bible's best ideas, the church's finest interpretations—to make sense of the Bible. I applaud Calvin and Luther for what they knew to be important: Bible readers need some basic ideas if they want to read the Bible well. Many leaders today seek to do something similar: alongside learning to read the Bible, a basic theological orientation is also taught to guide the reading of the Bible. This is where creeds and catechisms come into importance. But not all do this: some give people the Bible, tell them to read it, and basically say, "What you see in the Bible is exactly what is there." This is a case of pastoral neglect.

Because of this neglect, we are now living in a church with a myriad of interpreters.[4] And it has caused a mighty reaction today with many evangelical Christians bolting for more traditional churches. The major current in this stream is the appeal to *tradition*. There are two senses of tradition here, one that I adhere to strongly (Great Tradition) and one that repels me (traditionalism). The first is the Great Tradition. The Great Tradition is how the church everywhere has always read the Bible. (It can be pointed out that never has the church read the Bible always the same in every location, so this is hyperbole for a reality nonetheless: the Great Tradition affirmed by and large by all, such as the Nicene Creed.) There is a wonderful evangelical resurgence today of returning to the Great Tradition of the church, and I mention two examples: Thomas Oden's *The Rebirth of Orthodoxy*, and J. I. Packer's and Thomas Oden's *One Faith*.[5] Each of these is calling Christians to the core doctrines that the faithful in the church have always believed. They are urging evangelicals especially to take more seriously what I am calling the Great Tradition.

We may learn to read the Bible for ourselves, but we must be responsible to what the church has always believed. We can reduce the Great Tradition to the Nicene Creed, the Apostles' Creed, and the importance of justification by faith from the Reformation. These creeds point us toward the nonnegotiables of the faith; they point us to what God has led the church to see as its most important doctrines.

Some are going farther than this, though, and are giving too much authority to tradition. They are saying we need to read the Bible *through* tradition. The singular problem here is *traditionalism*. Traditionalism too often becomes the inflexible, don't-ask-questions, do-it-the-way-it-has-always-been-done approach to Bible reading. It reads the Bible *through* tradition. What happens then? Those who read the Bible *through* tradition always see the traditional way of reading the Bible. This approach is nearly incapable of renewal and adaptation.

What do we mean then by traditionalism? There are about six steps in this approach, and it occurs in every church and denomination I've been around. Rest assured, traditionalism occurs everywhere. You might say it's human nature. Here are the six steps, leading to traditionalism:

Step 1: We read the Bible.

Step 2: We confront a current issue and we make a decision about an issue—like baptizing infants or adults—or we frame "what we believe" into a confession, a creed, or a doctrinal statement.

Step 3: We *fossilize* our decision and it becomes a tradition.

(Somewhere around here we become absolutely convinced our tradition is the one and only perfect interpretation of the Bible.)

Step 4: We are bound to our tradition forever.

(It is now *traditionalism*.)

Step 5: We are bound to read the Bible *through* our tradition.

(Somewhere around here we become convinced that God's Spirit led us to our tradition and that it is nothing less than an accurate, God-prompted, don't-question-it unfolding in history of what God's Word says.)

Step 6: Those who question our tradition are suspect or, worse yet, kicked out of our church.

(Somewhere around here we become ineffective in our world and become increasingly cantankerous about how the youth are wandering away from the faith.)

The Bible itself points us away from traditionalism. The biblical authors and the early fathers didn't fossilize traditions. Instead—and here we come to a major moment in this book—*they went back to the Bible so they could come forward into the present.* They did not go back to stay there (the "retrieve-it-all" tendency); they didn't dismiss the Bible easily (the "retrieve-only-the-essence" approach); and they didn't fossilize their discernments (traditionalism). Instead, each one went back to the Bible, to God's Word, so they could come forward into their own day in their own ways. But they went back to the Bible in light of the fresh, unfolding revelation of God in Christ, and their adaptations were organically connected to the bedrock gospel ideas in their Great Tradition. This explains the variety of expressions from Genesis to Revelation; it alone explains how Paul and Peter could preach and preach and hardly quote a word of Jesus. It wasn't because they didn't know the words of Jesus. No, it was because they knew them so well they could renew Jesus's message in their day in their own ways—as God's Spirit prompted them.

I believe it is important to live within the Great Tradition and to interpret the Bible alongside that Great Tradition, but I also believe it has become nearly impossible for fossilization and traditionalism not to creep in. Is there a third way, a way that both returns to retrieve and also respects the Great Tradition? I believe there is, and it is the way of ongoing and constant *renewal* that returns, retrieves, and renews by reading the Bible *with* the Great Tradition.

3. Reading with Tradition

God was on the move; God is on the move; God will always be on the move. Those who walk with God and listen to God are also on the move. Reading the Bible so we can live it out today means being on the move—always. Anyone who stops and wants to turn a particular moment into a monument, as the disciples did when Jesus was transfigured before them, will soon be wondering where God has gone.

In the sixteenth century the citizens of the Italian city of Lucca, in Tuscany, sensed their security was threatened by the mighty nobles of both Pisa (famous for its leaning tower) and Florence (famous for what my dear wife, Kris, calls its "pictures"). The Lucchesi (folks from Lucca) hatched a plan in response to these surrounding threats—transform their thin walls into impregnable walls. So for one entire century, 30 percent or more of the taxes were used to fund the new walls. The Lucchesi built a tall and squat one-hundred-foot-wide wall of dirt, buttressed on each side with bricks. The irony of the story is that neither the Florentines nor the Pisans ever attacked Lucca. Happily, that wall did serve the Lucchesi by holding back a flood in 1812. Today, visitors to Lucca enjoy the 2.5-mile walk around the city atop the wall.

This wall might illustrate what happens when we convert the genius of a generation into fossilized, inflexible tradition. The wall, though it does get tourists like Kris and me to walk its entire length, is in the way. It is like reading the Bible *through* tradition. First you must scale it, traverse it, and descend it before you even have a chance of enjoying the inside of the city.

So how can we read the Bible with both a "return and retrieval" reading and a respect for the Great Tradition? I suggest we learn to read the Bible *with* the Great Tradition. We dare not ignore what God has said to the church through the ages (as the return and retrieval folks often do), nor dare we fossilize past interpretations into traditionalism. Instead, *we need to go back to the Bible with our eyes on the Great Tradition so we can move forward through the church and speak God's Word in our days in our ways.* When we do this, *we must also be conscious of keeping our fresh speaking of God's Word in our day connected organically to the Great Tradition.* We need to go back without getting stuck (the return problem), and we need to move forward without fossilizing our ideas (traditionalism). We want to walk between these two approaches. It's not easy, but I contend that the best of the evangelical approaches to the Bible and the best way of living the Bible today is to walk between these approaches. It is a third way.

In this approach we are to give the Bible primacy, like the "return and retrieval" crowd and the Reformers and (too often) unlike the traditionalists. The traditionalist approach too often swallows up the Bible with its tradition. But we are also to move forward by *setting the Bible loose to renew and keep on renewing* who we are, what we think, how we express the gospel, and how we live out the gospel in our world. Yet unlike traditionalists, we don't freeze or fossilize our expressions of the gospel. What we decide is our way for our day. We expect the next generation to do the same. Reading the Bible *with* the Tradition gives us guidance, but it also gives us freedom to reexpress the Tradition. In the last part of this book I will provide a few examples to show that reading the Bible *with* the Tradition sometimes means we will disagree with the Tradition even if we respect it.

Is there a danger here too? This approach, because it loves to return to the Bible, can easily slide into hyper-innovation. And because it reads the Bible *with* the Tradition, it can also fall prey to traditionalism. So what can we do to avoid this hyper-innovation weakness? It's simple, and we are seeing more and more today who are doing it. We need to have *profound respect* for our past without giving it the final authority. I have not said much about the Nicene Creed, but it will perhaps illustrate our point: When I read the Bible I keep my eye on the Nicene Creed, not because it is infallible but because it is the deposit of the church's wise and faithful interpretation of what the Bible says about God. I believe the final decision should always rest with the Scripture, but dismissal of the Great Tradition is foolish. Not so much respect that we fall into traditionalism, but enough to slow us down to ask how God has spoken to the church in the past. We show serious respect for our past when we learn our church history, when we learn how major leaders read the Bible in the past, and when we bring their voices to the table as we learn how to read the Bible for our time.[6]

Kris and I, along with our son Lukas and his wife, Annika, are now active members of an Anglican church in our area (Church of the Redeemer). Our church wonderfully combines the Great Tradition—we recite the Nicene Creed weekly, we use the church's lectionary for our Scripture readings and sermon, we celebrate Communion (called Eucharist) each week—with a flexibility that our pastors discern as they are prompted by the Spirit. The Great Tradition provides parameters and wisdom while the Spirit guides us to what we need for our church each week. All Spirit with no Great Tradition creates chaos; all Great Tradition with no Spirit creates traditionalism. Walking the balance beam is what life in the Spirit today is all about. That balance beam walks between *conservation* and *innovation*, about which I will say more in part 5 of this book.

Renewal carries forward God's timeless and historic message in a timely and cultured way for our day. We know that what we discern for our day is timely but not timeless. Making timeliness timeless is fossilizing. Our task is to take the timely timelessness of the Bible and make it timely timeliness for our world. We need to go back to the Bible's timely timelessness so we can come forward to live out the Bible in our timely timeliness. (Don't try to say that too fast.)

The Bible and I Story, Continued

I have to make a confession. Somewhere along the line while I was learning to read the Bible and while I was coming to terms with my own question, during seminary and doctoral research my wide-eyed wonder of Scripture diminished, and the jaw-dropping surprises were fewer and farther between. My desire to master the Bible and put it all together into my own system drained the Bible of its raw, edgy, and strange elixirs. I was caging and taming the Bible's blue parakeets.

Many Bible teachers go through a period when teaching the Bible is a job and studying theology seems to do little more than put bread on the table. Many of us will admit that at times the mystery, the thrill, and the intoxicating attractions fade. But most of us—and this happened for me—come out the other end of that dimly lit and foggy tunnel to find the light. Some call this life beyond the tunnel a "second naïveté." While teaching undergraduates—this was more of a process than an event—I gave up overpowering and silencing the blue parakeets in the Bible and began once again to listen to the Bible. The combination of students asking questions and those startling blue parakeet passages in the Bible awakened in me my earlier passions. Once again, as if drinking some eternal ambrosia, I found renewal and a renewing joy in the good news. I began to hear the blue parakeets again. The question came back with full force, and I embraced it as my own.

I now have no desire to tame blue parakeets. The Bible is what the Bible is, and I believe it. "Let the Bible be the Bible" is my motto, because teaching the Bible has taught me that the Bible will do its own work if we get out of the way and let it. Someone once said that the Bible needs no more defending than a lion, and I agree.

I have learned that when we take our hands off the pages of the Bible, read and listen to its words, and enter into its story by faith, something happens. It renews and continues to renew its powers. It becomes what it was meant to be, something both more intimate than an old pair of jeans and more unusual than alien creatures, something like a familiar stranger or an unpredictable neighbor or a pet lion whose presence invigorates its surroundings. Something like the glory of the ocean, which on the surface appears gentle and strolling and pleasant to observe, but under that surface there's a vibrant, teeming, swirling, dynamic world full of beauty and wonder. Or perhaps listening to the Bible is like having the most powerful person in the world sit down with you for coffee as a friend and chat with you.

Join me as we enter into the world of reading the Bible in such a way that it comes to life for us, in such a way that it is renewing and ever renewing, in such a way that we learn how to live it out. Three words tell us how to read the Bible, and we will devote a section to each:

Story

Listening

Discerning

That's all we need to know. It's all in those three words.

PART I

STORY

What Is the Bible?

In the past God spoke to our ancestors through the prophets at many times and in various ways, but in these last days he has spoken to us by his Son, whom he appointed heir of all things, and through whom also he made the universe.

Hebrews 1:1–2

CHAPTER 3

INKBLOTS AND PUZZLES

How, Then, Are We Reading?

In the 1990s, Kris heard about a new kind of book called *Magic Eye*, and she bought one for our kids for Christmas. Perhaps you remember the popularity of *Magic Eye* books. Whether you do or don't, I hope you can find one somewhere and look at its pictures, which really aren't pictures. They are autostereograms. The pictures in these books, if we let our eyes do what they can do, somehow transform from normal two-dimensional images into three-dimensional images. In front of you is what appears to be a flat picture, perhaps with some dots. But if you look at that picture just right—if you have eyes to see!—what you think is an ordinary picture of dots and an assortment of shapes begins to take on life. We see humans and flowers and planets in the sky in three dimensions. (I have to admit that this is pretty easy for me. I have been standing where men stand in designated rooms for men in public buildings and had the wall in front of me, nothing more than ordinary wallpaper, take on 3D!)

What we are looking for in reading the Bible is the ability to turn the two-dimensional words on paper into a three-dimensional encounter with God, so that the text takes on life and meaning and depth and perspective and gives us direction for what to do today. Gaining Magic Eyes ushers us into the renewal way of reading the Bible.

Perhaps another analogy will work. Who of us, once having read

C. S. Lewis's *The Voyage of the Dawn Treader*, can forget the scene where Eustace Scrubb and Lucy and Edmund Pevensie stare at a picture on a wall of a Narnian ship when suddenly the picture draws them into a whole new world. Suddenly that picture on the wall comes alive, and they begin to feel the breeze, smell the air, and hear sounds. The kids are magically drawn into the painting and find themselves in the water, where they are helped into a boat with the enticing name *Dawn Treader*. These kids, now in a new reality, travel to distant lands looking for the seven lost lords of Narnia. At the end of their adventures they find a lamb that turns into Aslan. Great story.

It is that sort of adventure with the Bible that we are looking for, the adventure of staring at the Bible's words on paper only to find ourselves drawn into the story itself. We feel it, taste it, hear it, and come to know it with such perspective and depth that it renews us. That kind of renewal gives us courage to begin living it all over again in our world, but in a new way for a new day. This is the way of renewal.

No Shortcuts!

We find our Magic Eyes and we are drawn up onto the *Dawn Treader* only *when we learn to read the Bible as a story*. The Bible's story, in the simplest of categories, has a plot with a

Beginning (Genesis 1–11), a (long, long)
Middle (Genesis 12–Malachi 4; Matthew–Revelation), and an
End (Matthew 25; Romans 8; Revelation 21–22).

I am tempted to dive right now into this story, to show that reading every passage in the Bible in light of the story draws us into the story. But we first have to point out some shortcuts too many of us have been taking. In our next chapter we will begin to look at the story of the Bible and its plot.

I wish I could explain it all, but I can't. Somewhere we've gone astray, and we've stopped reading the Bible as story. Our intent, and it is the right one, is to get something out of the Bible for our daily lives. I too want the Bible to be a "light on my path" (Psalm 119:105), and I'm sure you do as well. But, because reading the Bible as story takes more time, thinking, and discerning, we've developed routines and techniques that get us to our goal sooner. We've learned the CliffsNotes version of the Bible; we've developed shortcuts to grace. In my years of teaching the Bible, I've found five shortcuts to grace from listening to students and church folk who reveal how they read the Bible in the questions they ask.

One of my son's good friends, Kevin Patterson, is short and a little heftier than he'd like to be. Kevin, like a cairn terrier, is always up for a new challenge. Several years ago, Kevin acquired a desire to work on his body, but the old-fashioned way of running and lifting and doing sit-ups wasn't working for him, so he decided that AbTronic was the answer. Caught in the lure of a TV ad, Kevin became convinced that if he bought this contraption, a device that fit around his belly and sent short electronic impulses to contract his muscles, he'd lose weight. The rationale given was impeccable: "It's that easy and thirty minutes daily is usually all it takes to help improve figure problems." (So says the Internet ad.) Here's the pillow promise: "Muscles can be shaped while you are reading, relaxing, walking, or doing housework." Ergo, buy the thing!

So for about a month, whenever Kevin came by (to play on our son's Xbox), he wore his AbTronic device. After all, it said it "tones and tightens your upper abs, lower abs, and love handles with no sweat at all." The picture of a well-toned man in his mind didn't hurt. "Say good-bye to strenuous, time-consuming workouts. With the AbTronic, your muscles are moving but you are not." Just what Kevin wanted—he could play Xbox and lose weight. We've since learned that these devices don't accomplish what they say they will. Kevin will fess up that it didn't work.

Here's my point: many of us, instead of taking the longer but more rewarding path of reading the Bible as story, want a shortcut, an

AbTronic approach to Bible reading. We want to get the benefits—a toned body—without the effort of working out. We want the electronic impulse of contact with God and grace for the day without the effort of exercising our minds by reading the Bible and discerning how it all fits together and how we can live it out in our day in our way. Just as shortcuts in exercise prevent full health benefits, so also *shortcuts in Bible reading affect our spiritual health.*

Here are a few shortcuts that I've observed:

Shortcut 1: Morsels of Law

For some, the Bible is a massive collection of laws—what to do and what not to do. It is not difficult to understand how the Bible, which contains plenty of commandments and prohibitions—there are 613 in the Old Testament alone—can gradually give us the impression that it is a collection of legal morsels, a law book. Nor is it an uncommon experience, especially for the younger generation, to express the sentiment that "law book" is how they were taught the Bible, and it turned them off to the Bible.

Why? It begins with God. God becomes the Law-God, usually a little ticked off and impatient. Our relationship to God becomes conditioned by whether we are good citizens. There's another ugly element to the mistake of making the Bible a law book: what it does to us. We, the Obedient Ones, become insufferable. How so? We ...

> become intoxicated with our own moral superiority,
> become more concerned with being right than being good, and
> become judgmental.

In short, law-book readers become pompous, self-righteous, and accusatory. Sometimes we become resentful that others haven't caught up to our level of holiness. I use "we" because I, like the Delphic oracle, know whereof I speak.

I was a teenage legalist and considered myself one of the Obedient Ones. We happily tossed away a few of the Bible's commands, like loving our enemies and caring for orphans and widows, because we were crusaders and zealots for wholehearted obedience to the commands of God. In their place we added more commandments, and the ones that particularly appealed to me were "thou shalt not dance," "thou shalt not go to movies," "thou shalt not drink," and "thou shalt not play cards (except Rook or Dutch Blitz)." (God was still uttering his timeless commands in King James English in the sixties and seventies, at least he did in my church.) It was these "thou shalt nots" that made me particularly righteous because it convinced me, in front of God and the whole world, that I had joined an elite fraternity of the faithful. I could go on, but you probably get the picture.

There is, of course, an important place for the Bible's laws, commandments, and prohibitions. If you read Psalm 119 in one sitting, which is possible even if difficult, you will encounter an ancient Israelite who found utter delight in the Lawgiver and his laws. You will find a psalmist who loved God. You will find a man (I assume) who didn't see laws as a burden but as the good revelation of God on how to walk in this world with God in such a way that it would lead to the blessing of God. Yes, commandments aplenty can be found in the Bible. Commandments *as such* are good; they are God telling us how best to live.

But converting the story of the Bible, and we'll get to this in the next chapter, into a collection of little more than commandments completely distorts the Bible. We need to move on.

Shortcut 2: Morsels of Blessings and Promises

In 1551 a certain Stephanus divided the New Testament into numbered verses. We are thankful (with some groans). Thankful, because now it is much easier to refer to a specific part of the Bible. It is easier to say "John 1:14" than to say, "That line in the Bible where it says, 'The Word became flesh.'" Numbering verses is one thing, but when publishers provide a Bible where the only divisions are chapters and verses, as if each verse were a new paragraph, reading the Bible as a story is much more difficult. Take your favorite novel or book, photocopy a page, cut out each sentence, number each sentence, and then paste them back onto a page with each number beginning at the left margin, and you'll see the problem. It's much harder to read a book that way. One has to wonder what got into the head of publishers who started doing this. It's a colossal mistake.

Even more importantly, we need to observe what versification did to how we read the Bible. Dividing the Bible up into verses turns the Bible into morsels and leads us to *read the Bible as a collection of divine morsels, sanctified morsels of truth.* We pause for each one to see if we can get something from it. Now I want to meddle with a significant problem. For some morsel readers of the Bible, the Bible has become a collection of morsels of *blessings*, with calendars including one blessing for each day of the week.

On Monday we get Psalm 23:1.
On Tuesday we get Matthew 5:3.
On Wednesday we get Luke 11:2.
On Thursday we get Jeremiah 31:31.
On Friday we get Mark 14:24.
On Saturday we get Matthew 11:28.
On Sunday we get Romans 4:25.

Random verses, with generosity poured on top of generosity. On other calendars we get, instead of a blessing, a *promise* each day—promises about things like these:

God's faithfulness
God's grace
God's power
God's love
God's patience
God's listening to our prayers
God's eternal plans for us

Random verses, with blessing on top of blessing or promise on top of promise. (No one has yet composed a wrath-of-God calendar of warnings, though some seem poised to begin making such a calendar.)

What happens to the Christian who reads the Bible, day after day and week after week, as little more than a collection of morsels of blessings and promises? (You might want to sit down with a friend and talk about this.) For one, everything is good and wonderful and light and airy. These people become optimistic and upbeat and wear big smiles ... *until* something bad happens, until they enter into a period of suffering and feel distant from God, or until they hit a wall. For every hill, there is a valley. For every Joshua there's a Job, for every new church in the Pauline and Petrine missions, there's an imprisonment and a scar (a first-century tattoo).

One of the most important things about the Bible is that it tells realistic truth. Sure, there are all kinds of wonderful blessings surrounding Abraham, Moses, David, and Paul ... and there also are days of doubt, defeat, disobedience, and darkness. David was on top of the world at times, but he also asked God this question: "My God, my God, why have you forsaken me?" (Psalm 22:1). Edith Humphrey, a New Testament scholar, made this important observation of what happens when we focus solely on blessings and promises: "It is unfortunately the case that some contemporary expressions of Christianity have forgotten, or are embarrassed by, this moment of dark reflection, and instead espouse an unrealistic and warped view of spiritual victory." She also speaks of the "relentlessly upbeat" moods that lead to "false security and canned joy."[1]

It is important to know the blessings and to rely on God's promises. Please don't misunderstand my point. But the blessings and promises of God in the Bible emerge from a real-life story that also knows that we live in a broken world and some days are tough. The stories of real lives in the Bible reflect the truth that we are surrounded by hurting people for whom Psalm 22:1 echoes their normal day.

Those who read the Bible as story refuse to cut up the Bible into morsels of blessings and promises because they know the Story. They know that the David who found God's blessings and trusted in God's promises knew the dark side of life. Imagine how the God of the universe, who chose for some reason to communicate with us in the very thing that makes humans so distinct—sophisticated language in the form of a story covering spans of time—must respond as he observes his people seeking random sayings! It's a wonder that God hasn't at some point made the words disappear from the page so when we open our Bibles, nothing but blank paper stares us in the face.[2] We deserve it.

Shortcut 3: Mirrors and Inkblots

Hermann Rorschach (1884–1922), a famous Swiss Freudian psychiatrist, devised the inkblot test. You've probably seen one. What happens is quite straightforward: you (the patient) are shown a card on which is an inkblot; you tell the therapist that you see, say, a butterfly; and the therapist—with that special Mona Lisa smile—thinks to herself, "This person's normal." But if you say, "I see my neighbor's brain" or if you start mentioning a pelvis, the therapist—with that same Mona Lisa smile—begins to think in terms of deviancy and disorders. What a person sees in the inkblot gives the therapist information about a person's personality, emotions, and thought processes. It doesn't matter what the inkblot is—it really isn't anything. It gives a person an opportunity to reveal himself or herself.

Some people read the Bible as if its passages were Rorschach inkblots. They see what is in their head. In more sophisticated language, they project onto the Bible what they want to see. If you show them enough passages and you get them to talk about them, you will hear what is important to *them*, whether it is in the Bible or not. They might see in the "Jesus inkblot" a Republican or a socialist, because they are Republicans or socialists. Or they may see in the book of Revelation, a favorite of inkblot readers, a sketch of contemporary international strife. Or they may have discovered in the inkblot called "Paul" a wonderful pattern for how to run a church, which just happens to be the pastor's next big plan. You get the point—reading the Bible as an inkblot is projecting onto the Bible *our* ideas and *our* desires.

I used to give students in my Jesus class a test each semester on opening day. (The test can be found in Appendix 2 at the end of the book.) That test asks them to fill out a basic personality questionnaire about their view of Jesus and then to answer the same questions, now slightly shifted, about themselves. The amazing result, and the test has been field-tested by some professionals, is that *everyone thinks Jesus is like them!* The test results also suggest that, even though we like to think we are becoming more like Jesus, the reverse is probably more the case: *we try to make Jesus like ourselves.* Which means, to one degree or another, we are all Rorschachers; we all project onto Jesus our own image.[3]

Hardly a month goes by that I don't get an advertisement about a new book. Inevitably, the marketing department gives me the same song and dance: "Here, for the first time, we see what Jesus was really like. Here, for the first time, we get back to Jesus as he really was." Studies about Jesus are my professional specialization, and I am willing to say this: Anyone who says they are about to reveal what Jesus was really like is about to reveal not what Jesus was like, but *what they are like.* They've used Jesus as a Rorschach inkblot. You can count on it. I could list the books and name the names.

Instead of being swept into the Bible's story, Rorschach thinkers sweep the Bible up into their own story. Instead of being an opportunity for redemption, the Bible becomes an opportunity for narcissism. This is the problem with taking this shortcut: reading the Bible becomes patting ourselves on the back and finding our story in the Bible, instead of finding the Bible's story to be our story. Instead of entering into that story, we manipulate the story so it enters into our story.

I want to turn now to a different kind of shortcut, a hard-earned shortcut that also makes us rethink how we read the Bible.

Shortcut 4: Puzzling Together the Pieces to Map God's Mind

For some people the Bible is like a big puzzle. Once you've got the puzzle solved, you no longer have to work with the pieces. The shortcut is that once you've expended the energy to solve the puzzle, the job is done—forever and a day. These people know what the Bible says before they open it because they've already puzzled it together.

One of the English translations sitting on my desk has 1,153 pages. Spread over those 1,153 pages, in random order and with no clear clues as to where to begin or which pieces of information are most important, are Bible verses that contain information like pieces in a puzzle. God has scattered his mind throughout the Bible, and he gives to us, his readers, the challenge of putting the puzzle together. Puzzlers belong to what I call the Flat Bible Society. They work in a flat room, and they've scattered throughout the room these random puzzle bits of information from the Bible. If you pick up the right piece first and gradually work your way through every verse (the pieces of the puzzle) of the whole Bible, you will eventually get your Bible's puzzle pieces to look like the picture on the box ... but that's the problem. We don't really know what the picture looks like. We have to *imagine* what the complete, original picture really is.

Truth be told, this kind of pieced-together puzzle, the Grand System that we construct out of the pieces, is an act of theological imagination. And do you know what Mark Twain said about "imagination"? Speaking of Captain Stormfield, he said, "He had a good deal of imagination, and it probably colored his statements of fact; but if this was so, he was not aware of it."[4] Too many puzzlers don't know that the puzzle they believe in is an imagined system of thought.

What's wrong with this shortcut? First, *we need to think about what this Grand System, the solved puzzle, really is*: it is a system of thought that presumes that we know what God was doing before the Bible was written, and once we have this puzzle in hand, we've got the Bible figured out. At some level, these folks think they have *mapped the mind of God*. Their map, or their solved puzzle, is something no author in the Bible believes. Instead, the solved puzzle is something God was revealing over time that they put together. While we don't often think like this, the enormity of this claim boggles the mind (or it should).

Second, this approach nearly always *ignores the parts of the puzzle that don't fit*. Some evening, sit down with an encyclopedia and read the entries on the major groups in the church—Roman Catholics, Eastern Orthodox, Lutherans, Reformed, Congregationalists, Baptists, Episcopalians, Presbyterians, nondenominational, and so on. What you will undoubtedly see is that each one of these groups emphasizes something true and important in the Bible; you will also see that each one de-emphasizes or even ignores something important to the other groups. Each of these groups has a solved puzzle that guides their thinking—no one's puzzle is complete, no one's puzzle is perfect. Each of these groups ignores parts of the puzzle that don't quite fit their system.

Third, *puzzling together the pieces we find in the Bible into a system is impossible.* The Bible contains authors as diverse as Moses and David (who hardly ever quotes Moses), Isaiah and Ezekiel, Daniel and Matthew, John and Paul, Peter and James, as well as the author of Hebrews, and Luke. I have sometimes puzzled pieces together from all over the Bible in what I thought were clever, creative, and meaningful ways. Just as often, I have had a pit in my stomach with this worry: my puzzle is not the puzzle of anyone's in the Bible. It is *my* puzzle, not the Bible's.

Think about it this way: it is one thing to pull together the social thinking of Charles Dickens from his novels, and many would say that can be more or less accomplished. But now let's expand our efforts to include other novelists: Why in the world would we even try to pull together the social thinking of all nineteenth-century English novelists? This is not unlike what puzzlers are doing with the various authors of the Bible. Then why do we try to pull together all the authors of the Bible? Who ever told us that was the way to read the Bible? Some might say, "But the Bible is a unity because God is behind it all." I agree, but who says that our system is that unity? Our next concern might shed some light on that question for you. I know it does for me.

Fourth, puzzling *calls into question the Bible as we have it.* After all, had he wanted to, God could have revealed a systematic theology, chapter by chapter. But God didn't choose this way of revealing his truth. Maybe—this "maybe" is a little facetious—that way of telling the truth can't tell it the way God wants his truth told. What God chose to do was to give to you and me a story of Israel and the church, and we have a series of authors who tell that story and who contribute in one way or another to that story as the plot unfolds. Open a typical theology book and here are the major chapters: Introduction, God, Humans (or "Man"), Christ, Sin, Salvation, Church, Future. Open the Bible and what do you get? God, a swirl of chaos that God spins into beauty to compose a garden, into which he plops two humans and says, "Now take care of this for me." Which is more inviting? (Please don't say the first option.)

So, and here I anticipate something later in the book, maybe we should follow God's design and let the Bible be the Bible. What does that mean? Maybe it is the *story* of the Bible that is the system! No one has spoken more timely words here than Eugene Peterson:

> The most frequent way we have of getting rid of the puzzling or unpleasant difficulties in the Bible is to systematize it, organizing it according to some scheme or other that summarizes "what the Bible teaches." If we know what the Bible teaches, we don't have to read it anymore, don't have to enter the story and immerse ourselves in the odd and unflattering and uncongenial way in which this story develops, including so many people and circumstances that have nothing to do, we think, with us.[5]

What is the problem here? In one word, *mastery*. Those who solve the puzzle think they've got the Bible mastered; they have caged and tamed the Blue Parakeet who gave us the blue parakeets. God did not give the Bible in order that we could master him or it; God gave the Bible so we could live it, so we could be mastered by it. The moment we think we've mastered it, we have failed to be readers of the Bible. Of course, I think we should read the Bible and know it—but it is the specific element of reading for mastery versus reading to be mastered that grows out of this shortcut.

Now I present a final shortcut, a tasty but tempting one.

Shortcut 5: Maestros

I like to cook, and I consider myself an amateur specialist in making risotto, an Italian way of making rice. Kris and I recently spent a week in Italy on vacation, and I ate risotto every evening, sampling the recipe of each cook's way of making risotto. My intent was to see how a *maestro di cucina*, a master of the art of Italian cooking, makes risotto so I could improve my own risotto. In Stresa, near Lago Maggiore on the northern tip of Italy, we went to Hotel Ristorante Fiorentino. Carla Bolongaro welcomed, seated, and served us while her son, Luigino, the *maestro di cucina*, prepared our dinner. ("Dinner" seems hollow for what an Italian cook offers.) All risottos are prepared in thick-bottomed pans, the starches of the rice drawn out from the Carnaroli or Arborio rice with broth one ladle at a time. Luigino added saffron and some tasty prosciutto along with some bits of porcini mushroom (*mama mia!*). By the time we left, we knew we had tasted risotto at its finest.

I don't tell you this to make you hungry or to mention that I have several times done my best to imitate the risotto recipe of the Bolongaro family, but to say that many read the Bible the way they learn from a *maestro di cucina*. That is, they go to the Bible to find the master, the *über*-Rabbi—Jesus—at work. Then when they get up from their reading of the Bible, they imitate Maestro Jesus. "What would Jesus do?" is the only question they ask. The problem here is the word "only."

It is almost justifiable to make Jesus the Maestro. But more than a few of us are aware that Jesus has been eclipsed for many Bible readers by Maestro Paul. In this shortcut, Jesus is either ignored or overwhelmed by Paul's way of thinking. Some of us grew up in churches where the thought patterns, the lenses, the grid through which everything was filtered—however unconsciously—was the book of Romans or Paul's theology.

I'm one such person. I grew up in a Pauline world, and I went to a college and studied the Bible in a Pauline world. Even when we dipped into the Gospels, especially at Christmas and Easter, we used

Maestro Paul to inform us about what Jesus was really doing and saying. I cannot tell you what it was like when, as a first-year seminary student, I sat and listened—at 7:45 a.m. with my jaw agape—to Walt Liefeld, someone who could open the world of Jesus for me. Right then and there, in the deepest recesses of my soul, I knew I had found my life's passion—to study and teach about Jesus. I had been tutored under Maestro Paul and found Jesus.

The problem was not Paul. (I'll get to him soon enough.) The problem was that I was not taught to read the Bible as a story. Many of us weren't. I had been nurtured in a world that read the entire Bible as a solved puzzle that used Maestro Paul's categories to understand everything else in the Bible. Reading the Bible through a maestro's eyes gives us one chapter in the story of the Bible. One-chapter Bible readers develop one-chapter Christian lives.

Now that I've pointed out some shortcuts we all too often take, what is the long way? How can we learn to read the Bible as Story? How can we develop Magic Eyes and be drawn up onto the *Dawn Treader*? As the guide at the museum says as she moves on to the next room, "Step this way."

CHAPTER 4

IT'S A STORY WITH POWER!

How, Then, Shall We Read?

Blogging may be the world's most fascinating form of communication. Someone jots down their ideas, clicks "publish," and those ideas instantaneously appear for the whole world to see. The world does see. More importantly, the world sometimes comments back. Sometimes anonymously and sometimes bitingly and sometimes it hurts. The first lesson a blogger learns is this: anyone in the world can say anything they want at anytime on a blog. The second lesson is this: you may not know that person. In my first week of blogging (Google Jesus Creed), I learned these two lessons, and they shocked me. One of the first questions that wandered its way through my head when I began reading a comment on something I had written was: "Who is this person anyway?"

After years of teaching, preaching, and writing, comments and questions were common for me. I am used to being questioned. In fact, I enjoy it. But teachers know who is saying what and more often than not we also know where our students' questions are "coming from." But those who drop comments in the comment box on a blog can do so anonymously or with a fictitious name. Under the cloak of anonymity, they can become bold and brazen and can blast away. Incivility marks blogs far too often. To be sure, blogs form blog communities where most learn enough about other commenters that, even if we don't know the person personally, we recognize their electronic personality. Knowing one another restores civility. Still, until one discovers "who is who" and "where they are coming from," comments can sometimes startle and shock.

On my blog we have developed a simple protocol: no anonymous comments. Why? Since I believe "context is everything," contextless comments and faceless comments, which are what fictitious names or anonymous comments are, are not permitted. Anyone who speaks up anonymously or fictitiously is contextless. Until we know the context or until we know who is saying what and why, it is difficult to know how to respond.

Reading the Bible is the same: context is everything. Until we learn to read each text in its context—who said what, when, why, how, etc.—we run the risk of misunderstanding the Bible. I'll give an example. Do you pay interest on your loans? Do you participate in (or with) a company that charges interest? The Bible says some clear things about charging interest in Leviticus 25:35–38:

> If any of your fellow Israelites become poor and are unable to support themselves among you, help them as you would a foreigner and stranger, so they can continue to live among you. Do not take interest or any profit from them, but fear your God, so that they may continue to live among you. You must not lend them money at interest or sell them food at a profit. I am the LORD your God, who brought you out of Egypt to give you the land of Canaan and to be your God.

It's about as clear as the lenses on my glasses (which for some obsessive reason I keep clean). But, and I'm willing to bet on this one, none of us obeys this commandment. Interest was prohibited, full stop, no questions asked. God put his reputation on the line for this one. (That's the point of the last verse quoted above.) You might start fiddling around and say that since it was for fellow Israelites, this only means that we shouldn't charge interest or pay interest to fellow Christians. This only pushes us further into the corner, because—and I'm willing to bet on this one too—we don't bother to check on our mortgages to make sure Christians aren't charging us interest. Besides the effort it would require, we don't care because we aren't interested in this commandment in the Bible. Why is this? It all has to do with how you and I read our Bibles.

You probably read this prohibition of interest the way I do: *that was then, and this is now.* Reading the Bible like this is reading the Bible as Story. It unfolds and propels us to live out the Bible in our day in our way. But how do we know when the principle of "that was then and this is now" applies? It's easy when everyone agrees, and we all seem to have concluded without much conscious effort that charging and paying interest is how the system works (though we'd all be surprised how debated charging interest was in Europe in centuries past). But what happens when some disagree with the status quo? It's not so easy then. When some disagree, we suddenly notice the blue parakeet in our presence and begin to rethink how we read the Bible.

I believe those seven words are the secret to reading the Bible: "That was then, and this is now." They reveal that we have learned to read the Bible as Story, even though most of us never give this a minute's thought. We need to. That is why this first section of the book, devoted to "the Story," needs to be given the attention we give it. Until we learn to read the Bible as Story, we will not know how to get anything out of the Bible for daily living. We need to read each passage in its location in the Story, and then we will see how it all fits together. And unless we read the Bible as Story, we might be tempted to make "that was then" into "it's also now." But it isn't. Times have changed. God spoke in Moses's days in Moses's ways (about interest), and he spoke in Jesus's days in Jesus's ways, and he spoke in Paul's days in Paul's ways. *And he speaks in our days in our ways*—and it is our responsibility to live out what the Bible says in our days. We do this by going back so we can come forward, always proceeding into our world organically connected to what is in our past.

It's a Story!

As we go back to the Bible, we ask a big question: How would you classify and shelve the Bible in a library? Using the Dewey Decimal System, where would you put it? Since the architects of the DDS have already assigned it to Religion (200), where it has its own number (Bible: 220), the answer to our question might seem easy. But if we think about how people treat or read the Bible, and we think back to our third chapter where we talked about shortcuts, we might find ourselves in an interesting conversation. It seems to me that here is where some folks would shelve the Bible in a library:

Lawbook:	320 (Political science) → 340 (Law)
Blessings/promises for the Day:	150 (Psychology) → 158 (Applied)
Rorschach:	158 (Applied psychology) or 126 (The self)
Puzzle:	110 (Metaphysics) or 120 (Epistemology)
Maestro:	227.06 (Paul) or 232.092 (Jesus Christ)

Each of these locations on the shelves of the library tells us something true about the Bible. In fact, it is amazing how many locations could contain Bibles! Apart from its obvious location with Religion, the Bible properly belongs with History of the Ancient World, Palestine/Israel (933), and also in the Life of Jesus (232.092); and because the gospel spreads from the land of Israel throughout the whole world, it could also be moved to World History (909). But there's one element about the Bible that makes the DDS inadequate: the Bible claims to be God's telling of history. The Bible is the story of God's people. It is "*his*" story, and I doubt any library wants to assign a number to "God's Story"!

Going back to the Bible teaches us to read the Bible as God's story. Read, as an example, Acts 7. Here we have someone who puts the whole Bible together for us. Stephen, an early Christian deacon, was about to be put to death for following Jesus. The future apostle

Paul (then called Saul) chimed in with his judgment and approved the capital sentence for Stephen.

But first Stephen was put on trial. He was asked if the charges against him were true. Stephen's answer is an example of how to read the Bible. He didn't do anything other than tell the story of Israel that had opened a new chapter—a chapter called Jesus the Messiah. With Jesus, everything changed. Everything! Stephen had to follow Jesus even if it meant dying for him. If you follow along with Stephen's story, you are sucked into the Story, just as the Pevensie kids were drawn into the picture and onto the *Dawn Treader*. If you are looking for an argument, a kind of "point one, point two, point three, therefore do this," you may not find your Magic Eyes in Acts 7. It's there for those with eyes to see.

All across the spectrum today, experts are saying we need to read the Bible as Story. Robert Webber, formerly a Wheaton professor, offers us an invitation: "So I invite you to read the Bible, not for bits and pieces of dry information [pieces in a puzzle], but as the story of God's embrace of the world told in poetic images and types."[1] I add another voice, namely, the excellent Old Testament scholar John Goldingay: "The biblical gospel is not a collection of timeless statements such as God is love. It is a narrative about things God has done."[2] For a third voice, consider a Jewish scholar, Abraham Joshua Heschel: "The God of the philosopher is a concept derived from abstract ideas; the God of the prophets is derived from acts and events. The root of Jewish faith is, therefore, not a comprehension of abstract principles but an inner *attachment to those events*."[3]

Each of these scholars points us in the same direction. In your hand is a Bible that God gave you to read. God asks us to read the Bible as the unfolding of the story of his ways to his people. Stephen was killed for telling that story.

So was William Tyndale. Tyndale was put to death because he wanted to make a reality the Reformation's most dangerous idea[4]—putting the Bible and its powerful story in the hands of every Christian so each of us could read it. The Bible in your hand is there because of William Tyndale. You may not know what a privilege it is. For most of the first 1,500 years of the church, the average person did not have a Bible, and even if they did, most could not read. Tyndale was the vanguard for English translations.

I want to pause here to pay homage to one of our greatest Bible translators, because we need to be reminded that the Bible I am writing about in this book, the Bible that you and I hold in our hands, is a Bible that cost some people their lives just to translate.

William Tyndale Gives Us the Bible

I am surrounded by books and Bibles. Most of us read the Bible in English; I have a number of translations, and you probably do too. The roots of all English translations go back to William Tyndale.[5] Tyndale had a goal in life: "If God spare my life, ere many years I will cause a boy that driveth the plough shall know more of the Scripture than thou [a learned man] dost." His goal? To translate the whole Bible so clearly that even farm boys could read and understand it.

The Roman Catholic establishment of England was opposed to translating the Bible for fear that what was happening in Germany, namely, the explosive Reformation led by Martin Luther, might come to England. What was there to fear? The Bible. Nothing but the Bible. The clergy's knowledge of the Bible at that time would shock the reader today. Some did not know which book of the Bible contained the Ten Commandments (many thought they were found in Matthew's Gospel), some did not know where to find the Lord's Prayer (which was said constantly in Catholic services), some did not know who originally said it, and some could not even recite it. Tyndale's dream ran headfirst against the establishment. What Luther had done in Germany was about to take deep roots in England.

Tyndale began work on a translation of the Bible into plain English but could not find support for his work in England, so he crossed the English Channel to Germany, hoping to be carried by Luther's steam. In Cologne, Germany, in 1525, as Tyndale was translating Matthew 22 (he was on verse 12), he and his companion William Roye escaped an attempt to arrest and imprison them for their supposedly seditious work of translating the Bible.

Five years later, a certain Thomas Hitton was arrested in England for preaching heresy. "At his examination he confessed that he had smuggled a New Testament ... from abroad. After imprisonment he was condemned ... and on 23 February burned alive at Maidstone." The religious establishment meant business when they prohibited translation.

Tyndale translated most of the Bible, but before he was finished he was tricked "by a vicious, paltry and mean villain" who revealed Tyndale's location. In October of 1536, Tyndale was tied to the stake and strangled by an executioner. His last words were an expression of nothing less than his simple vision to translate the Bible into plain English: "Lord! Open the king of England's eyes!" We wonder if the crowd behind the barricade that watched the gathering of brushwood and straw, the crowd which stepped aside to watch Tyndale mount the place of execution, heard his prayer. Did they hear what he said when the authorities asked him that last time to recant his stubborn ways? They would have seen him tied to a stake and the rope gathered around his neck. After signaling that it was time to tighten the rope and letting it do what it was designed to do, the authorities judged him dead. They set the kindling afire to consume the body of a man who had but one goal—to make the Bible readable for everyone.

You and I have a Bible, and most of us read it without fear. To quote Augustine, *tolle lege*: "take, read." Tyndale's biographer said, "The bare text [of the Bible], if given whole, will interpret itself." But we must read it—and that means from Genesis to Revelation—as it is meant to be read.

A Confession

For many years, instead of grasping the Bible as Story, I was a maestro Bible reader. I learned to tame the blue parakeets—and there were plenty in the Bible to tame—by making them all sound like Maestro Jesus, the *über*-Rabbi. At times I sneaked into the cabins of others for a meal or two with other cooks; that is, I wrote commentaries on Galatians and 1 Peter. During this time I nursed a grudge against two authors who, for me, were blue parakeets: the apostle Paul and the apostle John. Why? I believed they had *ignored* the kingdom message of Jesus.

I was upset with Paul and Peter for using words like "justification" and "church" and "eternal life"—not that there is anything wrong with their terms. So devoted was I to the Maestro's verbal vision that I thought these other New Testament writers should have used Jesus's pet expression, namely, "kingdom of God." I could not understand why Paul dropped terms like "disciple" or why he seemed to ignore the Sermon on the Mount or why John translated "kingdom" into "eternal life." So I tamed them by using only Jesus's words.

Furthermore, as a maestro reader of the Bible, I also nursed a grudge against the puzzlers of this world, and my grudge emerged from two convictions about how to read the Bible. First (and I still sense this at times), those who have a solved puzzle rarely let Jesus's kingdom message be what it is. Second, every approach I've read by puzzlers somehow managed to avoid the Story and the Plot as the central categories for knowing the message of the Bible. Instead of creation and fall, exodus and exile, as well as community and redemption, the Story was flattened out. Categories like God, man, Christ, sin, salvation, and eschatology were pieced together from various authors. Unfortunately, the authors themselves were not given their day before the jury. I congratulated myself for being hyperbiblical about Jesus's message of the kingdom, which I thought was better than the puzzling approach. But while I was fair to Jesus, I didn't have an approach that let each author in the Bible tell their own story. In attempting to be faithful to the Bible, I was being unfair to the Bible as we have it.

But that all changed when I realized more theoretically that God chose to communicate with us in language. This may seem either profoundly obvious, on the level of the person who says the sky is above us, or "profoundly profound." For me this was profoundly profound.

Since—and this is why it changed how I read the Bible—God chose to communicate in language, since language is always shaped by context, and since God chose to speak to us over time through many writers, God also chose to speak to us in a variety of ways and expressions. Furthermore, I believe that because the gospel story is so deep and wide, *God needed a variety of expressions to give us a fuller picture of the Story.*

This liberated me from the maestro approach and drove me to the Story approach of reading the Bible. I now know that the various versions of the Story in the Bible need to be seen for what they are: "wiki" stories of the Story. (I'll get to this "wiki" idea if you'll read on to the next section.) To illustrate how often this Story is (partly) summarized, notice these passages in the Bible: Exodus 15; Leviticus 26:3–13; Deuteronomy 6:20–24; 26:5–9; 29; 32; Joshua 23:2–4; 24:2–13; 1 Samuel 12:7–15; 1 Kings 8; 1 Chronicles 1–9; 16:8–36; Ezra 5:11–17; Nehemiah 9:6–37; Psalms 78; 105; 106; 135:8–12; 136; Isaiah 5:1–7; Jeremiah 2:2–9; Ezekiel 16; 20; 23; Daniel 9:1–27; and Habakkuk 3:1–16. And now to the New Testament: Matthew 1:1–17; Acts 7:2–50; 10:36–43; 13:17–41; Romans 9–11; Hebrews 11; and Revelation 12:1–12. How can one not also include 1 Corinthians 15:1–28 and Revelation 21–22? Others might add other passages, but this list should make abundantly clear that the Bible has oasis stops that summarize where the Story has gotten to thus far.

In our Bible, God did what God has always done: he spoke in Moses's days in Moses's ways, in Micah's days in Micah's ways, and in Jesus's days in Jesus's ways. Which meant, when Paul came around, Paul got to speak in Paul's ways for Paul's days, and when John put quill to parchment, he was freed up to speak in John's ways for John's days. This discovery liberated me, and (to use some puns now, so catch them) it justified Paul and gave new life to John to take Jesus's kingdom story and make it their own story of the Story. I've come to see these stories of the Story to be like the seventh day of creation— very, very good. No single story, not even Jesus's story, can tell the whole Story. We need them all.

Why Wiki-Story?

So, you ask, why see the various authors as "wiki" stories? We are all familiar (if not intimate) with Wikipedia. Those who say they aren't will be sentenced to read Karl Barth's *Church Dogmatics* for ten consecutive hours for not telling the truth! Wikipedia has its detractors and its problems, but that won't keep the world or our students (or any of us) from using it. It is a collaborative, democratic, interactive, developing encyclopedia to which anyone in the world, ostensibly, can make a contribution.

Wikipedia is not like your father's encyclopedia, whether that was *World Book* or *Britannica*. Instead, an entry in Wikipedia can change daily: paragraphs can be deleted and entries can be completely rewritten or new entries added. It's sometimes called "open source." (Here's the path to the Wikipedia entry for "Open Source": http://en.wikipedia.org/wiki/Open_source.) Because it is truly "open," bad information can filter into the entries and render their quality suspect. In calling the Bible a Wiki-Story I will bracket off the problems of bad contributors to Wikipedia. All I want to focus on here is one element: *the ongoing reworking of the biblical Story by new authors so they can speak the old story in new ways for their day.*

If you'd like a more Jewish way of saying that each author is a writer of a wiki-story, I'd say the Bible contains an ongoing series of *midrashim*, or interpretive retellings, of the one Story God wants us to know and hear. Each biblical author—whether we talk of Moses and the Pentateuch, or the so-called Deuteronomic histories, or the Chronicler, Job, or Ecclesiastes, or the various prophets, or Jesus or Paul or John or James or the author of Hebrews or Peter—each of these authors tells his version of the Story. They tell wiki-stories of the Story; they give *midrashim* on the previous stories. Sometimes one author will pick up the story of someone else, as when the Chronicler picks up 1 and 2 Kings, and will recast it, or when Isaiah picks up Micah and Hosea. But other times we have more or less a new story, as with Daniel or Jeremiah or Ezekiel or the apostle Paul or the writer of Hebrews.

If you'd like to see this process in action, open your Bible to Matthew 4:1–11, Matthew's version of the temptations of Jesus. Matthew here tells a wiki-story, a new version, of an old story. Many— far too many, in fact—have been taught this passage in a blessings/ promises or Rorschach approach. They've been taught to read this text for themselves—as a method for responding to temptations to sin. The supposed biblical answer, which is never even remotely mentioned in the text itself, is to quote the Bible at Satan when we are tempted. This makes sense, but it has nothing to do with the text itself.

Here's the question the Story asks us, and it reveals what we mean by a wiki-story: Is Jesus's temptation the reliving of Adam and Eve's experience in Eden? (Jesus is then cast as the second Adam, only this time perfectly obedient, and thereby the pioneer of a new Adamic line.) Or, which is more probable, is Jesus's temptation by Satan the reliving of Israel's wilderness testings? (Jesus is then recast as the second Moses or a second Israel leading his people to a new promised land.) In either case, Matthew casts the story of Jesus's temptations as an updated version, a wiki-story, of an older story—either the Eden story or the wilderness story.

Many New Testament specialists will tell you that nearly every page of the New Testament is a wiki-story on an Old Testament wiki-story. In fact, the Old Testament scholar John Goldingay says the New Testament is nothing but footnotes on the Old Testament![6] He adds that "one cannot produce a theology out of footnotes." That is, if you don't have the Old Testament in your head, you can't grasp what the New Testament authors are saying. (Goldingay, as is typical with him, exaggerates to make a point—only he might not think he's exaggerating.)

Here's where we are:

- The Bible is a Story.
- The Story is made up of a series of wiki-stories.
- The wiki-stories are held together by the Story.
- The only way to make sense of the blue parakeets in the Bible is to set each in the context of the Bible's Story.

None of the wiki-stories is final; none of them is comprehensive; none of them is absolute; none of them is exhaustive. Each of them tells *a true story of that Story*. In our next chapter I want to sketch what the Story looks like.

CHAPTER 5

THE PLOT OF THE WIKI-STORIES

How Does the Bible Work?

Saying the Bible is Story is not saying it is make-believe or a fib or fiction or myth, nor is it to assert that gobs of the stories didn't happen. We say the Bible is Story because if we read it from beginning to end, we discover that it has three features: it has a *plot* (creation to consummation), it has *characters* (God—Father, Son, and Spirit—and God's people and the world and creation around them), and it also has many *authors* who together tell the story. So to discover the basics of the Story, I will ask you to sit back and imagine something with me.

Imagine Jesus reclining at the head of a table at a writers' banquet. To his right are more than thirty authors, the authors of Old Testament books.[1] To his left are more than ten authors of New Testament books. Each of these authors has his (or her) hand raised—not to ask a question but for permission to tell their story of the Story. Each one has a story to tell, or perhaps even better, each one has *a way* of telling the Story. Before they are given permission, however, Jesus gives them some instructions in the form of a plot to which they are to conform their story. We are only imagining Jesus at the head of this table, of course, and one can find theological reasons to put the Father or the Holy Spirit at the head of the table. Our point is that God directs the Bible along the line of the Story.

Where to Begin?

But where do we begin? One of the adventures of Bible reading is that it all depends on what questions you are asking. Yes, there is an overarching plot to the Bible—God's creating the heavens and earth to completing his creation work in the new heavens and new earth. But our Bible has so many themes and so many characters and twists and turns that we are suddenly confronted with an abundance of riches. We could tell the history of Israel and focus on events; we could tell a history of Big Influencers, beginning with Adam and Abraham and skipping to Moses and Isaiah before we get to Jesus, who eclipses the apostles. We could tell a history of culture making from Genesis to Revelation, as Andy Crouch has recently done.[2] We can tell the Bible's story of ongoing justice and liberation or the Bible's story about human nature or social organizations or politics. As a Bible professor, I've seen dozens of approaches to the Bible's Story, and nearly every one of them has something to offer to the Bible reader.

There is not just one and only one story in the Bible. But there are two nonnegotiables in the Bible's Story. First, there is **a general plot** from the creation of the heavens and the earth in Genesis 1–2 to the establishment of the new heaven and the new earth in Revelation 20–22. Second, there are **redemptive benefits** for those who participate in that "general plot" by declaring allegiance to the God of that plot. Before I get to the redemptive benefits (the story of the *Eikon*, the image of God, below), I want to sketch briefly the General Plot,[3] which I will call the King and His Kingdom Story.

The King and His Kingdom Story

What our parents and our grade school teachers taught us was true, but for a moment we have to go against their wisdom. To comprehend the Bible's King and His Kingdom Story, we have to go to the end of the Story, to the book of Revelation, to understand which direction we need to point ourselves as we navigate through the Bible itself. What we discover in Revelation 20–22 is that God's plan for creation is the kingdom of God. God's final kingdom here is called "a new heaven and a new earth" (Revelation 21:1). Descending down from God's dwelling place, this new city over the new Jerusalem has a king, the Lamb of God, who is not only king but the temple itself! God will be the people's God and the people will be God's people. There is something profoundly important in beginning with the end: we see that the plan of God is not just my personal salvation (I will discuss benefits below) but all of creation's benefits! Evil will be defeated, goodness will be finally established for all time, all jewels and glittery items will be donated to the glory of God, the Lamb is all the light the new Jerusalem will need, peace and safety and open doors will be the way of life, and all God's people will worship the one true God.

Knowing this end teaches us how to read the Bible's King and His Kingdom Story. I suggest there are three chapters in this Story:

1. **Theocracy:** The Creator God who makes a covenant with Abraham rules, no humans are to rule, and all humans are to trust and obey this one true God. This Story is found from Genesis 1 to 1 Samuel 8. Thus, the story extends from Adam and Abraham to Moses and Samuel, but a noticeable feature of this story is that humans constantly resist the will of God, God makes a covenant to redeem them, gives the law to guide them, and provides a sacrificial system to reconcile them to himself. But most importantly, God turns his gracious and guiding attention especially to one family, Abraham's, and to one nation, Israel. From Genesis on, the core of the Bible's Story is Israel, and in the New Testament it is the church. Noticeably, unlike the nations all around Israel, there is no king among the one true God's people. God alone is their king.

2. **Monarchy:** God permits, but only permits, his people Israel to have a king, a monarch. Why? Because as Samuel says to God, Israel wants a king so that they can be like the other nations. This

extends from 1 Samuel 8 to Matthew 1:1. This can be called the monarchical concession of God in order to discipline Israel to see that God's original way—theocracy—is the best way. God remains the one true God and King, but Israel gets a human king who is to be under God the King. Yet again, the kings act like the humans under Theocracy: they resist the will of God; God's covenant provides a way of reconciliation and restoration; the sages of Israel develop wisdom for the people of God so they will learn how to live well and flourish; the prophets become more central to announce God's will, to predict the future, and to declare that someday God will bring Israel back into a theocracy again. In the monarchy chapter, law, wisdom, and prophecy mature and become central to the community of God, Israel.

3. **Christocracy:** God calls a halt to the human rule of a monarchy, sends his royal Son—Jesus the King, the Messiah, the Son of God and Son of Man, and Wisdom incarnate. He lives with us, shows us how to live, teaches us the way of God, and then he dies for us, he is buried, he is raised for us, and he ascends to the right hand of the Father to rule. The Christocracy period extends from Matthew 1:1 to the end of Revelation, where the Lamb who is the Lion who is the Son rules with the Father over the new heaven and the new earth. Once again, God rules (Christocracy is the theocracy), but now the people of God expand from Israel to include gentiles in the one people of God, the church. This people too are not perfect. Church people sin, but forgiveness is now granted through the cross of Christ. This Christocracy, the church age, will be completed when Christ returns, all evil is defeated, and the ways of God are established forever. Christocracy will then turn, as 1 Corinthians 15:20–28 shows, back into **theocracy**.

This is the Bible's General Plot: from God creating the heavens and the earth to the completion of creation by establishing the new heaven and the new earth. I call this three-chapter Story the King and His Kingdom Story. This King and His Kingdom Story shapes every other story that can be told from the Bible, and stories that ignore the King and His Kingdom Story—any story where Jesus and his redemptive benefits are not central—fail to be consistent with the Bible's General Plot.

Once we know the King and His Kingdom Story, we can learn to read the Theocracy chapter and the Monarchy chapter in light of the Christocracy chapter. We learn to see that Adam and Eve, made in the "image of God" according to Genesis 1:27, were fashioned after the True Image of God, Christ (Colossians 1:15–20). We learn in the King and His Kingdom Story that every king and prophet and priest were anticipations of Jesus—Prophet, Priest, and King. We learn that Israel's wisdom in Proverbs and elsewhere points us to Jesus, the Wisdom of God incarnate, and that the way to live is to live in a Christlike way. We learn that the Passover and the sacrificial system of Exodus and Leviticus anticipate and are fulfilled in the death of Jesus on the cross. We learn that the exodus and the exile are fulfilled in Jesus's own death, and that the exile is ended by the return of King Jesus to the temple. We learn that Jesus absorbed that exile in his life, death, burial, resurrection, and ascension. God's law for Israel anticipates following Jesus in the New Testament: those who follow Jesus are the realization of following the law of Moses. It is then profoundly Christian Bible reading to read the whole Bible as fulfilled in King Jesus and His Kingdom. Each wiki-story in the Bible has its place in its time, but it also has its place in the King and His Kingdom Story.

The Gospel

The Bible calls the Christocracy chapter of the King and His Kingdom Story the *gospel*. The gospel, however, has too often been reduced to its benefits. That is, it is reduced to *what we get out of it* and to *salvation itself*. How is it reduced? When we say the gospel is about our salvation, we make the Story's *benefits* the whole Story, and in so doing a major mistake is made: the Story is no longer about the King but about us, about me. When we keep focused on the King and His Kingdom Story, Jesus (the King) remains central. But when we make the redemption central, it becomes about us, and Jesus becomes not the subject of the Story but the means of our redemption. This is why the Christocracy chapter of the Story is described as Paul transmits it to us in 1 Corinthians 15:1–5 as a Story *first and foremost about Jesus*:

> Now, brothers and sisters, I want to remind you of the gospel I preached to you, which you received and on which you have taken your stand. By this gospel you are saved, if you hold firmly to the word I preached to you. Otherwise, you have believed in vain.
>
> For what I received I passed on to you as of first importance: that Christ died for our sins according to the Scriptures, that he was buried, that he was raised on the third day according to the Scriptures, and that he appeared to Cephas, and then to the Twelve.

That is also why the gospel sermons in the book of Acts, preached by the apostles Peter and Paul, are so uniformly focused first on the story of Jesus and then, only after we focus on the King, can we talk about the redemptive benefits that the King offers to us. Here is one example, from Peter's sermon in Acts 10:34–43:

> Then Peter began to speak: "I now realize how true it is that God does not show favoritism but accepts from every nation the one who fears him and does what is right. You know the message God sent to the people of Israel, announcing the good news of peace through Jesus Christ, who is Lord of all. You know what has happened throughout the province of Judea, beginning in Galilee after the baptism that John preached—how God anointed Jesus of Nazareth with the Holy Spirit and power, and how he went around doing good and healing all who were under the power of the devil, because God was with him.

"We are witnesses of everything he did in the country of the Jews and in Jerusalem. They killed him by hanging him on a cross, but God raised him from the dead on the third day and caused him to be seen. He was not seen by all the people, but by witnesses whom God had already chosen—by us who ate and drank with him after he rose from the dead. He commanded us to preach to the people and to testify that he is the one whom God appointed as judge of the living and the dead. All the prophets testify about him that everyone who believes in him receives forgiveness of sins through his name."

For Peter, to preach the gospel is to tell the Story of the King and His Kingdom, and after he has told the Story of Jesus he tells his audience the redemptive benefits of salvation, which we will discuss in the next section.

There are many approaches to the Bible's Story, but we need to keep the General Plot—the King and His Kingdom—in mind for each approach. When focusing here on the redemptive benefits, the approach needs to recognize that the redemptive benefits come to us through this King, the benefits are designed for us to respond in faith and obedience with thanksgiving to the King, and these benefits are to become a blessing we share with others. God's grand Story graciously includes us and draws us into redemption and glory to God alone. The Story is not about us, it is about God. This God is the Redeemer and this King is the Agent of Redemption and His Kingdom Story is a story about those who are redeemed.

Redemptive Benefit Story

Here are the basic elements of the redemptive benefit plot inside the King and His Kingdom Story to which all Bible writers have been asked to conform, whether or not they choose to bring up each specific element. The elements of the redemption plot revolve around five themes.

Plot	Theme
Creating *Eikons* (Genesis 1–2)	Oneness
Cracked *Eikons* (Genesis 3–11)	Otherness
Covenant Community (Genesis 12–Malachi)	Otherness expands
Christ, the Perfect *Eikon*, redeems (Matthew–Revelation 20)	One in Christ
Consummation (Revelation 21–22)	Perfectly One

Each author must write their story within this redemption plot, but they are given considerable freedom to tell the Story in their own way. Whether you turn to Exodus or Ezra, Malachi or Mark, or Acts or Hebrews, you must read each book as a variation on this Story.

One of the most exciting findings of those who learn to read the Bible as Story is to see how each book or author shapes the various elements of this plot, emphasizing one element or another. We cannot do this for each book of the Bible in this book, but a good place for you to begin is with one of the minor prophets, say Micah or Haggai, and see what you think each writer does with each of these elements of the plot. Once you get the hang of reading the Bible this way, you can then map the story of each author. Before long you will have a notebook full of ideas about each of these points ... but especially the ones in the middle.

The most important thing I have to say here is this: *The unity of the Bible is the King and His Kingdom Story that brings redemption. It is this Story that puts the Bible together.* Our grand systems of theology, however helpful they are, do not form the unity of the Bible; the Story that God tells forms and frames that unity. The plot I sketch below is not simply mine, though I have put my own stamp on it here and there. Essentially, this is the plot the church has always used to understand the narrative flow of the Bible's redemptive story. Recently I read a book called *On the Apostolic Preaching* by a second-century saint, Irenaeus of Lyons (in France). His book is the oldest commentary on how to read the Bible, and the plot I sketch below is essentially the same as the one Irenaeus sketches.[4] It is the only plot the church has ever had. The Bible's plot is the King and His Kingdom Story that brings redemption.

CREATING *EIKONS*: Designed for Oneness

We begin at the beginning (Genesis 1–2), which begins with God, who creates everything. The instant someone uses the word "create" in the Christian world, however, we face a problem: evolution and creation, faith and science. These debates have made it enormously difficult for modern readers to see what these two chapters are really about.[5] If we drop that concern so we can engage this text, we will discover a window onto the whole Bible.

The pinnacle of God's speaking things into existence was creating human beings. To clarify what God says about this event, I will translate two important words in Genesis 1:26–27 with unfamiliar words to grab our attention and lead us to the heart of what creation is all about. "Let us make *The Adam* [human beings] in our *Eikon* [image, likeness of God]."[6] Here are the verses set out in full:

> Then God said, "Let us make *The Adam* in our *Eikon*, in our likeness, so that they may rule over the fish in the sea and the birds in the sky, over the livestock and all the wild animals, and over all the creatures that move along the ground."
>
> So God created *The Adam* in his own *Eikon*,
>   in the *Eikon* of God he created them.

Then the Bible informs us (in Genesis 2) that God chose to "split *The Adam*" into two, into an *Ish* (man) and into an *Ishah* (woman). Thus, Genesis 2:23 reads:

She shall be called *Ishah*, for she was taken out of *Ish*.

The choice to make *The Adam* as an *Eikon* and to split *The Adam* into two, male and female, is profoundly important for understanding the story of the Bible.

The Trinitarian

God creates

The Adam

then splits the lonely *The Adam* into

Ish   in communion with   *Ishah*

and brought together
by God to form

One Flesh

In brief, the point of Genesis 1–2 is this: God wanted *The Adam* to enjoy what the Trinity had eternally enjoyed and what the Trinity continues to enjoy: perfect communion and mutuality with an equal. *The Adam* was in union with God and itself and Eden. But in another sense, *The Adam* stood alone in Genesis 2. As *The Adam* sorts through all the animals, *The Adam* was without communion with an equal. So to make the need for communion and love abundantly clear, God openly reveals that this aloneness is not what God wants for *The Adam*. God wants *The Adam* to be two in order to experience the glories of communion of love and mutuality.

Several elements in the creation story make the communion-intent of splitting *The Adam* of God clear. Unfortunately, since we've been fighting about creation and evolution for so long, we miss this stuff. One of the most important themes of Genesis 1–2 is God's creation of Adam and Eve to enjoy loving mutuality and communion. Others include God designing the entire cosmos as a temple, and our responsibility to worship God and to govern this world on God's behalf. But our love for one another is also important to Genesis 1–2. Notice these elements illustrating that God made Adam and Eve so they could enjoy one another in glorious, loving communion.

- God creates the *Ishah* from the man's rib, from his side, a symbol of companionship and mutuality rather than subordination.
- The *Ishah*, the woman, is called an *ezer kenegdo*, a companion, in Genesis 2:18: "I will make a helper [companion] suitable for him."
- After splitting *The Adam* into *Ish* and *Ishah*, God brings them back together to become "one flesh." Marriage symbolizes the union of oneness in love. Marriage completes creation. Marriage restores *The Adam* and reveals mutuality. Marriage unleashes procreation to multiply more and more *Ish*es and *Ishah*s in God's good world.

The creation story is a story of what we were made to be and do:

> *God is a Trinity, three equal persons in one(ness).*
> *God designs* Eikon*s for oneness in love.*
> *God makes* The Adam, *who isn't one with an equal.*
> *So,*
> *God splits* The Adam *into two so Adam and Eve can enjoy oneness.*

The relationship of Adam to Eve is like the relation of Father, Son, and Spirit. That is why the Bible says they are "one flesh." This word "one" is the same word used in Israel's famous daily confession, the *Shema*: "Hear, O Israel: The LORD our God, the LORD is *one*" (Deuteronomy 6:4, emphasis added). As God is "one," so Adam and Eve are "one." If you get anything out of Genesis 1–2 this is it:

> *The loving oneness of God finds earthly expression*
> *in the loving oneness of Adam and Eve.*
> *When* Eikon*s are at one with God, self, others, and the world,*
> *the glory of the One God illuminates all of life.*

Nothing in the Bible makes sense if one does not begin with the garden of Eden as a life of oneness—human beings in union with God and in communion with the self, with one another, and with the world around them. The King and His Kingdom Story redeems us into "oneness"—oneness with God, with ourselves, with others, and with the world. When this oneness is lived out, God is glorified and humans delight in that glory. When we keep focused on the end of the Story—the new heaven and the new earth—we see that the *Ish* and the *Ishah* were created for the kind of life seen in the new heaven and the new earth. That was their purpose and that is their destiny. This is our Creator's intent, but oneness was about to take a hit in the second element of the Story.

CRACKED *EIKONS*:
Distorting Oneness, Creating Otherness

Mr. and Mrs. *Eikon*, Adam and Eve, in these first two chapters of our Bible are in four oneness relationships: with God, with the self, with one another, and with Eden, the ducky little garden given to them to enjoy. But in Genesis 3, Eve, with her husband clearly in tow, chooses to do what God said not to do. As a result, they "crack the *Eikon*" and jeopardize oneness. Again, if we sit down with Genesis 1–3 and forget about evolution, creation, and scientific origins and just read this text for what it says, we learn something profound about who we are and what we are designed to do. What we learn in Genesis 3 is that sin distorts oneness because the *Eikon* is now cracked. What we learn is profoundly common to all human experience: humans do bad things to one another because humans are curved in on themselves instead of curved toward God.

The first impact of rebelling against God according to the Bible is experienced within the self, in Adam and Eve's self-consciousness. The Bible says they were ashamed of themselves because of their nakedness (Gen 3:7; cf. esp. 2:25, "Adam and his wife were both naked, and they felt no shame").

The text in Genesis then continues this march of distorting oneness in that Adam and Eve hid from God (3:8–9). Mark Twain describes their moral relation to God: "It is very difficult to look as if you have not been doing anything when the facts are the other way."[7]

Third, their oneness with each other shows the impact of sin, and they begin to blame others for their decision: Adam blames Eve (and God?), and Eve blames the serpent (3:11–13).

Fourth, to complete the march toward madness, God must open the gates into the real world and send the two cracked *Eikons* east of Eden (3:21–24). The fourfold relationship of oneness, previously enjoyed in the glorious oneness of love, was now completely cracked: they were at odds with God, with self, with one another, and with the world. *Oneness had become otherness.* Instead of dwelling in Eden, they dwelled in exile from Eden.

Instead of experiencing one another in oneness, they began to experience one another as "others." In fact, Genesis 3 predicts something that tells the story of human relationships: "Your desire will be for your husband, and he will rule over you" (3:16). This is not a curse as if this *must happen forever and always.* Instead, the desire to rule rises in the human heart because oneness is cracked. Instead of loving one another as they love themselves, they will now desire to climb over the other and on top of the other in order to control and dominate. This fallen story of otherness leads to death.

But the good story of oneness leads to life. The entire rest of the Bible, aiming as it will toward Jesus Christ because he is its King, is about turning *Eikons* bent on otherness to *Eikons* basking in oneness with God, with self, with others, and with the world. The benefit of the King's redemption is a life of being restored, as it were, to Eden. Better yet, it is a life of being prepared for the final Eden, the new heaven and the new earth, the Kingdom of God.

The problem that the fall creates can be called "sin," though that word is not used in Genesis 3. Sin is a cracked relationship of otherness with God, with self, with others, and with the world. The redemptive plan of the Bible is to restore humans into a oneness relationship with God, self, others, and the world. *This otherness problem is what the gospel "fixes," and the story of the Bible is the story of God's people struggling with otherness and searching for oneness.*

COVENANT COMMUNITY:
The Struggle for Oneness

Here too many Bible readers lose their way and jump ahead because they've limited the otherness problem to God and self, not to mention they lose contact with the King and His Kingdom Story. Many Christians want to skip from Genesis 3 to the Gospels or Romans 3. Let's remind ourselves of how many of us read the Bible: our plot is creation, fall, and redemption. So now that we've got the fall, let's get to redemption.

I like this creation-fall-redemption plot, but there's something missing. (Like 1,033 pages!) It is right to see the plot move from creation and fall to redemption, but *how* God chooses to redeem is a giant (three-hundred pound!) blue parakeet in the Bible for many readers. The story of the Bible is creation, fall, *and then covenant community*—page after page of community—*as the context* in which our wonderful *redemption* takes place. That redemptive story about the covenant community gains its shape from the King and His Kingdom Story: our focus is to be on God, who at this point in the Story is the sole King (Theocracy). This King designs immediately a way for cracked *Eikons* to experience communion with the King and with others in the covenant community called Israel, called "the kingdom" often enough in the Bible.[8]

Reading the Bible as Story teaches us one thing—that it is the *otherness with others* that most concerns God. Otherness of the self and God is the assumption, but otherness with others is the focus of the Story. We in the Western world are obsessed with our individual relationship with God, which leads us to read the Bible as morsels of blessings and promises and as Rorschach inkblots. But reading the Bible as Story opens up a need so deep we sometimes aren't aware we need it: oneness with others under the King who rules his Kingdom.

Not so fast, God must be saying to the many individualistic Bible readers who want to shake the fall loose by making a beeline to the cross and resurrection. That's not the way God wants us to read the Bible. What does God do after the fall in the Story? God lets his cracked *Eikons* foolishly fiddle around for a few chapters. At the end of this time, God does a do-over with Noah and the flood. Then—and I can't emphasize this enough—God forms a *covenanted community*—a community in which they are to find oneness with God, with self, with *others*, and with the world. Here we discover God as King over God's people, the kingdom of his people.

This covenanted community, which focuses on oneness with others, will shape the rest of the Bible. God's idea of redemption is community-shaped. Oneness cannot be achieved just between God and self; rather, oneness involves God, self, *and others, and the world around us.* There are pages and pages about this stuff. If we don't care about how Israel is faring, about how Judah is faring, about kings and prophets and worship centers, or about how Israel longed for the Messiah when oppressed by Rome, we will find the Bible boring indeed. Only after this lengthy set of stories about Israel do we arrive at the New Testament.

Then, in the New Testament, we get the same emphasis as in the Old Testament because we now read about how God's Spirit invaded that little messianic community and drove it out into the Roman Empire—and we are asked to care about how these local communities (i.e., churches) did in the Roman Empire.

Just pick up your Bible and start in Genesis 12 and skim through Esther, some 450 pages in my Bible, and you will observe the story of God's people in the realities of otherness with others and oneness with others. God cares deeply about this—for pages, for centuries. Creation, fall, redemption—yes. But, and here's what so many miss, the *way* God works redemption in this world is *through his covenanted community—first Israel, then the church.* The redemptive benefit of the King and His Kingdom finds concrete embodiment in the covenant community, the people of the kingdom.

Otherness Gets the Last Word

But there is a massive problem staring at us as we read this Story: *God's people don't get the job done.* I don't know if this strikes you, but I believe it should: something is terribly wrong with God's covenant people. While there are some high points, like the exodus from Egypt and the return from exile, the people never truly achieve the design God has for them. Here are just a few of the lowlights:

- Only Noah and his family survive the flood and then the man messes things up immediately.
- Abraham is God's chosen father of his people and he lies about his wife.
- Moses murders, rescues Israel at the exodus, gives them the Torah and a worship center, and then sins in the desert.
- Israel gets into the promised land, but they can't shake off idolatries.
- David is the king, and he can't control himself.
- David's son builds a great temple, but he can't control himself either, so within a generation the "oneness" nation becomes a "twoness" nation.
- One of those nations gets deported to Assyria while the other, Judah, hangs on longer but finds itself eventually in Babylon.
- Then God, in his rich mercy, ends the exile and leads Judah back to the promised land and they rebuild the temple and ... the whole thing starts all over again. Otherness seemingly gets the last word.

Woven into this story is a deep thread of failure that creates otherness. How to resolve the deep thread of failure drives the story onward. Deep within the fabric of this story is that *Israel won't get the job done until the job is done for them.* That job won't get done until Jesus, Israel's long-awaited Messiah, comes. The King will bring oneness in His Kingdom.

CHRIST, THE PERFECT *EIKON*:
Oneness Restored

The Bible's story has a plot headed in the direction of a *person*. And that same story is headed in the direction of a *community* "in" that person. This is a way of repeating that in the story there is a redemptive benefit—salvation—but the focus of that redemptive benefit is the King himself.

Everything God designed for *Eikon*s is actually lived out by Jesus. Everything *Eikon*s are to do comes by being "in Christ" or by becoming "one" with Jesus Christ.

The good gospel things of becoming one with God, self, others, and the world happen to us only *when we are united to Christ, when we become "one" in Christ.* Let me say this succinctly: The story of the Bible then aims at Galatians 3:28:

> There is neither Jew nor Gentile, neither slave nor free, nor is there male and female, for you are all one in Christ Jesus.

The story of the Bible takes the otherness of cracked *Eikon*s and directs us toward Jesus Christ, in whom alone we find oneness.

God accomplishes four things in Christ, each of which contributes to the restoration of oneness. These four moments do the job, end the otherness, and create the oneness that the story of the Bible has been yearning for. We need each other; without that, otherness continues to reign; but when the strength of each is tapped into, oneness can be found.

Incarnation of the King

In his *incarnate life*, when he becomes one with us, King Jesus recapitulates, or relives, Israel's (our) history. He becomes one of us. In fact, he becomes *all of us* in one divine-human being. Jesus is all Adam and Eve were designed to be and more; he loves the Father absolutely and he loves himself absolutely and he loves others absolutely and he loves the world absolutely. The King in the Kingdom Story is the Oneness Story in one person.

Death of the King

Humans are guilty before God according to Genesis 3; the punishment for that guilt is *death*. Notice how Eve tells the serpent what God had said to her: "You must not eat fruit from the tree that is in the middle of the garden, and you must not touch it, or you will *die*" (v. 3; emphasis added). Otherness leads to death; *the* problem to resolve is death. Thus, because God's intent is to make the *Eikons* what he designed them to be, God takes on our death—our punishment for sin—so that we don't have to die eternally.

God did push Adam and Eve out of the garden of Eden lest they should "live forever" in their "otherness condition." That act of God was an act of mercy—an act that ultimately anticipates the cross of Christ. Jesus's act of dying our death *forgives* us of our complicity in Adam and Eve's sin by assuming what we deserved: death. Three prepositions tell the Story of Jesus's death:

- Jesus dies *with us*—he dies our death and we die with him. He becomes one with our death and we become one with his death.
- Jesus dies *instead of us*—that final death is taken on board by him and we don't have to die that final death.
- Jesus dies *for us*—by assuming our death, we are forgiven of our sin.

But forgiveness is only the beginning of restoring us to oneness.

Resurrection and Ascension of the King

Eikons, forgiven as they are, are now only in neutral. They are no longer dead. That's not enough. What do humans need? Life. Jesus is raised *for us*. I wish more of us would see how significant the resurrection is for God's redemptive plan, for the story that unfolds in the Bible. By becoming one with the Resurrected One through faith, we are raised to new life. Why? So that we might stand up and walk again as *Eikon*s are designed to live—with God, with self, with others, and with the world. The resurrection creates dead *Eikon*s walking again.

Above I sketched briefly what the Bible means by "gospel"; in these points now I am rehearsing the gospel itself. We are telling the story of Jesus as the King and His Kingdom Story that brings redemptive benefits: the King became one of us, the King died for us, and the King was raised for us. Entering into that King's story brings us into the Kingdom and all its benefits.

Pentecost of the King and the Spirit

And now the only need left is the power to create oneness, which is precisely what Pentecost is all about. God sends the promised Spirit of the new covenant so that the covenant community can be empowered to be glowing *Eikon*s, people who are restored to oneness with God, self, others, and the world. The most decisive impact of Pentecost, where the gift of the Spirit is made clear, is not speaking in tongues but community formation (oneness). Read Acts 2. Here you can glimpse a view of the new heaven and the new earth, the kingdom of God taking shape in the world among God's people, and you can see that the King and His Kingdom bring redemption and empowerment to be what God wanted Adam and Eve to be in Eden.

It is no surprise, then, that Luke's account of Pentecost returns to this theme of oneness. Acts 2:42–47 focuses on the oneness that was achieved now that God's work was finished. "All the believers were together and had everything *in common*" (2:44). Acts 4:32 says this: "All the believers were *one* in heart and mind. No one claimed that any of their possessions was their own, but *they shared everything* they had" (emphasis added in both passages). This is the story the whole Bible was designed to tell: otherness overturned and oneness restored. It happens in the covenant community that is "one" in Christ. The King and His Kingdom bring a redemption called "oneness."

But again, notice that the focus of this oneness in the Bible is oneness with *others*. Once oneness is restored between God and the self, it begins to work itself out into oneness with others and this world. Love of God is joined with love of others. These words of Paul reveal the plan:

> All this is from God, who reconciled us to himself through Christ and gave us the ministry of reconciliation. (2 Corinthians 5:18)

It's all right here: we (the self) are at one with God, and this leads to oneness (reconciliation) with others in this world.

CONSUMMATION: Oneness Forever

The Perfect *Eikon*'s work, however, is a two-stage work, not unlike the blind man who first saw what he thought were trees and then, once Jesus applied a second dressing of Deep Magic, could see fully. King Jesus's first work, the accomplishment of oneness in his first coming, stands now as partial redemption as it moves us toward the Kingdom, the new heaven and the new earth. The fullness of that work, complete union and perfect oneness, when God once again opens the gates to Eden for Adams and Eves, will be consummated only when Christ returns to establish the new heaven and the new earth. When that happens, Mr. and Mrs. *Eikon* will bask in the glory of union with God, where they will themselves be so radiant as to draw attention to God's oneness as the origin of it all.

This, or something quite close, is the plot of the story that Jesus expects everyone to use to tell their wiki-stories. I am tempted as a Bible teacher to work this out now for every book in the Bible, for each wiki-story of the Story. But this book is not an introduction to the Bible. Instead, it is about how we are to live the Bible out and how blue parakeets force us to rethink how we read the Bible. This means that we need an example, and I have chosen how women are gifted to perform ministries in the church as our example. This issue will reveal how reading the Bible's General Plot (the King and His

Kingdom) and its redemptive benefits as a oneness-otherness-oneness story gives us discernment for today. It will give us the desire to go back to the Bible with respect for the Great Tradition so we can have the courage to make the Story real in our world. But before we get to that discussion, we want to delve into an element of Bible reading that is nearly always neglected:

> If the Bible is Story, how do we read it?
> The answer: We listen to God.
> Thus the question might better be stated: What is our relationship to the Bible?

Turn the page.

PART 2

LISTENING

What Do I Do with the Bible?

"Therefore everyone who hears these words of mine and puts them into practice is like a wise man who built his house on the rock. The rain came down, the streams rose, and the winds blew and beat against that house; yet it did not fall, because it had its foundation on the rock. But everyone who hears these words of mine and does not put them into practice is like a foolish man who built his house on sand. The rain came down, the streams rose, and the winds blew and beat against that house, and it fell with a great crash."

Jesus, according to Matthew 7:24–27

He said to them, "Therefore every teacher of the law who has become a disciple in the kingdom of heaven is like the owner of a house who brings out of his storeroom new treasures as well as old."

Jesus, according to Matthew 13:52

Blessed Lord, who caused all Holy Scriptures to be written for our learning: Grant me so to hear them, read, mark, learn, and inwardly digest them, that I may embrace and ever hold fast the blessed hope of everlasting life, which you have given us in our Savior Jesus Christ, who lives and reigns with you and the Holy Spirit, one God, for ever and ever. Amen.

"But when he, the Spirit of truth, comes, he will guide you into all the truth."

Jesus, according to John 16:13

CHAPTER 6

FROM PAPER TO PERSON

How Do We Read
God's Words?

A student of mine majoring in art brought a piece of her artwork to class. Before others had found the way to their seats, she brought it to me, placed it in front of me, and with a little flush in her face said, "I thought you might like to see this."

Well, of course, I did, and because the artist was standing next to me and because I wanted to be sensitive to her personal creation, I took a good, long look at it and said, "I really like this." Then I asked her the common question art students don't want to answer: "What are you trying to say in this?"

Again, a little more flush in the face, and her response: "What do you see?" Two things were going on here. First, she cared deeply what I saw in that piece and wasn't about to tell me what she was trying to say. Second, and even more important, this piece of art was deeply personal to her. It said something from the depth of her soul. It was a revelation of her heart. She put her soul on display in her piece of work in order to evoke response from others.

The Bible is like this. It is the creation of God, who is the Artist, and the Artist stands next to us as we read the Bible. I sometimes think we forget what we are reading. The Bible is *God's* story. When I say this, I am making a claim so extraordinary we may be tempted to skip

93

over it. The Bible, so we believe, is unlike all other books because these words are *God's* words, this book is *God's* book, and this story is *God's* story. The overarching King and His Kingdom Story with its inner story of redemption is *God's* story and *God's* redemption.

Knowing that the Bible is God's story and that God stands next to us as we read it leads to an important question: How do we read a story that we claim is *God's* story? To dig deeper than these questions, we need to ask a better one: "What is my *relationship* to the Bible?" This question is one of the most important questions we can ask about reading the Bible, and I am a little startled that so many who talk about the Bible skip over the question. Too many stop short by asking only, "How can I learn to understand the Bible?"

But even that question is not good enough. The real question at the bottom of all of them is this: "What is my relationship to the *God* of the Bible?" Our relationship is not so much with the Bible but with the *God* of the Bible. There's a difference that makes a big difference.

Deep Inside

I grew up with a specific kind of approach to the Bible, and it has taken me a long time to develop a more complete understanding of the Bible. I grew up with what might be called the "authority approach" to the Bible. Simply put, it works with these words: God, revelation, inspiration, inerrancy, authority, and submission. Let me summarize: God *revealed* himself in the Bible. To make sure the Bible's authors got things right, God's Spirit was at work *inspiring* what they wrote. Because God, who is always true, produced the Bible, it is *inerrant* (without error). As God's true Word, therefore, it is our final *authority*, and our response to the Bible must be one of *submission*. I believe this is an approach that fosters a specific but inadequate kind of relationship with the Bible.

Deep inside I knew there was something wrong with framing our view of the Bible like this. It took me years to put my finger on it. Perhaps I can say it like this: When I read my Bible, the words "authority" and "submission" don't describe the dynamic I experience. It is not that I think these words are wrong, but I know there is far more to reading the Bible than submitting to authority.

As a college student, one of my favorite chapters of the Bible was Psalm 119. Why? Because the psalmist and I shared something: we both loved God's Word, and we both loved to study its words. But the psalmist's approach to his Bible—and you can just sit down and read it—is not expressed like this: "Your words are authoritative, and I am called to submit to them." Instead, his approach is more like this: "Your words are delightful, and I love to do what you ask." The difference between these two approaches is enormous. One of them is a relationship to the Bible; the other is a relationship with God.

Here are some of my favorite lines from Psalm 119, and it is out of words like these that a "relational approach" to the Bible can be formed:

- I delight in your decrees; I will not neglect your word (v. 16).
- My soul is consumed with longing for your laws at all times (v. 20).
- Your statutes are my delight; they are my counselors (v. 24).
- Direct me in the path of your commands, for there I find delight (v. 35).
- I will walk about in freedom, for I have sought out your precepts (v. 45).
- For I delight in your commands because I love them (v. 47).
- Your decrees are the theme of my song wherever I lodge (v. 54).
- You are good, and what you do is good; teach me your decrees (v. 68).
- The law from your mouth is more precious to me than thousands of pieces of silver and gold (v. 72).
- How sweet are your words to my taste, sweeter than honey to my mouth! (v. 103).
- Your statutes are wonderful; therefore I obey them (v. 129).

Here is perhaps the entire psalm in one line: "I have sought your face with all my heart" (v. 58). God's face! How cool is that? A relational approach to the Bible finds room for words like "delight" and "my soul is consumed" and "counselors" and "freedom" and "love" and the "theme of my song" and "good" and "precious" and "sweet" and "wonderful." The view of Scripture I grew up with didn't have room for such words. Deep inside I knew there was more.

What I learned about the authority approach to the Bible was that it is not personal enough or relational enough. It does not express enough of why it is that God gave us the Bible.

What Do You Teach?

I'm a professor, and every November, Bible and religion professors gather together for an academic conference. Truth be told, the best thing about this conference is that we get to see our academic friends. Gathering with friends introduces us to our friends' friends. Such casual conversation leads to a common question: "What do you teach?" I've been asked this question hundreds of times. We wear name tags, but they have only our name and the school we teach at.

One time, as a young professor, I asked the common professorial question to a wise and gentle professor: "What do you teach?" His response stunned me: "I teach students. What do you teach?" He made me realize in a new way what I am actually called to do. I wager that about 99 percent of professors who have been asked that question will give you the subject matter they teach—Old Testament, New Testament, Judaism, church history, systematic theology, and the like. That wise professor's answer and question changed how I approach what I do. I need to remind myself of this as I enter the class: I'm not teaching a *subject* (Jesus's temptations) but *students* who need to come into contact with the subject matter (Jesus's temptations).

The standard approach, where the focus is teaching a subject, is not relational and personal enough. Teachers are teaching *students* a particular subject matter. They are not teaching a subject matter to students. The difference is a big difference.

What I'm saying is that the authority approach to the Bible is not enough. There is more to the Bible than its subject matter. In fact, the dynamic involved is earth-shattering and ought to revolutionize how we approach the Bible. It is, as noted above, the *relational approach*. So let me build a relational approach to the Bible, one that finds resonance with the delightful obedience of the psalmist, one that sees God's words as personal words, and you can see what you think. I will focus on five ideas that will fill out what we mean by reading the Bible as Story so we can learn to live it out. The relational approach turns the Bible from facts-only to facts-that-lead-to-engagement with the God of the Bible.

The Relational Approach to the Bible

God and the Bible

The relational approach *distinguishes God from the Bible*. God existed before the Bible existed; God exists independently of the Bible now. God is a person; the Bible is words on paper or on a screen. God gave us this papered Bible to lead us to love his person. But the person and the paper are not the same.

The distinction between a person's words and the person is an important one, but I am not sure we Christians have always made that distinction. Perhaps this will make it clear: I love my wife, Kris; I do not love Kris's words. I encounter Kris through her words, but I am summoned to love her, not her words. Sometimes I say to her, "I love what you say to me," but that is a form of expression. What I'm really saying is, "I love you, and your words communicate your love for me."

We need to see the same distinction with the Bible. If we don't, we set ourselves up for problems. Even when the psalmist says he loves God's commands, the larger context shows that it is God whom he loves, and God's words extend the person onto paper. Notice how often the psalmist says "you" in Psalm 119; my NIV has forty-one such occurrences, as in "You are my portion, LORD" (Psalm 119:57). Notice also how often he says "I" (109 times). This combination of "you" and "I" is a revelation of the relational approach. A relational approach seeks a relationship with the person behind the paper words "I" and "you" in Psalm 119.

Missing the difference between God and the Bible is a bit like the person who reads Jonah and spends hours and hours figuring out if a human can live inside a whale—and what kind of whale it was—but never encounters God. The book is about Jonah's God, not Jonah's whale. Or it is like the athlete who becomes enamored with her soccer uniform and forgets that she's got a game to play regardless of what the uniform looks like. Or perhaps it is like a college student who, like, forgets that the point of college is, like, studying and learning and not (only) finding a wonderful social life. Or it is like the person who is obsessed with the appearance of the church building and misses the point that the building is facilitation of worship and fellowship, of loving God and loving others.

True, you can't have Jonah's prophecy without the whale, you can't have a soccer game without some uniforms, you can't have college without social relations, and it is harder to conduct a worship service without some sacred space; but the first element is distinguishable from the second. So it is with God and the Bible. Once again, God speaks to us in words, but God is more than the Bible.

Here, then, is our first step in a proper relationship with the Bible: we must distinguish God from the Bible.

God ≠ Bible

The Bible as God's Written Communication

A relational approach also focuses on the Bible as *God's written communication with us.* The Bible is like a spoken message or a letter from God addressed to God's people, not unlike the words we might speak or write in order to communicate something to someone we love. Once again, we must pause briefly to consider what we are saying. God is not the Bible. To make the Bible into God is idolatrous.

The Bible is God's communication—in the form of words—with us. We can trot out all the important words about the Bible—inspiration, revelation, truth, etc. But those are not enough. Behind all of these words is the astounding claim we Christians make: the Bible is God's communication with us in the form of words. For the papered book to be what it is intended to be, God's communication with us, we need to receive those words as God's words addressed to God's people.

God communicates → Bible → with God's people

Listening

If we are invited to love God by reading the Bible as God's communication with us, then a relational approach to the Bible invites us *to listen to God (the person) speak in the Bible and to engage God as we listen.* The relational approach knows the Bible is filled with wiki-stories—timely stories of the Story by human authors. But our approach believes the Bible is more than human wiki-stories. These authors are *divinely guided so that their wiki-stories tell God's story.* If we once admit this, we are summoned to stand in front of the Bible as *those listening to God's story.* (We may argue with God and the Bible and we may ask questions, but that all comes after we listen. Our next chapter will explore the theme of listening.)

God communicates → Bible → with God's *listening* people

The Bible and the Big Conversation

One of my favorite discoveries about the relational approach is that we enter into *the Bible's own conversation and the conversation the church has had about the Bible.* The Bible is a lively conversation of one author or prophet or apostle with another as each listens to God speaking. If you read Deuteronomy and then read Job—I know, that is not a typical evening's reading—you observe that Job is engaging Deuteronomy in a serious conversation. Yes, Job says to Moses, there is a correlation between obedience and blessing, but there is more to it than that. Job learned, and God reveals to us, that sometimes God is at work outside the correlation of obedience and blessing.

Another example: Most of us, after reading James, say that we are justified not by faith alone but also by works (James 2:24). We recognize that James is in conversation with Paul, with someone like Paul, or with someone who is distorting Paul. Paul emphasizes justification by faith and James emphasizes works, and reading these two in the web of an ongoing conversation puts each in its proper context.

And there's a second conversation going on. Just as the biblical authors converse with one another, so Christians in the history of the church have conversed with one another—about the Bible's own conversation. Church history is a series of conversations about The Conversations in the Bible. Some, as we sketched in the second chapter, believe we can ignore what God has said to others; they leapfrog over the history of the church to return to the Bible alone. This approach, sadly, ignores the conversation God has directed throughout the history of the church. But if we learn to read the Bible *with* tradition—and it's a bit like sitting down at a table with three or four generations in our family on Christmas holiday—we can enter into this big conversation in which we can learn from the wisdom of the past. Our privilege and our challenge are to carry on that conversation in our world today.

God communicates → Bible → with God's listening people
in conversation

Relationship with God

I bring it all together into one central focus now: A relational approach believes *our relationship to the Bible is transformed into a relationship with the God who speaks to us in and through the Bible.* We come back now to our first observation: If we distinguish God from the Bible, then we also learn that in listening to God's words in the Bible we are in search of more than a relationship with words on paper, we are seeking a relationship with the person who speaks on paper. *Our relationship to the Bible is actually a relationship with the God of the Bible.* We want to emphasize that we don't ask what the Bible says, we ask what God says to us in that Bible. The difference is a difference between paper and person.

God communicates → Bible → with God's listening people
in conversation
↓
relationship with God of the Bible

Let me put this now one final way: God gave the Bible not so we can know *it* but so we can know and love God through *it*.

Professors and Their Administrators

Maybe another analogy will point us in the right direction. My relationship to the president and provost and dean of my university, Northern Seminary, might be called a relationship of authority. William Shiell, our president, and Jason Gile, our dean, are in one sense authority figures. They have more authority than I do—and they should have. Frankly, knowing the kind of life an administrator is called to live, I am quite happy to cede that authority to them. Actually, I'm not ceding anything to them. They are given authority by the board of trustees, and my responsibility is to acknowledge their authority. However you look at it, they have a kind of authority I don't have.

However, it's all about framing the relationship. If I frame their relationship to me in terms of authority—as in "They are my authority figures"—then I have to frame my relationship to them in terms of sub-mission—as in "I do whatever they say." If a professor's responsibility is simply one of submission—which it isn't at our school—the whole relationship is framed by words like "hierarchy," "authority," and "obedience."

Is this a proper way of framing the relationship of an administrator and a professor? I hope not. In fact, if an administrator chooses to frame his or her relationship to professors in terms of authority—as in "I am in charge. Listen to me. Do this or that!"—then the dynamic heart of the relationship has gone south. Administrators who find this approach appealing are usually in trouble or they are saying the professor is in trouble. If a man or woman frames his or her relationship to a spouse or to children in terms of the word "authority," you can bet your sweet bippy that the relationship is not what it should be.

What if we frame our relationship differently? What if, instead of framing a professor's relationship to the administration in terms of authority, we frame it in terms of love, trust, and conversation? To be sure, within that frame there is authority and sometimes debate and disagreement. I've had my share of that. But the point we are making is that the framing of the relationship is very important. What words do we use that best frame such a relationship? I am certain of this: authority and submission are not the best terms.

Let's extend this to another realm. For reasons better left untouched right now, some traditional Christians have framed the relationship of a husband and a wife in terms of hierarchy, authority, and submission. Why? Because Paul and Peter use such terms in their letters (see Ephesians 5:21–33 and 1 Peter 3:1–7). Apart from studying these passages more carefully in their own contexts, which story reading of the Bible insists on in light of passages like Galatians 3:28 or Colossians 3:11, we are apt to frame a husband-wife relationship in such terms, but we would be making a serious mistake. There's a lot more to it than this. Any relationship of a husband and wife that is not foremost a frame of love will distort the relationship.

The story of the Bible has one book devoted to husbands and wives, the Song of Songs, and before one ever reads Ephesians 5 or 1 Peter 3, one should dip deeply into the Song's intimate secrets. The framing of a husband and wife relationship in terms of love—the kind of delightful, playful love found in Song of Songs—completely changes things.

So too if we frame our relationship to the Bible in terms of authority, we will inevitably have authoritarian issues emerging as theology. Here is a conclusion that has taken me years to come to: without denying the legitimacy of the various terms in the authority approach, those who have a proper relationship to the Bible *never need to speak of the Bible as their authority nor do they speak of their submission to the Bible.* They are so in tune with God, so in love with him, that the word "authority" is swallowed up in loving God. Even more, the word "submission" is engulfed in the disposition of listening to God speak through the Bible and in the practice of doing what God calls us to do.

Once we come to terms with the relational approach of the Bible and we frame the Bible as God's story in the form of a plot with wiki-stories, we begin to think about our *relationship to the Bible.* If submission falls short of how we respond to the Bible, what word best captures our response to the Bible? Turn the page.

CHAPTER 7

GOD SPEAKS, WE LISTEN

What Is Our Relationship to the God Who Speaks to Us in the Bible?

One day in my office a student turned our conversation to the right set of beliefs about the Bible. He asked, "Why does my youth pastor ask me all the time if I still believe in the 'inerrancy' of the Bible?" I was about to explain to him the history of the doctrine of Scripture and the battles Christians have waged over the Bible when he interrupted me with these words (and this is how he said it): "You know, Scot, I really don't give a d—n what my youth pastor's view of the Bible is because he doesn't give one frickin' dime to the poor and he's never met a homeless person in his life and he didn't even know about Darfur when I mentioned it to him at Christmas." This student obviously was a bit worked up, so I sat back to listen.

He continued, "My view of the Bible is this: I read it often—not every day—and I *do* what I think God tells me to do. I don't make much money, but I give . . ." He was about to tell me what percent he gave to the poor but stopped himself because, he told me later, he thought it might be self-congratulatory. Then he asked a pointed question, a good one: "What good is 'inerrancy' if you don't *do* what God says?" His next question shook me a bit: "If I do what God says to me through the Bible, doesn't that show that my view of the Bible is the right one?" Students. You gotta love 'em.

How many of us know our *doctrine* about the Bible but don't *do what the God of the Bible says*? To paraphrase our Lord's brother, "What good is it, my brothers and sisters, if people claim to have [the right view of the Bible] but do not practice what it says?" (James 2:14, retooled). Believing in inspiration, revelation, infallibility or inerrancy, and authority describes one's *view* of the Bible. Fine. We need to talk about our view of the Bible. But that isn't enough.

We have too many today who say, "Now that you've got the right view of the Bible, you're on the side of the angels." Having the right view isn't the point of the Bible. We need to have not only a "view" of the Bible but also a "relationship" to the God of the Bible. *Knowing* water will hydrate the body and *believing* that drinking five bottles of water daily is healthy are not the same as *drinking* the water until one's body is properly hydrated. Those who drink the water are the ones who really know and believe. Having the right view of the Bible is knowing and believing, but we need to move to the next step: engaging the God of that Bible.

Jesus told a parable that teaches this point. It is called the parable of the two sons (see Matthew 21:28–32). Here's the parable part:

"What do you think? There was a man who had two sons. He went to the first and said, 'Son, go and work today in the vineyard.'

"'I will not,' he answered, but later he changed his mind and went.

"Then the father went to the other son and said the same thing. He answered, 'I will, sir,' but he did not go.

"Which of the two did what his father wanted?"

"The first," they answered.

Agreeing-and-not-doing and not-agreeing-but-finally-doing are two different things. A relational approach focuses on the second.

We must begin an entirely new conversation that gets us beyond the right *view* of the Bible to one that seeks to answer this question: "What is our *relationship* to the God of the Bible?" I suggest that the answer to that question, and one that comes to mind immediately for the one who reads the Bible attentively, is simple: Our relationship to the God of the Bible is *to listen to God so we can love him more deeply and love others more completely.* If God's ultimate design for us is to love God and to love others, we can acquire that love only by learning to listen to God.

Listening and loving are intimately connected.

Yo, Scot, You Doin' Anything?

A student knocked on my door one fall during the first week of classes. "Yo, Scot, you doin' anything?" she asked.

"No, of course not," I said in what has to be one of my more common understatements. "Come on in." You should know that the average college student spends nine hours a week studying. If that same student were taking sixteen hours of credit, that means she would be occupied with being a student twenty-five hours a week. You do the math.

She sat down in a chair next to me and asked me without a moment's hesitation, "What do you think about homosexuality?" To which I thought to myself, *Wow, that's a big question to ask a teacher you've seen exactly once.* She must have realized that and quickly asked another, "What do you think of the war in Iraq?"

Now I had a flashing insight. I knew this student wasn't in my office to ask questions or to look for answers to big questions. She wanted to talk to one of her professors. Having had experience at this, I sensed she was homesick and wanted to be with a parent-like figure. So I asked her about herself, and she asked me a brief question about my blog and my wife and my kids. I then asked her a question, and for the next twenty minutes she went on in a nonstop prattle. Suddenly looking at her cell phone, which doubles as a watch, she exclaimed, "Ohmigosh [that's one word nowadays]! I'm late for class." She slung her backpack over her shoulder, hurried out the door, down the steps, and then, as if realizing she hadn't quite made closure, yelled back, "This was fun. Let's do it again sometime!" *Sure*, I thought.

This student grew to see me as one of her favorite professors for one reason: I had enough time to listen to her. I never quite knew what she saw in me, but I was all ears for her on many occasions. She would stop by—"Yo, Scot, you doin' anything?" (No, of course not)—and we would chat and I would listen and then she would leave. Sometimes that's all it takes. Listening and loving, we must never forget, are connected.

Kris and I talk all the time; she asks me about my day and I talk my way through the day. I ask her about her day, and she talks her way through her day. Then we're done. I don't think we say to ourselves, "Now I'm listening; listening is loving; therefore, I'm loving now." Instead, listening to each other is our mode of existence. (I must confess that I'm nowhere near the listener Kris is.)

Reading the Bible is an act of listening. Listening, to quote the title of a popular book, is an act of love.[1]

Listening as Love of God and Others

The most perceptive book about how to listen to the Bible is by Alan Jacobs, a professor at Wheaton College. Jacobs reminds us that *words matter because words flow out of persons*. In *A Theology of Reading: The Hermeneutics of Love*, Jacobs articulates a theory of reading that emerges from two important observations:

1. Written words are *personal* communication from one person to another.
2. The proper relationship of a Christian to a person's communication is to *love* that person by *listening* to their words.[2]

Words on a page, Jacobs informs us over and over, are not just little squiggles of information on paper. Written words are personal exchanges, personal deposits of a person. Our words come from the depth of our heart and soul, and they extend who we are. That is why we care what others think of what we say. Not everything we say is this serious, of course. When I say "How much?" at the grocery store, not too much is on the line (unless, of course, I don't have enough money in my pocket). But statements like "I love you" and questions like "Will you be here for me?" and promises like "I will be with you" are personal exchanges. Words matter because they represent persons. *Because words represent persons, how we respond to words matters.*

When someone writes me an email, it is far easier for me to disagree with the words, scan what has been said, or even casually dismiss the words than if the person were standing in front of me and saying the same thing. I am much more likely, and you probably are too, to listen to a person than to an email. In fact, it would be unchristian to refuse to listen to, to ignore, or to dismiss a person facing me. Jacobs reminds us that the Christian summons to love our neighbor as ourselves, what I call the "Jesus Creed," teaches us that *written words are as serious as the spoken word.*

Jacobs calls this Christian understanding of words "the hermeneutics of love." "The hermeneutics of love requires that books and authors ... be understood and treated as neighbors."[3] This means that when our neighbors speak, we listen. Love listens.

Listening in the Bible

Did you know that the words "listen" and "hear" are found more than 1,500 times in the Bible? Klyne Snodgrass, a friend and former colleague, studied each of these references and came to this realization: "The biggest complaint in Scripture is that people do not listen to God. Theirs is a freely chosen deafness." Choosing not to listen contradicts the *Shema*: "*Hear*, O Israel: . . . Love the LORD your God" (Deuteronomy 6:4–5, emphasis added). Klyne then reached this insightful conclusion: "The greatest command is to love God; the prior command [to loving God] is the command to hear."[4] Love of God and love of others can happen only when we have ears to listen to God speak.

The words "hear" or "listen" in the Bible operate on at least three levels (I will provide my own translations): attention, absorption, and action. *Attention* opens our ears. If you've ever been around a group of people speaking a language you don't know, you instantly recognize what Paul meant in 1 Corinthians 14:2: "For those who speak in a [spiritual] tongue do not speak to other people but to God. Humans do not *attend to* what they are saying [because they cannot understand it]; they are speaking mysteries by the Spirit" (my translation).

A second, deeper level of meaning can be found in Solomon's great prayer request after he became king. This expression pertains to *absorption*, when our ears let God's voice in so that it fills our being: "So give your servant a [*hearing*] heart" (1 Kings 3:9). And God did give him a "wise and discerning heart" (3:12), a heart that fully absorbed what God was saying.

The third level puts legs on the ears as *action*, as Jesus says: "Therefore everyone who *hears* these words of mine and puts them into practice is like a wise man who built his house on the rock" (Matthew 7:24). Or as when the Father says to the disciples of Jesus when he was transfigured: "*Listen* to him!" (17:5, emphasis added in both passages). Both of these speak of a listening that has ears that lead to certain behaviors.

When we read the Bible as Story and develop a relationship with the God of the Bible,

- we learn to *listen* to and for God in the Bible as we read it;
- we are *attentive* enough to recognize God's voice and let it in;
- we *absorb* what God says so that it floods our inner being; and
- we *act* on what we have heard from God.

Listening to our fellow humans is an art, and you need to get better at listening. So do I. Listening to the Bible is also an art, and you need to get better at that as well. So do I. Sometimes we don't listen. Another way of saying this is that sometimes we listen but not well—there is some attention, but no absorption or action.

Not Listening

I was fifteen. My driver's education instructor had directed me to drive to Reed Park in Freeport, Illinois. The park was near the Little League diamond, where there was a parking lot with a series of graveled ovals around which and through which we beginners all learned to turn a vehicle safely and accurately. On this day it was my turn to drive backward, which I was about to learn was not easy.

At the far end of the parking lot, my instructor directed me to stop the car and begin backing up. I listened (in the sense of attended) and began to do what I thought he had instructed me to do. To my left was a slight hill, maybe three feet high, extending the length of the lot. Somehow I managed to get both wheels on the driver's side on that hill and the instructor's side still on the level gravel oval. We were both leaning left to maintain our balance.

He gave me more instruction, I listened (in the sense of attended to), but I did not absorb what he was saying. The situation got worse as I backed even farther up the hill. I was frustrated, as only a fifteen-year-old male (now shamed in public) can be.

I stopped the car, put it in park, and offered a suggestion that indicated I was not listening to his instruction—in the sense of attention, absorption, and action. I said I should drive forward out of this mess and start all over. My teacher, convinced I wouldn't learn from this mistake, refused to let me. I "listened" to his advice, put the car in reverse again, began moving backward, and made the situation worse. Now all four tires were on the hill.

I said it was impossible to back out, quickly put the car in forward, and began to drive. My instructor slammed on his brake and said, "Put it in reverse!"

I had stopped listening and was seeing everything my way. I argued, my frustration heating up into stronger words. I demanded that I drive forward.

He said, "Listen to what I say and you will get out of this mess."

I said, "No way, it's impossible."

With his foot still on the brake, I did a fifteen-year-old thing. I put the car in park, pushed open the door, got out of the car, shut the door, and began to walk home. I had had enough. Up the street about a half a block, my teacher drove by, gave a little honk, and waved at me. I nodded and kept walking.

About two weeks later, my instructor suggested we continue my driver's education lessons. He didn't have to mention that the lesson would be on how to drive in reverse. I was now ready to listen and I absorbed and acted on his words. (I never back up without thinking of that event in Reed Park.)

Did I mention the driver's education teacher was my father?

David, a Nonlistener

The Bible is filled with people who, by *not* listening to God, became saintly folks acting sinfully. Take David as an example. David knew what Moses said in Deuteronomy 17:17: the king "must not take many wives, or his heart will be led astray. He must not accumulate large amounts of silver and gold." David heard this (attentiveness), but he didn't listen (absorption, action). Instead, David accumulated wives and concubines:

Michal, daughter of Saul
Abigail, widow of Nabal of Carmel
Ahinoam of Jezreel
Maakah, daughter of Talmai king of Geshur

Haggith
Abital
Eglah
Ten concubines according to 2 Samuel 15:16
Bathsheba, intentionally widowed from Uriah the Hittite
    (2 Samuel 11:14–17)
Abishag (1 Kings 1:1–4)

A colossal example of not listening. His son Solomon had 700 princess wives and 300 concubines (1 Kings 11:3). He must have been on steroids!

Love Listens

The Bible is also filled with examples of good and godly folks who paid attention to, absorbed, and then acted on the words of God. Abraham, Joseph, and Josiah are the first ones who come to mind for me. You may think of others. It's all about listening, the kind of listening that leads us to love God and to love others. The apostle Paul did not put the word "listen" in his list of what love is like in 1 Corinthians 13, but he would agree with any of us who join Alan Jacobs by saying, "Love listens."

Alan Jacobs's fine study, mentioned above, leads me to this question: "What would Bible reading look like if it were to be governed by 'the love chapter'?" I read Paul's words in 1 Corinthians 13:4–8 and see in these words a blueprint for reading the Bible. If love listens, then listening to God in the Bible will look like Paul's virtues of love. Add the word "listening" to each of these lines and see what happens:

[Listening] love is patient;
[listening] love is kind.
It does not envy,
it does not boast,

it is not proud.
[Listening love] does not dishonor others,
it is not self-seeking,
it is not easily angered,
it keeps no record of wrongs.
[Listening] love does not delight in evil but rejoices with the truth.
It always protects, always trusts,
always hopes, always perseveres.
[Listening] love never fails.

Good reading is an act of love and therefore an act of listening. But good listening—good attentive listening, good loving listening—is more than gathering information. It is more than just sitting around the back porch with God as we sip tea while God tells us his story. God speaks to us for a reason—I call this "missional" listening. In brief, God tells his story so we can enter into a relationship with him, listen to him, and live out his Word in our day and in our way.

CHAPTER 8

THE BORING CHAPTER (ON MISSIONAL LISTENING)

What Does God Want to Happen to Listeners?

After reading this chapter, Kris referred to it as "the boring chapter" and kept asking me if I had made it better. It was not that she thought it had bad ideas, but she thought it was too theoretical and more than once asked me if I really needed this chapter. I can say I have hacked away and reshaped this chapter a number of times, and I know one thing: it's not as boring as it once was. If you get bored, skip to the next chapter. But let me begin with a story; maybe that will help.

A few years back I taught a course at North Park called "Methods in Bible Study." I believe it is important to read the Bible *with* tradition, so one of our textbooks, by the great fourth-century church father St. Augustine, was titled *On Christian Doctrine*.[1] Augustine's book was the ancient church's equivalent of our *How to Read the Bible for All Its Worth*.[2] What I read in Augustine's book annoyed me and delighted me at the same time. It gave a method that undid everything I was teaching my students and yet told them everything I ultimately wanted to say. Why? Because it made the bold claim that if the Bible leads the reader to be more loving, then the Bible has accomplished its mission. What annoyed me was that the mission was accomplished whether or not we interpreted the passage with historical precision and contextual accuracy.

Of course, someone would have immediately called good ole Augustine on the spot for suggesting accurate interpretation doesn't matter. Augustine anticipated that, so he offered a graphic image. Getting the right result of becoming more loving, even if we aren't as accurate in our interpretation as he'd prefer, is like a person on a journey who gets lost but somehow finds the way to the right destination.[3] It's not as if Augustine thought every interpretation was as good as any other. Augustine wrote shelves of commentaries on books of the Bible; he knew how to turn his finger into a pointer and his quill into a torch when he thought he had to. But Augustine knew the Bible's main mission: so we can become people who love God and love others. If our reading of the Bible leads to this, the mission is accomplished. If it isn't . . .

Here is a sad fact: many of those who teach us how to read the Bible teach us how to gather information and find the right path from A to B. They teach us about words and paragraphs and book outlines, and they point us to sources and resources for understanding the historical context. Each of these is important. But what Bible study books don't focus on is church and personal transformation. Any method of Bible study that doesn't lead to transformation abandons the missional path of God and leaves us stranded.

So what is God's missional focus in giving us the story of the Bible? In one expression, it is to give us facts so that we will move those facts into relationship, character, and action.

The Relational Approach Is Missional

The relational approach to the Bible goes beyond normal methods to take us to the heart of what reading the Bible is all about. What is that heart? I can think of no better place than Paul's words to Timothy in 2 Timothy 3:14–17. This and Psalm 119 are the most significant passages in the Bible when it comes to the Bible talking about itself. It tells us that God gave the Bible a mission: God speaks to us so we will be the kind of people he wants and will live the way he wants us to live. Read the verses below quietly until you get to the beginning of verse 17, and then forcefully announce (unless you are in a public place) the first two words of verse 17:

> But as for you, continue in what you have learned and have become convinced of, because you know those from whom you learned it, and how from infancy you have known the Holy Scriptures, which are able to make you wise for salvation through faith in Christ Jesus. All Scripture is God-breathed and is useful for teaching, rebuking, correcting and training in righteousness, [17]SO THAT the servant of God may be thoroughly equipped for every good work. (emphasis added)

Everything leads to verse 17, where we come face-to-face with a big fat "so that." Educators know that teaching *begins at the end, with outcomes,* with the "so thats" of education. Outcome-based education means we ask this question as we prepare and teach: "What do we want our students *to be* and to be able *to do* at the end of this assignment, this course, this major, and this degree?" We no longer ask just what we want students *to know*—measured normally by exams and papers—but we want to know what students are able *to do with what they know.* Typically, theological schools have three major outcomes or something like them, three major "so thats":

- knowledge of Bible, theology, and church history
- critical thinking skills
- spiritual formation in both identity and behavior

That is, we want our students to know some facts, we want them to be able to think reasonably about faith, and we want them to be internally formed so they can practice what they believe. We cannot promise they will achieve each of these, but we shape our courses toward these "so that" outcomes. By the way, the word "outcome" for me is gobbledygook English from a group of people I call "educrats," whose job it is to run from school to school to make sure professors are accomplishing something measurable. The word "outcome" makes me think of what our plumber pulls out of our sewer. But "educrats," most of whom must not have done well in English classes, have worked themselves into a position to decide which terms teachers must use. We now use this word as often as our students use the word "like," as in "she was, like, so late to class," and as often as our politicians use the gobbledygook "single-payer."

God too is interested in "outcomes," though I'm not sure he'd approve of the word, so the Bible uses "so that." To get to the outcomes, we have to go through a sequence of thoughts for Paul, unmasking the four stages for missional listening as he writes to Timothy. Just remember that everything is aimed at "so that." Everything! Any reading of any passage in the Bible, the whole Story, that doesn't end up with the "so that" of 2 Timothy 3:17 is not done.

Missional Listening

Missional Listening Begins with the Wisdom of the Ages

Paul begins where we left off in an earlier chapter: he exhorts Timothy to read the Bible *with* the tradition, not *through* the tradition, and certainly not all by himself. Timothy has been formed by those who knew the gospel. Here's what Paul says to him in 2 Timothy 3:14–15.

> But as for you, continue in what you have learned and have become convinced of, *because you know those from whom you learned it*, and how from infancy you have known the Holy Scriptures, which are able to make you wise for salvation through faith in Christ Jesus. (emphasis added)

117

As Phil Towner, who has written the finest commentary we have today on this letter from Paul, deftly observes, "The teaching is only as good as its teachers."[4] I would add, "The teaching is also *just* as good as its teachers."

Judaism is known for its mastery of Torah and Talmud. It is also known for teachers who not only *know* but *observe.* Such was the world in which Jesus and Paul lived. When we think of teaching in the first century, we dare not let ourselves think of a classroom with desks and inkpots and papyrus scrolls bundled up on a library shelf at the back of the room. Or of a teacher in the front of a room lecturing away as students were doing what they could to stay awake and memorize their lessons so they would pass the next test. Nor should we think of learning as simply amassing information. Instead, we need to think of a Jesus and a Paul who were out and about engaging folks in conversation, with disciples hanging around them, asking questions, and studiously watching the behaviors of Jesus and Paul. In other words, education for them was not simply information; it was also formation. Education was training in righteousness and in good works. It was more like a golf lesson than a classroom lecture. Don't forget the apostle Paul said, "I urge you to imitate me" (1 Corinthians 4:16), and he also said that he and his co-workers had offered themselves to the Thessalonians "as a model for you to imitate" (2 Thessalonians 3:9).

Timothy's teachers were two women—his mother and grandmother (2 Timothy 1:5; 3:14)—and the apostle Paul (3:10–11). Missional listening begins with wise mentors, such as Timothy's.

Slide and Land

You have no doubt either been to or seen a waterslide in a big theme park. Confession time: I've been to water parks, I've watched my children at water parks, but—here's my excuse—sliding down a slide (or swinging on a swing) is not a thing I do; it easily disrupts something my doctor calls the "inner ear" and "labyrinthian canals." I get nauseated sliding down slides. My illustration here comes from watching my kids when they were young.

Waterslides are long and wide and curvy and have wonderfully banked sides. Water runs down the waterslide freely and abundantly to increase the speed of the slider. What we might not observe is that everything about a trip down the slide and into the pool of water at the bottom is determined by the slide itself. Even more important for our safety is that where we land is shaped by the slide. Without banked, steep sides, we would fly off the slide and … well, we'd get hurt.

Reading the Bible *with* our wise mentors is like sliding down a waterslide. The gospel is the slide; the Bible is one wall, our teachers and our Great Tradition are the other wall; the water is the Holy Spirit. The pool at the bottom of the slide is our world. If we stay on the slide and inside the walls as we slide down, we will land in our own water world. If we knock down the walls of the slide or get too careless and tumble out of the safety of that slide, we could injure ourselves. However, observe this: our life is lived in the pool. Here's my point: God asks us to listen—attention, absorption, and action—to the gospel story and to read the Bible *with* our wise mentors who have gone before us. When we do that, we will land in the pool in our day and in our way.

But we are getting ahead of ourselves. Missional listening begins with the wisdom of the ages, but there is a special dynamic at work in missional listening that has the capacity to change who we are and how we live.

Missional Listening Is Empowered by Inspiration

Scripture is also *God-breathed,* or "inspired." Paul didn't have a New Testament, so when he says "Scripture," he probably means the Old Testament and perhaps some gospel traditions about Jesus and some early apostolic writings (1 Timothy 5:18; cf. 2 Peter 3:15–16). What is most important here is the dynamic Paul is pointing at: the presence of the Spirit who takes words on paper and turns them into the living presence of God speaking to us. Here is where the relational approach reminds us that Scripture, as God-breathed, is God the person speaking to us on paper.

What makes missional listening powerful, what leads the reader into a life of righteousness and good works (the outcomes Paul mentions), is the promise that the Spirit who hovered over the author is the same Spirit at work in the reader.[5] Unfortunately, too many of us spend too much time arguing about the meaning of "inspiration" and not enough on the point of it all. The Spirit who guided the author through a history and a community to the moment when he put quill to papyrus is the same Spirit at work when you and I sit down with our Bibles.

What gives us the power for the outcomes is the Spirit.

Missional Listening Is a Process

For years Kris would get home from her office as a psychologist and ask me how my day went. She always asked me what I was studying, and sometimes I would bubble up in a flourish of words. Now before I say anything further, I need to insert this thought: I live and breathe and eat and sleep and walk and play and converse with a woman who is unflaggingly committed to what matters and to what is useful. She knows that "theories" can only go so far; she knows that theology is supposed to involve a *process* leading to real life changes.

One day when she asked what I had studied, I told her I had been studying the participle "going" in the Great Commission and informed her that after hours of study, a good translation would be "Go make disciples!" That, I thought (and still do think), is better than "By going, make disciples" or "Go and make disciples." I had discovered something. Not earth-shattering, of course, but my hard work paid off. Kris thought my translation was clever and, for all she knew, accurate. Then she made another point by asking a question, just the sort of question a psychologist might ask: "So, did you go make any disciples today?" Bingo! The "So what?" question got me. If what I learned wasn't "useful," if the process didn't lead to the "so that" of 2 Timothy 3:17, it wasn't much good. Kris's questions have changed my career interests.

My book, *The Jesus Creed: Loving God, Loving Others*, which discusses the significance of loving God and loving others as the heart of spiritual formation, emerged from a string of Kris's "So what?" conversations. The point of the book is to get us to recite the Jesus Creed so often that it digs its way into our very bones. One time I said something out of impatience (my besetting sin) to Kris, and she observed in the far room that what I had said "wasn't very Jesus-Creed-like." Ouch. So a week or so later, Kris said something to me I didn't like, so I informed her that her comment was not very Jesus-Creed-like. Her defense: "I didn't write the book!"

We've played with this banter for a few years now, but underneath it all is a conviction we both have that God designs all biblical study to be a "useful" process that leads us to the Bible *in such a way that it creates a person who loves God and loves others*. Anything less fails to achieve why God speaks to us in the Bible. God's got a mission in giving us the Bible, and that mission is "useful."

Paul too knew the Bible was designed to be "useful." "All Scripture," he wrote, "is God-breathed and is *useful* for ..." (2 Timothy 3:16, emphasis added). Missional listeners discover we are in a process of being transformed from what we are into what God wants us to be. Here's the process:

> We become informed;
> we get rebuked;
> we are restored; and
> we become instructed in righteousness.[6]

If we are committed to missional listening to God as we read the Bible, we will learn, we will be rebuked about our failures, and we will be restored. What is the outcome of this process? *Righteousness*. To be "righteous" means our minds, our wills, and our behaviors will be conformed to God's will. It means holiness, goodness, love, justice, and good works.

It takes time, but missional listening leads to righteousness.

Missional Listening Blossoms into a Life of Good Works

" ... SO THAT the servant of God may be thoroughly equipped for every good work" (2 Timothy 3:17).[7] The divine outcome, the divine "so that" of missional listening to the God of the Bible is *good works*. Any reading and any interpretation that does not lead to good works, both as the practical application and as the behavioral result, aborts what the Bible is designed to produce. I know, "aborts" is a strong word, but we need such a word here. God's "so that" is "good works."

What are good works? Peter urged the Christians in Asia Minor to be benevolent in their cities; Paul exhorted the Roman Christians to love their neighbors as themselves; John urged his readers to walk in the light and to love one another; James reminded followers of Jesus to care for widows and orphans, to feed the hungry, and to clothe the naked. Good works are concrete responses to the needs we see in our neighbors.

I don't think any person reading this book wonders *what* good works are. The question is not what they are but whether we are doing them. This passage written by Paul in 2 Timothy 3:17 leads me to the following two conclusions—and they stare at each of us:

If you are doing good works, you are reading the Bible aright.
If you are not doing good works, you are not reading the Bible aright.

If you are in the first group, keep it up; if you are in the second group, make some changes.

Earlier in this chapter I likened missional listening to sliding down a waterslide at a theme park. The slide is the gospel, the walls of that slide are the Bible and our wise mentors (tradition), and the water is the Holy Spirit. I also said that our joy, our delight, our challenge is to enter the slide, to enter the Bible as Story, and to let it take us where we are supposed to go. When that happens, we become people of good works.

I want to turn now to the landing, to what happens to us when we slide down the waterslide. Where will we land? How do we land? Our landing in the water is a process of discernment of learning how to fly from the story of the Bible into our world. Each of us, in fellowship with our community of faith, is called to enter the slide and follow its faithful contours so we can land in the water of our world.

PART 3

DISCERNING

How Do I Benefit from the Bible?

Though I am free and belong to no one, I have made myself a slave to everyone, to win as many as possible. To the Jews I became like a Jew, to win the Jews. To those under the law I became like one under the law (though I myself am not under the law), so as to win those under the law. To those not having the law I became like one not having the law (though I am not free from God's law but am under Christ's law), so as to win those not having the law. To the weak I became weak, to win the weak. I have become all things to all people so that by all possible means I might save some. I do all this for the sake of the gospel, that I may share in its blessings.

The apostle Paul, according to 1 Corinthians 9:19–23

For this reason, since the day we heard about you, we have not stopped praying for you. We continually ask God to fill you with the knowledge of his will through all the wisdom and understanding that the Spirit gives, so that you may live a life worthy of the Lord and please him in every way.

The apostle Paul, according to Colossians 1:9–10

CHAPTER 9

THE YEAR OF LIVING JESUS-LY

What Do We Do and What Do We Not Do?

So how do we apply the Bible to our lives? How do we live out the story of the Bible today? Do we open up a passage, read it, and live it just as it says? Most will admit that it's not that easy, at least not all the time.

Let's take a quick look in our Bibles at Leviticus 19. Somehow we know what to "pick" and what to "choose" and what "not to pick" and what "not to choose" when we read this chapter. (If you do this in a class, which I have done, ask everyone to vote on those they think we should do and those they think we shouldn't do. You might be surprised by the results.) I call this list of blue parakeet commandments from Leviticus 19 ...

The Commands We Mostly Don't Keep

Check the boxes of the commands you believe we should observe today.

☐ 1. Be holy because I, the Lord your God, am holy (19:2).

☐ 2. You must observe my Sabbaths. I am the Lord your God (19:3).

☐ 3. When you reap the harvest of your land, do not reap to the very edges of your field or gather the gleanings of your harvest. Do not go over your vineyard a second time or pick up the grapes that have fallen. Leave them for the poor and the foreigner. I am the Lord your God (19:9–10).

☐ 4. Do not go about spreading slander among your people (19:16).

☐ 5. Do not plant your field with two kinds of seed. Do not wear clothing woven of two kinds of material (19:19).

☐ 6. Do not eat any meat with the blood still in it (19:26).

☐ 7. Do not cut the hair at the sides of your head or clip off the edges of your beard (19:27).

☐ 8. Do not . . . put tattoo marks on yourselves. I am the Lord (19:28).

☐ 9. Stand up in the presence of the aged (19:32).

☐ 10. Keep all my decrees and all my laws and follow them. I am the Lord (19:37).

Other than #1 and #4, most of us don't follow any of these commands literally. Think about this list carefully because it really does make us rethink how we read the Bible.

- We don't keep the Sabbath (Friday night sundown to Saturday night sundown; Sunday is not the same as Sabbath).
- We don't harvest only some of our crops (if we even harvest).
- We don't worry about planting two kinds of seed (if we plant at all).
- We don't worry about wearing garments made of more than one substance—cotton and polyester blends, for example (if we even pay attention).
- We don't hesitate to eat medium to rare meats (unless vegetarian).
- We don't have moral issues in cutting our earlocks (at least I don't).

- We (most of us that is) don't think tattoos are sinful.
- We don't always (or ever!) stand up when older folks walk into the room.

These ten commands are never part of a discipleship program; yet they are commanded by God in the Bible. Furthermore, it's not like Moses is just giving a few good suggestions for special students who want to imitate him. In fact, these commandments are propped up with a profoundly theological comment—"I am the Lord your God." And they all start with an even more profound comment: "because I, the Lord your God, am holy." Moses anchors these commands in the holiness of God. Since God's holiness doesn't change, doesn't it make sense to think God's rules for his people don't change either?

The quick answer to this question is that while God's holiness doesn't change, his will for his people does. This, then, leads to one of my favorite questions: How do we know which of those commandments change and which ones don't? How do we choose? Who gets to choose? When is there to be conservation and when is there to be innovation?

Either we are completely wrong in our dismissal of these commands, or we have some categories in our Christian minds to help us know what to apply to our lives and what not to apply. (I think it is the second option.) To make this more complex, in spite of near-universal dismissal of most of these commandments, some Christians disagree on which of the ten to follow and which not to follow, so some have practiced these since the beginning of the church. Still, most of us would wipe most of these commandments off our moral map. Why? Here I give some typical answers:

They are from a bygone era.
They are from the Old Testament.
They are from Leviticus.
They are from what many call the Holiness Code.
They are from ceremonial codes and we follow only the moral codes.
They are fulfilled in Christ (which might mean any number of things).

Or they provide another set of reasons that really say, "That was then, but this is now."

Oddly enough, smack-dab in the middle of this chapter is Leviticus 19:18, one of Jesus's and the early church's favorite commands: "Love your neighbor as yourself." Somehow we know, perhaps because Jesus and the early Christians repeated it so often, that this command applies to us but many of the others don't. How do we know this?

Essentially, the church has always taught that the *times have changed and we have learned from New Testament patterns of discernment what to do and what not to do.* Often it is easy; sometimes we have to have a discussion but can agree. Other times it gets difficult. So ...

What about Sex before Marriage?

Most of us believe that premarital sexual intercourse is contrary to God's will. The New Testament doesn't say a thing about this. However, we know the prohibition in Exodus 22:16–17 and Deuteronomy 22:28–29, we believe premarital sexual intercourse is wrong, and we conclude that the laws of the Old Testament prohibiting such are to be applied today. Exodus comes at this from a specific angle, the angle of the disgruntled father of the seduced virgin:

> If a man seduces a virgin who is not pledged to be married and sleeps with her, he must pay the bride-price, and she shall be his wife. If her father absolutely refuses to give her to him, he must still pay the bride-price for virgins.

The Old Testament teaches that premarital intercourse is wrong (we accept that), and it obligates the couple to marriage (we're not sure about that one). We like the father's choice, and some of us wish the woman would get a voice in this text. But overall we think this text gets it permanently right. To make this point abundantly clear to university students in whom hormones are pounding into one another, I often say that there is no such thing as "premarital" intercourse in the Bible. Intercourse, I show them from this text, *constitutes the sexual union that we call marriage.* Perhaps it is an overcooked way of saying it, but I get my point across.

Every now and then a historically minded student will ask questions like this: "Well, didn't they marry younger? Isn't it harder for us?" What the student is saying is this: "Haven't the times changed?" What they are implying is this: "Is the regulation the same for us?" I think that's a good question.

Listen to this letter from a reader of my blog, Dianne Parsons, who also knows that the times have changed since the times of the Bible and that these changes, she is suggesting, have enormous implications for the sexual temptations of young adults.

I would like to see someone thoughtfully address the issue [in today's culture] of the gap of many years between the age of sexual maturity and age at which people enter into marriage. Assuming sexual maturity between age 10 and 15 (and often earlier) and marriage between 25 and 30, there is anywhere between 10 and 20 years of the strongest hormonal influence on sexuality. Yet churches still preach celibacy [she means the traditional view of waiting until marriage] with a straight face to the emerging generation, who mostly turn away.

I see four options for those in the emerging generation:

1) Remain celibate for one to two decades of the most sexually intense time of their lives;
2) Marry at a much earlier age than their contemporaries;
3) Stay away from church [and engage in intercourse] until married and/or with children;
4) Attend church and compartmentalize that part of their life and keep sexual intercourse "private."

A few choose #1, but let's be honest, most do not. Statistically, it's clear that many do not choose #2, except for those at seminary or Christian colleges. So what about all the others? Do ministry leaders assume that many in the emerging generation can or will be convinced to join group #1? How? By simply preaching "just say no"?

Dianne then asks what I think is a fundamental question that those who want to learn how to "apply" the Bible today are asking:

> How can we take a Bible that forbids sex outside of marriage, that was written in a time where there was little or no time that passed between sexual maturity and marriage, and apply it to today's situation? I see this as a significant challenge in ministering to the emerging generation, and I don't see it discussed much.

There it is. Some think of the Bible like this: "God says it, I believe it, that settles it." They treat the Bible the way many treat a troubleshooting chart at the back of a manual.

Problem: Premarital sexual temptation.
Solution: Just say no!
Response: "That was then, *and* it is *also* now!"

Others, however, are pressing the issue from a different angle. They say something like this as they approach the Bible as a troubleshooting chart:

Problem: Work on the Sabbath.
Solution: Keep the Sabbath by going to church or by taking one
    day off from work!
Response: "That was then, but this is now!"

With a genuine cry of the heart as well as a genuine intellectual question, these same persons get together and ask one another, "Why do we say the rule about premarital sex is to be applied but not the Sabbath one?" They are really asking this question: "Was the prohibition of premarital intercourse shaped exclusively for a culture in which young adults got married at the onset of puberty?"

If you think these are easy questions to answer, I would recommend getting your ear closer to the ground. The issue of "applying" the Bible is not that simple. We are learning that there's a lot more *discerning* going on than we thought. It is all about adopting and adapting, and we need to get our leaders together to start thinking more about this.

A Year of Living Biblically

The inspiration for this book came from years of reading, wondering, living, and teaching the Bible. The inspiration for this next section comes from A. J. Jacobs's funny, insightful, and suggestive (for me) book, *The Year of Living Biblically: One Man's Humble Quest to Follow the Bible as Literally as Possible*.[1] Jacobs grew up in an "extremely secular home" and is "officially Jewish." But he confesses, "I'm Jewish in the same way the Olive Garden is an Italian restaurant. Which is to say: not very." He continues, "The closest my family came to observing Judaism was that paradoxical classic of assimilation: a Star of David on top of our Christmas tree!"[2]

Jacobs decided to see what it would be like to live for an entire year by observing the Bible *literally*. "Millions of Americans say they take the Bible literally," he observes. But, "according to a 2005 Gallup poll, the number hovers near 33 percent; a 2004 *Newsweek* poll put it at 55 percent." What did Jacobs think?

> But my suspicion was that almost everyone's literalism consisted of picking and choosing. People plucked out the parts that fit their agenda, whether that agenda was to the right or to the left. Not me. I thought, with some naïveté, I would peel away the layers of interpretation and find the true Bible underneath.

I would do this by being the ultimate fundamentalist. I'd be fearless. I would do exactly what the Bible said, and in so doing, I'd discover what's great and timeless in the Bible and what is outdated."[3]

For five hours each day over four months, Jacobs reads the whole Bible—from Genesis to Revelation. Every time he comes upon a commandment, he types it into his Apple PowerBook. (He's with the angels on that one!) Seventy-two pages long, more than seven hundred rules. As he reads, he realizes something if he practices every commandment: "All aspects of my life will be affected." He ruminates, "I'll be the Gandhi of the Upper West Side." Some will make him weird: "Bathe after sex. Don't eat the fruit from a tree planted less than five years ago. Pay the wages of a worker every day." Some of the commandments are, in fact, banned by law: "Kill magicians." He's right: "This is going to be a monster project."[4]

You get the picture. If you want more, read his book. It's delightful. The whole book is a blue parakeet. It will make you rethink how we read the Bible.

What about Applying Jesus's Teachings Today?

I have no serious desire, though every now and then the idea does pass through my head just to see what it would be like, to observe all of Moses's laws "to a T." And I suspect 99.99 percent of you, if not more, stand alongside me in my lack of desire to do so. But I am quite willing to say that most of us do want to follow Jesus. Many of us, in fact, claim we do apply Jesus's teachings, literally to some degree, to everything we do.

Why talk about this? Because it is the *claim* that we follow Jesus alongside the obvious reality *that we don't follow Jesus completely* that leads us to *ponder how we are actually reading the Bible*. The passages we don't follow are blue parakeets that make us rethink how we read the Bible. All I really want to accomplish in this chapter is to get us to think more carefully about:

- the reality that we do pick and choose, even with Jesus and the New Testament, and
- the reasons we have for our adopting and adapting.

I've given away my secrets, so let me state them clearly: we don't follow Jesus literally, we do pick and choose what we want to apply to our lives today, and I want to know what methods, ideas, and principles are at work among us for picking what we pick and choosing what we choose. It is my belief that *we—the church—have always read the Bible in a picking-and-choosing way. Somehow, someway we have formed patterns of discernment that guide us. The deepest theme in our discernment is that we have a Great Tradition—a set of methods and beliefs and a culture that holds them together—that gives us instinct for knowing how to read the Bible.*

Picking and choosing, or reading the Bible with the tradition, is how the church has always read the Bible! It is no doubt safer to call this "adapt and adopt" or "conserve and innovate." Whichever expression we use, it all comes down to one word: *discernment*. We have learned to discern how to live out the Bible in our world today; we have discerned what to do and what not to do, what to keep as permanent and what to see as "that was then." We do more than read and apply; we read, we listen, and we (in connection with God's Spirit and God's people) discern.

Perhaps your response to these claims is the same as that of A. J. Jacobs: "Once you acknowledge that we pick and choose from the Bible, doesn't that destroy its credibility? Doesn't that knock the legs out from under it? Why should we put stock in any of the Bible?"[5] These are good questions, and many ask them. Just recently a student asked me those questions. But before any of us who claim to be Christians and who claim to follow Jesus can answer such questions, we need to look a little more closely at our practice of application. When we see how we actually live, we have two choices: either to become radical biblical literalists and apply everything (and I mean everything), or to admit that we are "pickers and choosers." Since the evidence reveals that we are all adopters and adapters, we need to admit it and then seek to explain ourselves. That is what this book attempts to do. I hope others will join the conversation.

I plan to give three examples from Jesus; we will explore other examples in the next chapter. I was tempted to go through example after example to bring out all the nuances, but that would have made this book too long. In most examples, I don't even give my opinion. Instead, I discuss how *we already discern* how to live the Bible and, in most cases, without much consciousness of what we are doing.

Jesus, Prayer, and Today

One day the disciples asked Jesus for some practical advice about prayer. "Lord," they said, "teach us to pray, just as John taught his disciples." In reply Jesus said to them (and I translate Jesus's words literally for effect): "*Whenever* you pray, *recite* this prayer ..."; then he gives the shorter form of the Lord's Prayer (see Luke 11:1–4). The NIV, emerging as it does from a world that does not believe in recited prayers, translates these words this way: "*When* you pray, *say* ..." I have translated "when" with "whenever" as a more literal rendering of the Greek expression. And instead of "say," a more accurate rendering would be "recite." I do so because Luke uses a present imperative; Jesus expects this very prayer to be repeated over and over—*whenever* they pray. The best way to translate something that is said over and over is "recite."

NIV	Literal
When you pray, say ...	Whenever you pray, recite this ...

Here is a fact from church history: to the best of our knowledge, the followers of Jesus have always recited the Lord's Prayer whenever they have gathered for worship and prayer. The evidence for this is universal—every major denomination in the world prior to the nineteenth and twentieth centuries recited the Lord's Prayer every Sunday. Why? Because Luke 11:2 taught them to do this. But many evangelical churches I have worshiped in and preached in do not recite the Lord's Prayer *whenever* they pray together. We have "applied" the words of Luke 11:2 differently, so differently that our translations reflect our own non-recital of the Lord's Prayer. Why? Because there is an unwritten, contrary-to-what-Jesus-taught principle at work that reciting set prayers leads to vain repetitions.

I have no desire to engage that debate. What needs to be realized is that this practice of *not reciting* the Lord's Prayer *whenever* we gather together is contrary to what Jesus said (and what the church has historically done).

Not reciting the Lord's Prayer is our *application of what Jesus said*. We have chosen, for pastoral reasons, not to do what Jesus commanded us to do and have chosen instead to apply these words in another way. How? We take them as a *general principle* instead of a specific commandment. This permits us to gather together in prayer without reciting the Lord's Prayer. This decision permits us to see the Lord's Prayer as a "model" prayer instead of a recited prayer. (For what it's worth, I think the Lord's Prayer is both a model and the precise words we should use *whenever* we gather in prayer. I recite it several times a day.)

Let's be honest: we treat this commandment of Jesus the way we treat most of the commands in Leviticus 19; we ignore it or dismiss it.

Jesus, Conversion, and Today

A second example is what Jesus requires or expects of those who want to enter the kingdom of heaven, all from the Gospel of Matthew.

> They must have surpassing righteousness (Matthew 5:20).
> They must do God's will (7:21).
> They must become as a little child in humility (18:3–4).

They must cut themselves off from whatever is in the way (18:8–9).
They must abandon riches (19:23–24).
They must separate from the teachers of the law and the Pharisees (23:13).

How do we "apply" these so-called entrance requirements of Jesus? We mostly don't apply them. We have discerned what they meant and how we can make use of them in our world.

For many Christians, these statements by Jesus sound far too much like "works righteousness." That is, we prefer a similar kind of saying in John 3:3: "No one can see the kingdom of God unless they are born again." How is one "born again"? Many answer that from the same chapter, verse 15: "that everyone who believes may have eternal life in him."

Here's a question: What would the gospel look like—in a four-point gospel tract—if the "abandon riches" statement was the basis for the framework? How about this?

Point 1: God created the world for all of us.
Point 2: Some out of greed have established systemic injustices.
Point 3: Jesus calls us to abandon all of our riches to rectify this.
Point 4: If you abandon your riches, the kingdom will come and the world will be what God wants.

Most in the history of the church have not believed that such a four-point gospel tract expresses the gospel. Some, thinking more historically, see these entrance requirements as no more than statements by Jesus to fellow Jewish contemporaries who needed to hear those words to see what repentance and faith looked like. Regardless of what we do, we, in effect, minimize what Jesus said.

While I do think we can offer a more robust gospel than we do today,[6] the intent here is to get us to think about how we are reading the Bible. How do we know whether we are doing the right thing when we, in effect, suspend Jesus's commands?

Jesus, Ethics, and Today

How do we apply Jesus's moral expectations? In particular, how do we apply the kinds of moral demands of Jesus we find in the Sermon on the Mount? We should be marked by a righteousness that (greatly) surpasses the righteousness of the Pharisees and teachers of the law (Matthew 5:20); we should avoid anger because Jesus teaches that anger is murderous (5:21–22); married folk should avoid lusting after others sexually because Jesus teaches that lust is adulterous (5:27–30); and we should, apart from the one exception for sexual infidelity, neither divorce nor remarry (5:31–32). To put all of this in one attractive container, we should be "perfect ... as your heavenly Father is perfect" (5:48). Even the disciples wondered if words like these were too much to handle; when Jesus said something similar sometime later, his best followers blurted out: "It is better not to marry." (19:10).

How do we apply words like those in the Sermon on the Mount today? Let's look at the different approaches in the history of the church to just one saying in this sermon: "Be perfect" (Matthew 5:48). What have we done with this statement of Jesus?

- Some say Jesus is exaggerating, raising the standard higher than we can achieve, but if we strive for it we'll do better than we are now.
- Others say that "being perfect" is what our moral life will be like in the eternal kingdom, and Jesus is teaching the final and eternal ethic God designs for us.
- Still others suggest that "being perfect" forces us to look inside to our heart of hearts to see our sinfulness.
- Yet others think Jesus means exactly what he says: he expects us to be perfect.
- Another: some think "perfect" actually means "whole" or "mature," so that being whole and mature is what Jesus really wants.
- One final one: some think "perfect" means to love our enemies and all we encounter.

We probably will not agree on how to read the word "perfect" in Matthew 5:48, but I hope this little section gets us to think harder about how we are reading the Bible. We are not trying to resolve all these issues. Instead, we are intent on demonstrating that we apply some of what Jesus says and we choose not to apply other things Jesus said. In other words, there is some adopting and adapting, some conserving and some innovating involved even with the sayings of Jesus. If there are two choices—totally literal or discerning a pattern—most of us will choose the latter every time.

By now I hope you are a bit unnerved about what I have said. This chapter is intended to provoke in order to get you to think about *how you are actually reading the Bible.* Some of you may want to turn back to a much more literal take-it-all-or-nothing approach, but I'm guessing most of you are now becoming aware that you do in fact adopt and adapt. What we must now pursue are the answers to this question: *What principles do we use to adopt and adapt the Bible?*

To answer this question we must broaden our vision from applying Jesus's teachings to applying those of the whole Bible. When we do, we will discover that we use various patterns of *discernment.* In the next chapter we will go through seven more examples, each of which startles us as Bible readers, just like the sudden appearance of a blue parakeet in the yard.

CHAPTER 10

FINDING THE PATTERN OF DISCERNMENT

Why Do We *Not* Follow the Bible Sometimes?

O ur all-too-glib and frequently heard Christian claim to practice whatever the Bible says annoys me. You might be annoyed that I just said this, but I'd like a fair hearing. I ask you to consider the following clear teachings of the Bible that few, if any, Christians practice. Perhaps you can ask yourself this question as you read through these passages: *Why do I* not *do what this passage in the Bible teaches?*

As you look at these examples, you will discover what I am calling a *pattern of discernment.* The pattern of discernment is simply this: as we read the Bible and locate each item in its place in the Story, as we listen to God speak to us in our world through God's ancient Word, we *discern—through God's Spirit and in the context of our community of faith or the Great Tradition—a pattern of how to live **in our world.*** The church of every age is summoned by God to the Bible to listen so we can discern a pattern for living the gospel that is appropriate for our age. *Discernment* is part of the process we are called to live, and discernment sometimes means conservation and at other times it means organic innovation.

DISCERNMENT: General Thoughts

In general, I am thinking of what a *local church or a local denomination does in order to discern* how best to live out the gospel in its day and in its way. While personal discernment for my own life is important, that is not what I have in mind here. Instead, I am concerned with how a local church, often in deep conversation with a denomination, discerns how to live. In fact, often the discernment process occurs at the denominational level to guide each local church.

We do not need to get into all the ways various Christian churches make decisions. Rather, our concern in this book is about discernment at the local church level. Part 5 will probe how churches (locally or denominationally) make decisions about women in church ministries. A tension occurs when a young woman believes she is called to preach or teach publicly but a local church or denomination has "discerned" that to be unacceptable. The young woman's belief is important to me, and I will deal with this, but our main concern is not so much with her discernment as with the church's.

A second general issue concerns *diversity*. Every culture will decide its own patterns for living out the Bible. Turkish Christians will not have the same pattern as that of Southern Californian Christians. Russian Baptists will live out the gospel in ways that differ from Brazilian charismatics. Anglicans in India will choose ways that differ from Anglicans in Wheaton. This is perhaps obvious to many, but we must remind ourselves of the vibrant diversity of the church at the local level. Seeking unanimity on all things is unwise; permitting discernment at the local level can sometimes create too much diversity, but it is wiser to have decisions made on some problems at the local church level than to have everyone under lock and key.

Discernment can be very *messy*. Discernment is called for on issues that are obviously unclear in the Bible, the gray and fuzzy areas.

No one argues with the clear and unmistakable teachings with which most Christians agree. No one believes it is right to murder. No one believes spousal abuse is right. No one thinks selling off children is acceptable. And in spite of the question about premarital sex that my reader asked on my blog, detailed in the previous chapter, most don't think premarital sexual intercourse is Christian behavior. These are the clear teachings in the Bible.

Churches, for instance, do need to discern if they want women to preach on Sunday. They will also have to decide how gays and lesbians will participate. These are messy areas. Here's the rub: to avoid the messiness, some revert to seeing the Bible as a law book. Eventually, though, a day will come when it becomes clear that discernment is going on. Decisions are being made. And that's what I'm most concerned about in this book.

DISCERNMENT: Specific Examples

Let's look at some examples—some of them quite messy—and we will learn about the unstated principle of discernment at work in the church.

1. Divorce and Remarriage

Let me make five quick observations to get in our minds what we mean by discernment in divorce and remarriage.[1] First, Jesus was against divorce, as is clear from Mark 10:11–12: "Anyone who divorces his wife and marries another woman commits adultery against her. And if she divorces her husband and marries another man, she commits adultery."[2]

Second, on another occasion Jesus "discerned" there is, in fact, an exception—sexual immorality.[3] Look at Matthew 5:32: "But I tell you that anyone who divorces his wife, *except for sexual immorality*, makes her the victim of adultery, and anyone who marries a divorced woman commits adultery" (emphasis added). Now we've got clarity: divorce is wrong except in the case of sexual immorality. If you want to know what Jesus and Jews of his world understood by "sexual immorality," turn to Leviticus 18 where you can read a list of sexual sins. All those, and probably more, were in Jesus's mind when he said "sexual immorality."

Third, the apostle Paul encountered a new situation in which he had to *discern* how the teachings of Jesus could be lived out when a non-Christian spouse deserted a Christian spouse. Was divorce also permissible for this situation? In 1 Corinthians 7, Paul discerned it was permissible. Paul knew precisely what he was doing—adding to what Jesus had taught. In 7:12 he says: "To the rest I say this (I, not the Lord)." What did he discern? "But if the unbeliever leaves, let it be so. The brother or the sister is not bound in such circumstances; God has called us to live in peace" (7:15).

Being true to Jesus, Paul is not looking for exceptions. He prefers that husband and wife stay together because the Christian might "save" the partner (7:16). But if the nonbeliever deserts, Paul discerns divorce is permissible, and he does so because we are called "to live in peace," which probably means Paul wants the Christians not to be disruptive in society.

Fourth, churches are called to enact similar discernments today, and long, hard, prayerful sessions have been directed at discerning whether abuse and desertion and immaturities are permissible grounds for divorce among Christians. No one says it is easy, but we have the following confidences: the guidance of the Spirit is promised us as we pray, as we study Scripture, and as we join in the conversation *with* church tradition. There will be both conservation and some innovation. It would be much easier for God to have given us rules and regulations for everything. But God, in his wisdom, has chosen not to do that. Discernment is an element of what it means to walk by faith.

Fifth, I believe our discernments should never become *rules or laws*. The moment we turn our discernments into rules or the moment we elevate them to the level of official positions, they are headed in the direction of fossilization, inflexibility, and the near impossibility of rethinking, renewing, and reforming. Instead, we need to render discernments with all the wisdom we can muster and let them remain as discernments and judgments, not rules or laws. At times churches and denominations will have to produce a "white paper" or a "statement" or even give a press release, but such official statements are needed only rarely, and probably less often than rarely.

In our discussion of examples, we will find some patterns at work in our discernment, but these are not rules we apply; rather, they are discernments. I am nervous about anyone who thinks we can find a mechanism that will guide our path. Instead, we need attentiveness to the guiding of the Spirit as we read the Bible together.

I accept the reality that churches disagree over discernments. I also accept that the process will be difficult. Even within a church where a sensitive process of discernment has been followed, there will be folks who disagree. That's the way it is, the way the church has always read the Bible. Longing for a day of certainty and uniformity in that certainty in this life may propel us into deeper discussions and the search for greater unity, but certainty and unanimity in discernment are not the world in which we live.

What the New Testament trajectory teaches us about divorce and remarriage is the need to remain firmly committed to marriage while permitting divorce in cases where the marital covenant has been destroyed. The pattern is to discern *the underlying reason for the fractured relationship and then to judge if that reason is acceptable.*

2. Circumcision

God told Abraham to make the covenant between them official by circumcising every male child *forever*. We need to read all these verses to see how serious this circumcision issue was:

> Then God said to Abraham, "As for you, you must keep my covenant, you and your descendants after you *for the generations to come.* This is my covenant with you and *your descendants after you,* the covenant you are to keep: *Every* male among you shall be circumcised. You are to undergo circumcision, and it will be the sign of the covenant between me and you. *For the generations to come* every male among you who is eight days old must be

circumcised, including those born in your household or bought with money from a foreigner—those who are not your offspring. Whether born in your household or bought with your money, they must be circumcised. My covenant in your flesh is to be *an everlasting covenant.* Any uncircumcised male, who has not been circumcised in the flesh, will be cut off from his people; he has broken my covenant." (Genesis 17:9–14, emphasis added)

Circumcision had been a big deal for the Jewish community for centuries. For this reason converts to Judaism were required to undergo circumcision. It was therefore natural for Jewish followers of Jesus to expect gentile converts to go all the way and go under the knife for Jesus (Acts 15:1–5). The question of whether converts should be circumcised was the pressing question that "cut like a knife" through the early churches. Think of this like a debate room with each party sitting together facing the other and a large group of undecideds surrounding both groups. Here are the options:

Pharisee-type Christians: "By all means! Circumcision is God's command."
Pauline Christians: "No, the times have changed!"
Undecided group: "What should we do?"

The early Christians were at a stalemate. To deal with their differences and discern how to live, they convened the first church conference in Jerusalem.

What we find in Acts 15 is *the pattern of discernment.* The early Christians discerned that circumcision, the (*don't forget this*) ageless command to Abraham, was not necessary for gentile converts. This was an innovation. James, brother of Jesus and now leader of the church in Jerusalem, came to the conclusion that gentile converts needed only to offer a minimal respect for those commandments that had always distinguished the Jews from the surrounding nations (15:16–21). Here we find a pattern of discernment, a pattern of listening to the old, understanding the present, and discerning how to live that old way in a new day. What we find in Acts 15 is a way of conservation (a "resident-alien" like understanding of gentiles) and innovation (no need for gentiles to be circumcised).

Yet what was decided in Jerusalem wasn't innovative and practical enough for Paul, who developed his own pattern of discernment for his churches. In fact, Paul went further than James with *three innovations on the Old Testament commandment to circumcise every boy forever.* First, in one of the most innovative positions Paul ever took, he said *circumcision really didn't matter*: "For in Christ Jesus neither circumcision nor uncircumcision has any value. The only thing that counts is faith expressing itself through love" (Galatians 5:6). I don't know how that strikes you, but it doesn't take a professional historian to imagine how Paul's opponents and Jewish friends would have responded. Paul's opponents knew, or thought they knew with certainty, that Paul was disagreeing with God's word! In terms of this book, Paul's statement was a blue parakeet observation, and this whole book converges right here. How did Paul discern that circumcision didn't really matter?

Second, conserving a theme in Moses and Jeremiah, Paul argued that *circumcision, even in the Old Testament, was ultimately an image of the heart* and not simply surgery on the body. Thus, Moses says in Deuteronomy 10:16: "Circumcise your hearts, therefore, and do not be stiff-necked any longer." And Jeremiah 4:4 says: "Circumcise yourselves to the LORD, circumcise your hearts, you people of Judah and inhabitants of Jerusalem." Paul puts it like this: "A person is not a Jew who is one only outwardly, nor is circumcision merely outward and physical. No, a person is a Jew who is one *inwardly*; and *circumcision is circumcision of the heart, by the Spirit, not by the written code*" (Romans 2:28–29, emphasis added).

If this didn't confuse some of Paul's criticizers, what about this? "Circumcision is nothing and uncircumcision is nothing. Keeping God's commands is what counts" (1 Corinthians 7:19). His opponents would have said, "Isn't circumcision one of those commandments?" For Paul, circumcision was clearly a commandment of God for all time, but paradoxically it was now no longer necessary for those who were "in Christ" because real circumcision was a matter of the heart. Which means circumcision is forever, but it morphs from a physical to a spiritual act. (You're not alone if you think Moses would have muttered and shook his head when Paul said these things.)

And third, Paul went one step further in an innovative direction: *baptism fulfills and replaces circumcision.* Notice these words from Colossians 2:11–12: "In him you were also circumcised with a circumcision not performed by human hands. Your whole self ruled by the flesh was put off when you were circumcised by Christ, having been buried with him in baptism, in which you were also raised with him through your faith in the working of God, who raised him from the dead." We might argue, then, that for Paul circumcision was eternal because it morphed into baptism.[4]

We who are Christians today no longer circumcise for reasons of the covenant because what was at one time expressed as a universal, eternal commandment was understood by early Christians—*in a pattern of Spirit-led discernment and innovation*—to be an external rite that would eventually find its fulfillment in the Christian rite of baptism. By the time Paul was done with this Old Testament commandment, the knives of circumcision were, to play with his terms, tossed into the water. So should we practice circumcision? No. Why not? Because we believe circumcision was a temporary entrance requirement that found fulfillment in baptism. And we believe this because we believe the Spirit who told Abraham to circumcise also told the early Christians that the day of circumcision had come to an end. The pattern of discernment can be called *theological development.* In other words, "That theology was then, but this theology is now."

I wish examples like this were all so clear. They're not.

3. The Style of Christian Women

> Wives, in the same way submit yourselves to your own husbands
> so that, if any of them do not believe the word, they may be won
> over without words by the behavior of their wives, when they see

the purity and reverence of your lives. Your beauty should not come from outward adornment, such as elaborate hairstyles and the wearing of gold jewelry or fine clothes. Rather, it should be that of your inner self, the unfading beauty of a gentle and quiet spirit, which is of great worth in God's sight. For this is the way the holy women of the past who put their hope in God used to adorn themselves. They submitted themselves to their own husbands, like Sarah, who obeyed Abraham and called him her lord. You are her daughters if you do what is right and do not give way to fear.

This text, from 1 Peter 3:1–6, contains three basic commands to women in first-century Asia Minor who had unbelieving husbands. They should:

- submit to their non-Christian husbands in order to convert them;
- avoid elaborate hairstyles and gold jewelry or fine clothing; and
- address their husbands with the word "lord."

Even if some conservative Christians today want to emphasize wives submitting to their husbands no matter how countercultural it may seem, they don't usually insist on Peter's commands about elaborate hair and nice clothing and fine jewelry, and they don't, so far as I know, insist on wives calling their husbands "lord."

Why do we not follow these explicit words of the apostle Peter? The only answer I can give is that over time the church has worked out a pattern of discernment that comes to this: women (and men I might add) should dress modestly. Even this pattern is not entirely accurate; for some the pattern of discernment is more radical. For them Peter's words are simply passé, outmoded. "That was then, but this is now. Peter's words are 'then.'" Many Christian women dress in the most fashionable clothing, pay considerable fees for coiffure, and have no qualms about expensive jewelry. Furthermore, they wear such things to church on Sunday morning where everyone can see them and where, by and large, no one puts up a fuss. I will avoid any sense of judgment on this matter except to say that men too are often dressed to the nines. Some who aren't pay big dough for their underdressed style.

What I am curious about is the pattern of discernment we now use. Let's say that we think Peter's intent is to encourage Christian women to be modest. My question, then, is this: How do we discern that his intent can be reduced to the principle of modesty instead of timeless commands? This pattern of discernment might be called *the deeper principle*. This approach knows that the principle is transcultural, but the specific expressions of that principle are not.

Let's press on.

4. Sun-Centered or Earth-Centered Cosmology

The Bible assumes that the earth was the center of the universe, but we now know, in spite of the strife it caused Galileo and the back-pedaling required of the church since his days, that the sun is at the center of the solar system. Our cosmology is heliocentric (sun-centered) whereas the Bible's is geocentric (earth-centered). Frequently the Bible speaks of the earth's foundation. The earth, the biblical authors say, sits atop a stable foundation with pillars: "He shakes the earth from its place and makes its pillars tremble" (Job 9:6; see 38:4–7; Proverbs 8:27–29). As if assuming the earth is flat, the biblical authors speak of its four corners. So, for example, the seer of Revelation says: "After this I saw four angels standing at the four corners of the earth, holding back the four winds of the earth to prevent any wind from blowing on the land or on the sea or on any tree" (Revelation 7:1).

In the biblical perception of the world, we have a principle at work we must admit: God spoke in those days in those ways, and one of those ways was a three-deckered universe of below the earth, the earth, and the heavens (e.g., Philippians 2:9–10). I suspect that's how they thought the world was really constructed.

How do we deal with a geocentric, flat-earth, three-layered universe? Science, which now factors into our patterns of discernment, rules for most of us, and we revise our view of what the Bible is actually saying. We have discerned that the Bible is actually using "phenomenological" language—language that expresses what the ancients observed, heard, and felt. Their language, then, is metaphorical. Are we bound to think that because the Bible implies the earth is flat and rests on pillars with a foundation that the earth is flat and sits on pillars? Some do, but most of us adjust and take the Bible with us into our modern scientific world.

Most of us also believe that what we thought the Bible was saying is not, in fact, what it was saying. That is, at times we have innovative interpretations because we have learned to listen well to science. The pattern of discernment here is simply *growth in knowledge, scientific and otherwise.* It need only to be mentioned that some think the same scientific development can be applied, say, to Genesis 1 and 2, while others want to stop short of such an implication. Some of us are willing to give it more freedom than others.[5]

5. The Death Penalty

Here we walk on thinner ice into a more-debated issue. Some Christians, *knowing full well what the Old Testament says and knowing that Romans 13 might be sanctioning death sentences,* believe that Christians should not support capital punishment. They believe a better way is possible for our world. For such persons, prosecution and life in prison is enough. Who knows, they ask, if this person might be reconciled to God, restored by grace, and made anew?

There are all kinds of texts and issues that come into play. Here are just a few: the Old Testament sanctioned capital punishment for the witch (Exodus 22:18), the idolater (22:20), the blasphemer (Leviticus 24:16), the rebellious son (Deuteronomy 21:18–21), adultery (22:22), and the one who broke Sabbath (Numbers 15:32–36). The breadth of behaviors that led to capital sentence has been innovatively shrunk in our world.

There are, however, some other tendencies and trends in the Bible. Cain was not put to death for murdering his brother (Genesis 4). There were cities of refuge where someone guilty of unintentional murder was both protected from blood revenge but yet somehow confined (Exodus 21:12–14; Numbers 35:10–13, 22–32; Deuteronomy 4:41–43; 19:1–13). Importantly, the guilty person in a city of refuge (analogous to our prisons) was released when the reigning high priest died (Numbers 35:25). Jesus didn't demand capital punishment for the woman caught in adultery (John 7:53–8:11).[6] Even more important, Jesus may well have undercut the foundation for capital punishment when he demanded that his followers turn the other cheek (Matthew 5:38–39).

Humans have done centuries of thinking about deterrence—does capital punishment actually deter crime? Protection—doesn't a criminal's death make for a safer society? Life—does or doesn't capital punishment demonstrate the value of life? Money—isn't it cheaper to put some to death than pay for confinement for life? Statistics—does not capital punishment weigh more heavily for the African-American and the poor than for the wealthy who can afford lawyers? And problems—we know some on death row have been proven innocent. Doesn't that force us to rethink the whole system? I could go on.

The fundamental argument against capital punishment goes something like this: "That was then, but this is now." Christians are split on this one. Jesus's teachings unleashed a new system of grace and forgiveness. In addition, society has developed in law, in enforcement, and in restoration to such a degree that capital punishment is no longer needed. The pattern of discernment for those who oppose capital punishment combines *social progress, historical development, legal development, and theological development that climaxes in Jesus's own teachings*. That development continues into our own day.

6. Tongues

Our sixth example is speaking in tongues, more often now called by its Greek term *glossolalia*. Here are the simple facts: the early Christians spoke in tongues (Acts 2), Paul spoke in tongues frequently (1 Corinthians 14:18), and Christians throughout the church have spoken in tongues. But—and here's the important point—since most Christians don't speak in tongues, because in the history of the church most haven't spoken in tongues, and because speaking in tongues was often isolated into small pockets of Christians, a pattern of discernment arose that "tongues aren't for today, they were a sign gift of the first century." And the pattern of "that was then, but this is now" was fine until the Pentecostal movement in the early 1900s, the charismatic movement of the 1960s, and the Vineyard movement of the 1970s and 1980s. At that time the "pattern" was discerned as a "no longer not for us" pattern. In other words, "that was then, but this is now" became a "that was then, and it is also now" pattern. The innovation was a form of conservation: speaking in tongues recovers the early church's way of life.

What we have here is a *variation in contexts*. Some think *glossolalia* was a manifestation of God's Spirit at the birth of the church but is no longer a pattern for the church. Others find a *normative pattern of discernment*: *glossolalia* is a permanent gift of the Spirit to the church. As a seminary student I routinely rode to school with a fellow seminarian who was Assembly of God. Often we chatted about charismatic gifts, and I will never forget what he said when I asked why I didn't speak in tongues but he did—and that everyone around him did and no one around me did. His answer: "Those who grow up *with it* are more likely to speak in tongues." Evidence backs him up, whether we like it or not. Those who grow up with tongues are more likely to speak in tongues. Variations in context, then, reveal to us that our own context shapes in part not only our interpretations but also our practices.

It is not my intent to resolve this issue. Instead, we conclude on an important note: *the pattern of discernment varies from age to age and from church to church and from person to person within a church.* This illustrates that the pattern of discernment can sometimes be messy.

We have two options:

uniformity of all in all things, or
diversity in the striving for unity.

This is precisely what Paul means by the verses in our final example, which is next.

7. All Things to All

First Corinthians 9:19–23:

> Though I am free and belong to no one, I have made myself a slave
> to everyone, to win as many as possible. To the Jews I became like
> a Jew, to win the Jews. To those under the law I became like one
> under the law (though I myself am not under the law), so as to win
> those under the law. To those not having the law I became like one
> not having the law (though I am not free from God's law but am
> under Christ's law), so as to win those not having the law. To the
> weak I became weak, to win the weak. I have become all things
> to all people so that by all possible means I might save some. I do
> all this for the sake of the gospel, that I may share in its blessings.

Paul's adaptability to context has drawn attention. Gordon Fee,
a New Testament scholar, speaks of Paul's "apparently chameleonlike
stance in matters of social relationships."[7] The apostle began a sermon
to philosopher types by exploring the gospel in philosophical terms
(Acts 17:16–34). When it came to traditional Jewish food laws, he
evidently just turned his head (see 1 Corinthians 8; also, written later,
Romans 14:2–3, 6). Why did Paul do this? Because of the gospel,
because Paul knew the King and His Kingdom Story. If one wants to
be completely faithful to Paul today, one would have to submit every
act and every idea to the principle of what furthers the gospel the most.
Because of that principle, Paul adopted and adapted.

Yes, Paul was a chameleon—he changed colors everywhere he
went—but he kept the same body. His gospel mission shaped everything he did. His gospel was the same, but his circumstances shaped
how he went about his business of spreading the gospel. Paul's process
looked messy to outsiders but was recognized as Spirit-led to insiders.

Some are a bit taken aback by Paul, but reading the Bible as the
King and His Kingdom Story makes me think Paul is doing nothing
new here. Adaptability of message and lifestyle is a theme written into
the fabric of the ongoing development of the Bible itself. God spoke in:

Abraham's days in Abraham's ways (walking between severed animals)
Moses's days in Moses's ways (law and ceremony)
David's days in David's ways (royal policies)
Isaiah's days in Isaiah's ways (walking around nude for a few years)
Ezra's days in Ezra's ways (divorcing gentile spouses)
Jesus's days in Jesus's ways (intentional poverty)
Peter's days in Peter's ways (strategies for living under an emperor)
John's days in John's ways (dualistic language—light and darkness)

Adaptability and development are woven into the very fabric of the Bible. From beginning to end, there is a pattern of adopting and adapting. Any attempt to foist one person's days and ways on everyone's days and ways hampers the work of the Holy Spirit. Can we be biblical if we fail to be as adaptable for our world as the Bible itself was for its time? Is this messy? Sometimes it is. Was the Jerusalem Council messy? Yes, it was. Did they discern what to do for that time? Yes, they did. Was it permanent, for all time, for everyone, always, everywhere? No. What gives us discernment for our world is listening to the Spirit in our times in light of the redemptive benefits of the King and His Kingdom Story.

All genuine biblical faith takes the gospel message and "incarnates" it in a context. The following observation unmasks all that we are advocating.

What is good for Abraham, Moses, David, Isaiah, Ezra, Jesus, Peter, and Paul is also good for us. But the precise expression of the gospel, the King and His Kingdom Story, or the manner of living of Abraham, Moses, David, Isaiah, Ezra, Jesus, Peter, and Paul may not be our expression or our manner of living. Living out the Bible means living out the Bible in our day in our way by discerning together how God would have us live. To do this, we need to baptize each wiki-story and each moment of our life into the King and His Kingdom Story as the large encompassing Story of the Bible.

We can be firmer: since it is clear that each of these persons adapted the Plot and the Story for their day, it is unlikely that their message or manner of life will be precisely the same as our message and our manner of life. We are called, as they were, to learn the Plot and the Story of the King and His Kingdom and its redemptive benefits, to listen to God, and to discern what to say and how to live in our day in our own way. We will speak to our world only when we unleash the gospel so that it can speak *in our day in our ways*. We are called to be faithful, and we do this by reading the Bible and knowing the Bible and living out the King and His Kingdom Story in our world today.

What this book is advocating is not new. It is my belief that most Christians and churches do operate with a pattern of discernment, but it is rarely openly admitted and even more rarely clarified. Discernment, I am arguing, is how we have always read the Bible for our world; in fact, it is how the biblical authors themselves read the Bible they had. I want to begin a conversation among Bible readers about this very topic: What pattern of discernment is at work among us?

I want now to dig a little deeper into a few examples in a brief fashion (slavery, atonement, and justice) and then concentrate more on one example: women in church ministries. I am not asking you to agree with me in the next few chapters, but I am asking you to admit that everyone today is using a pattern of discernment when it comes to theological topics like slavery or women in church ministries. Passages in the Bible about slaves, about atonement, about justice, and about women are often blue parakeet passages. Perhaps we need to ask how many of these blue parakeet passages we are silencing today.

The next few chapters will illustrate what it means to read the Bible *with* tradition instead of reading the Bible *through* tradition. It will illustrate how we practice the principles of conservation alongside innovation. In essence, I think the church has at times stayed on course but at other times it has gotten off track, misread some passages in the Bible, ignored others, and then fossilized that reading of the Bible into the Great Tradition. Sometimes the innovation needs to end and we need to back up into conservation. Other times we need an instance of organic innovation. While I respect that tradition, I have learned that reading the Bible *with* tradition encourages each generation to think for itself by returning to the Bible, confessing the Bible's primacy, and unleashing the power of the gospel in our day in our way.

PART 4

READING THE
BIBLE AS STORY

Three Examples

CHAPTER 11

SLAVES IN THE KING AND HIS KINGDOM REDEMPTION STORY

Learning the theory of reading the Bible as Story is one thing. Doing it is another. In this section I give three examples of reading the Bible as Story. I look at slavery, at atonement, and at justice. Each one illustrates reading the Bible in light of the King and His Kingdom Story and its redemptive benefits and is illuminated by thinking of them through the Bible's Story. Each illustrates both conservation and innovation, both adoption and adaptation.

Slavery in the Bible's Story

To read the Bible well we need to read it not just in terms of its redemptive benefits—are slaves redeemed?—but in terms of the King and His Kingdom Story. We need to look at the Bible's end goal when it comes to slavery and slaves and to read the Bible in light of that end goal. This makes for a huge difference in our thinking and understanding. But if we stop with the redemptive benefits we might just conclude: "As long as slaves hear the gospel and get saved, they're fine as slaves." Instead, when the kingdom of God becomes the larger story and vision in our reading of the Bible, we must conclude: "Slavery falls way short of God's reconciled, peaceful, just, and loving society."

The Vision of Redemption in the King and His Kingdom Story

There is no slave, and there is no slave owner in the great and final vision of redeemed creation in Revelation. I'm mistaken: the "slaves" of the final scenes in Revelation are servants of the Most High God. Which is to say, no humans have servants and there are no slave owners or slaves. Thus, the Bible tells us in the new heaven and the new earth all of God's "servants will serve him" (Revelation 22:3) and to these servants God is revealing his future plans (22:6). There is no slave and no slave owner because the vision described by the apostle Paul in Galatians 3:28 and Colossians 3:11 will become a reality:

> There is neither Jew nor Gentile, neither slave nor free, nor is there male and female, for you are all one in Christ Jesus. (Galatians 3:28)

> For we were all baptized by one Spirit so as to form one body—whether Jews or Gentiles, slave or free—and we were all given the one Spirit to drink. (1 Corinthians 12:13)

> Here there is no Gentile or Jew, circumcised or uncircumcised, barbarian, Scythian, slave or free, but Christ is all, and is in all. (Colossians 3:11)

The oneness of redemption that we have already discussed comes to completion in Christ: slaves and free are "one in Christ," and slave and free distinctions are erased in "one body," and there is in Christ "no . . . slave or free." That's the final paragraph in the King and His

Kingdom Story about slaves. To read the Bible in light of this Story means to see that God's aim for humans is the abolition of slavery.

It was not always that way, though, and one of the noisiest blue parakeets in the whole Bible is what it says about slavery.

The Need for Redemption

What is slavery? We must get this clearly understood before we can even begin to see how the Bible's Story shapes the story about slavery. These are the basic elements of slavery: a slave is (1) someone who is owned by a slave owner, (2) who uses that slave for profit (or pleasure) (3) against the will of that slave or, in unusual cases, (4) by the decision of the slave in order to pay off debts or because the slave loves the slave owner and his family. Slavery, then and now, describes almost always an involuntary labor force and the power to enforce ownership of someone without their consent. A good slave owner treats slaves better than a mean slave owner. In the history of the church there has been a mistaken contention that New World slavery in the colonies, the Caribbean, and South America was worse than ancient slavery in Israel, Egypt, Greece, or Rome. The evidence, however, is against this: slavery in both situations was about involuntary ownership, and brutality was found both in the ancient world and in New World slavery.

As we have seen in the various wiki-stories of the Bible, God spoke in those days in their ways, and one of their ways was slavery. Nearly every statement about slavery in the Old Testament can be challenged by what Paul says and especially by the absence of slave owners and their slaves in the kingdom of God. This is why we need to learn to read the whole Bible through the King and His Kingdom Story. The Bible's march is toward the eradication of slavery, but the march was slow, and that eradication didn't occur. Many times in reading the Bible we will be tempted to say, "Way too slow!"

To make a long listing of details short, here are some clear indicators of the brutality of slavery in the Bible—besides the obvious fact that a slave is a slave is a slave, that is, a slave is a human being involuntarily owned by a person powerful enough to own another human.[1]

> If a man sells his daughter as a servant, she is not to go free as male servants do. If she does not please the master who has selected her for himself, he must let her be redeemed. He has no right to sell her to foreigners, because he has broken faith with her. If he selects her for his son, he must grant her the rights of a daughter. If he marries another woman, he must not deprive the first one of her food, clothing and marital rights. If he does not provide her with these three things, she is to go free, without any payment of money. (Exodus 21:7–11)

> Anyone who beats their male or female slave with a rod must be punished if the slave dies as a direct result, but they are not to be punished if the slave recovers after a day or two, since the slave is their property. (Exodus 21:20–21)

> When you go to war against your enemies and the LORD your God delivers them into your hands and you take captives, if you notice among the captives a beautiful woman and are attracted to her, you may take her as your wife. Bring her into your home and have her shave her head, trim her nails and put aside the clothes she was wearing when captured. After she has lived in your house and mourned her father and mother for a full month, then you may go to her and be her husband and she shall be your wife. If you are not pleased with her, let her go wherever she wishes. You must not sell her or treat her as a slave, since you have dishonored her. (Deuteronomy 21:10–14)

There were slaves in ancient Israel; they were "property"; a father could sell his daughter into slavery but the slave owner could not then sell that daughter to gentiles; slaves could be beaten and treated harshly; slaves could be taken as war brides.

There is nothing pretty here, and it is not wrong for us who know the King and His Kingdom Story vision of the eradication of slavery in the kingdom of God to be irritated or depressed or even angry about these instances of slavery in the Bible. They are nothing less than shocking blue parakeet passages.

Signs of Redemption Anticipating the King and His Kingdom

There are signs of redemption in the Old Testament, and I want to point out a few of them. I begin with creation itself in which *all humans, male and female, are created as an "image of God"* (Genesis 1:26–27). The expression "image of God" refers to the vocation of Adam and Eve as representatives of all humans: they are to rule, as the Bible says in Genesis 1:26, over all creation under God who is the one true God and ruler of all. Humans are sub-rulers. The shocking (blue parakeet) reality is that the minute humans begin to *rule over other humans*, which is what slavery is, they have usurped God's rule. But the sin of Adam reveals itself immediately in his desire to "rule" over Eve (Genesis 3:16), and slavery is but an extension of that sinful, idol-atrous desire to rule other humans. That sinful choice to rule others on the basis of power, then, contradicts the order of creation we see in Genesis 1:26–27: Adam and Eve are to rule over animals, but not over other humans. Why? Because *only humans are "Eikons" of God.*

Israel developed a sympathy for slaves because Israel spent 400 years in slavery in Egypt. This is a second sign of redemption in the Bible's story. From the moment of the exodus, God told Israel over and over to Remember! Notice these verses:

Remember that you were slaves in Egypt and that the LORD your God brought you out of there with a mighty hand and an out-stretched arm. Therefore the LORD your God has commanded you to observe the Sabbath day. (Deuteronomy 5:15)

> Then you shall declare before the LORD your God: "My father was a wandering Aramean, and he went down into Egypt with a few people and lived there and became a great nation, powerful and numerous. But the Egyptians mistreated us and made us suffer, subjecting us to harsh labor. Then we cried out to the LORD, the God of our ancestors, and the LORD heard our voice and saw our misery, toil and oppression. So the LORD brought us out of Egypt with a mighty hand and an outstretched arm, with great terror and with signs and wonders. He brought us to this place and gave us this land, a land flowing with milk and honey; and now I bring the firstfruits of the soil that you, LORD, have given me." Place the basket before the LORD your God and bow down before him. (Deuteronomy 26:5–10)

The children of Israel were slaves in Egypt; they were treated harshly; God looked with favor upon them and rescued them at the exodus. They were guided through the wilderness where they received the law at Mount Sinai, and eventually they crossed the Jordan River and settled in the land. But they were to remember their slavery, and this *memory of slavery written into the fabric of their own Story gave them opportunities to be kind and compassionate to slaves.* Yet being kind to their own slaves is not the eradication of slavery. These passages remain blue parakeets in our Bible. Humans have an incurable drive to rule, and ruling over other humans forced to submit is called slavery. We resist their ruling over others as we observe a few signs of redemption in their laws about slaves.

So the third sign is the redemptive moments in the laws. A small step in the right direction of full redemption in the Story of the King and His Kingdom is seen when ancient Israel limited enslaving fellow Israelites to six years:

> If you buy a Hebrew servant, he is to serve you for six years. But in the seventh year, he shall go free, without paying anything. If he comes alone, he is to go free alone; but if he has a wife when

he comes, she is to go with him. If his master gives him a wife and she bears him sons or daughters, the woman and her children shall belong to her master, and only the man shall go free. (Exodus 21:2–4)

Restriction on the years of slavery is good; the children born to slaves who are not freed with a parent who is freed is not good. An even better sign of redemption is the Israelite slave owner treating the fellow Israelite slave and his family so well that the slave chooses to remain in the household of the slave owner.

But if the servant declares, "I love my master and my wife and children and do not want to go free," then his master must take him before the judges. He shall take him to the door or the doorpost and pierce his ear with an awl. Then he will be his servant for life. (Exodus 21:5–6)

Another sign of the King and His Kingdom redemption is glimpsed when fellow Hebrews—male or female—sold themselves into slavery to pay off a debt. When they were released, again after six years, they were not to be sent away with nothing to begin life anew:

If any of your people—Hebrew men or women—sell themselves to you and serve you six years, in the seventh year you must let them go free. And when you release them, do not send them away empty-handed. Supply them liberally from your flock, your threshing floor and your winepress. Give to them as the LORD your God has blessed you. Remember that you were slaves in Egypt and the LORD your God redeemed you. (Deuteronomy 15:12–15)

There is here a profound recognition of the status and condition of a slave and a strong sympathy on the basis of Israel's own story of being enslaved. Yet this remains a blue parakeet passage, for slavery itself is not condemned. This passage glimpses the King and His Kingdom from afar.

Yet another sign, another small step forward, is discovered. In Leviticus 25:39–46, *words are used in a potentially revolutionary manner.* How so? First, once again Israel is reminded that they were slaves (25:42). Second, the purchasers of fellow Israelites are *not to call them "slaves" but "hired workers or temporary residents."* Third, they are commanded not to treat such persons "ruthlessly," but "fear your God" (25:43). Fourth, these fellow Israelites are to serve only to the Year of Jubilee, another indication of reducing the time of their service (25:54).

Drawing upon Israel's own story of redemption is what Israelites were to do when a fugitive slave arrived in the land of Israel, a passage that should have more impact on Christians in the US than I hear in the conversation. What did Israel do? Here is what Moses tells them: "If a slave has taken refuge with you, do not hand them over to their master. Let them live among you wherever they like and in whatever town they choose. Do not oppress them" (Deuteronomy 23:15–16). Here again is a sign of redemption, the kind of redemption that will become a powerful vision in the King and His Kingdom Story, and here again the grace shown toward the fugitive slave is a grace experienced by Israel in Egypt.

A final sign of redemption that anticipates the vision of the King and His Kingdom Story stands tall out of the pages in the book of Job. In his own defense, Job confesses before his friends that he lives solely before the judgment of God (31:4) and so sets out a series of conditions: "If I have . . . let God" judge me. One of these concerns is how he has treated his own slaves and recognizes that his slaves are, like him, made in God's image:

> If I have denied justice to any of my servants,
>> whether male or female,
>> when they had a grievance against me,
> what will I do when God confronts me?

> What will I answer when called to account?
> Did not he who made me in the womb make them?
> Did not the same one form us both within our mothers?
> (Job 31:13–15)

This is the closest passage in the entire Bible, including the New Testament, between "image of God" in Genesis 1:26–27 (notice "male or female" in Job 31:13's second line) and enslaved persons. Job here candidly recognizes that though he has slaves, those slaves are no different than he is: they are creations of God and made in God's image.

I must say once again: a slave is a slave is a slave. A slave is a person owned by another person who has sufficient power to own another human being. A good slave owner is better than a mean one, but a slave remains an owned person. Slavery was practiced in ancient Israel. Slavery was regulated and modified in redemptive directions, but slavery was not repudiated in Judaism except—so far as I know—among the Essenes who lived at Qumran.

Moments of Redemption in the King and His Kingdom Story

There are two major moments of redemption in the New Testament. (There are actually three, but the third is so big I want to make it a separate point.) The first is with Jesus, who does not eradicate slavery nor does he denounce slavery, but he does something important: he *turns the language of following Jesus, knowing Jesus, loving Jesus, and obeying Jesus into the metaphor of slavery.* This can be looked at from two radically different angles: either Jesus accepted slavery as a given in his society, a sign of accommodation, or Jesus turned slavery into a positive image, turning it upside down by connecting it to one's relationship with himself. Here are a few glimpses of Jesus transforming the language of slavery into a positive image:

No one can serve two masters. Either you will hate the one and love the other, or you will be devoted to the one and despise the other. You cannot serve both God and money. (Matthew 6:24)

The student is not above the teacher, nor a servant above his master. It is enough for students to be like their teachers, and servants like their masters. If the head of the house has been called Beelzebul, how much more the members of his household! (Matthew 10:24–25)

Not so with you. Instead, whoever wants to become great among you must be your servant. (Matthew 20:26)

The greatest among you will be your servant. (Matthew 23:11)

All of this is connected to the image of Jesus as the Servant, both from Isaiah 53 and from Jesus's own words:

For even the Son of Man did not come to be served, but to serve, and to give his life as a ransom for many. (Mark 10:45)

Jesus connects the metaphor of slavery to his parables, to his relationship with God and the relationship of his disciples to himself, to the relationship of his disciples to one another, and through them all he reveals the status theme of God being King and himself as his earthly King and those in his Kingdom as those who serve Jesus the King. But in the parable of the prodigal son, Jesus tells us that the father welcomed the prodigal son back home and turned him from a servant/slave in a foreign land into a son with inheritance blessings (Luke 15:22–24). It is not a stretch to see Jesus here revolutionizing the slave theme into a son-of-God theme.

The second moment of redemption in the King and His Kingdom Story in the New Testament concerns the passages we mentioned above: that in Christ there is no such status as slave or free. Why?

Because in Christ all are redeemed into equality with one another as they become children of God (Galatians 3:28; 1 Corinthians 12:13; Colossians 3:11).

The Moment of Kingdom Redemption in Colossae

The third moment is a dramatic display of when the kingdom's great redemption became an invitation, plus some. Tucked away in your Bible is the last of Paul's letters in the canon of the New Testament. It is found just before the letter to the Hebrews and is a one-page letter from Paul to Philemon.[2] Two facts about the people: Philemon is a slave owner and his slave's name is Onesimus, which one famous New Testament scholar translates "Mr. Useful."[3] (Onesimus in Greek means "useful.") Another important fact: Paul is in prison.

Onesimus is a slave, which aligns him with millions in the Roman Empire. It is said that some 250,000 human bodies were sold as slaves in Rome's forum *every year*, and each slave was shown to purchasers with a necklace hanging down with a sign that explained the slave's defects. Most slaves were not bought, but were born into slavery. Because his mother and father were slaves, Onesimus was born into slavery. As such, neither his parents nor Onesimus when he became a "man" could be married. He could be semilegally connected to a "wife," but the children would be owned by Philemon, and there was no inheritance to be passed on when Onesimus died. Roman male slaves were always called "boys" because calling a male a "man" entitled him to marriage and inheritance. The sordid side of slavery, as if being owned by another human and being physically beaten were not sordid enough, was that some slave owners used their slaves for sexual pleasure—male slave owners who spent time with male or boy slaves was common in the Roman Empire. Onesimus and Philemon lived in Colossae (see Colossians 4:9).

The complication is that Onesimus, for some reason, ran away, though it is possible that he did not so much run away to escape forever but ran away to Paul because he believed Paul could be his advocate with Philemon over something Onesimus thought was an injustice. The letter itself is not clear enough for us to know for sure. For whatever reason, Onesimus ran away. What is odd is that he comes into contact with Paul, Paul preaches the gospel to Onesimus, Onesimus becomes a convert to King Jesus, and he was so gifted that the apostle Paul began to find him "useful" in ministry (read Philemon 10, 13). Paul develops a special relationship with Onesimus and in the letter to Philemon calls him his "heart" (v. 12) and his "son" (v. 10) and someone who is very dear to him (v. 16).

Now we will learn if Philemon knew how to put into practice the vision of the King and His Kingdom when it came to the redemptive benefits of a slave. The letter Paul sends to Philemon is nothing less than a test case to see if Philemon understands what it means to embrace the gospel story about Jesus. We might envision the event as one in which Paul kicks the door open and says to Philemon, "Here's Onesimus! He's a Christian! What do you think you should do with him?"

When Paul sent this letter to Philemon, the one who would read the letter to Philemon probably was Tychicus; see Colossians 4:7, 16. Paul would have instructed Tychicus about how best to "perform" this letter in front of Philemon. Paul wants this letter to make an impact not only on Philemon but also on the whole church of Colossae as well as on its neighboring churches in Laodicea and Hierapolis. So his instructions to Tychicus would have included when to make which gestures, when to pause and look people in the face, when to speed up, and when to raise the voice and when to soften the voice. We don't know specifics, but it is certain that Paul didn't let a hack read this letter and blunt the force with poor diction and reading skills.

Here's what Paul does in this letter because on the line is whether the church will have slaves or not. On the line is whether the vision of the King and His Kingdom is redeeming slaves in a way that sets them free into equality in Christ. On the line is whether Philemon will be able to sustain the slave owner's power over a slave who has become a Christian.

Paul begins by having this letter read in front of the whole church and not in a small room in private (Philemon 1–2). Next Paul publicly affirms Philemon in front of everyone in the house church by saying these things about him: Paul thanks God for Philemon, affirms Philemon's love for "all" his holy people (little did Philemon know that "all" was about to include a runaway slave), affirms Philemon's faith and partnership in the gospel work as well as Philemon's own growing knowledge of the gospel (which was about to grow in new ways!), and he affirms how Philemon has "refreshed" Christians with his various acts of grace (vv. 4–7).

Then Tychicus turns toward Philemon with Paul's appeal (vv. 8–21). Paul denies himself the power to command Philemon, but he appeals to him because of their mutual love. He works at getting Philemon's sympathy for himself because he's in prison as an old man, and he then announces that Onesimus has become his "son" and a Christian and is useful to Paul and (potentially) useful to Philemon. At this point Paul, having stunned Philemon with this news, backs off softly and says he's sending Onesimus back because the matter is legally in the hands of the slave owner. Paul wants Philemon's own approval. He even explains the departure of Onesimus as a divinely orchestrated event because now Philemon gets his slave back both as a slave and . . . *this is the most dramatic moment in this entire letter . . .* as a "dear brother." At this moment we can imagine Philemon's eyes are on Tychicus and then on Onesimus and back on Tychicus, but he's really seeing the face of Paul. He wonders, mutters, fumbles, stutters, and says to himself, "What in the world?!? A 'brother'! How can the slave be my family member?"

Paul continues in the letter, calling Onesimus someone who is "no longer . . . a slave, but better than a slave" (v. 16). That is, he's not a slave because his status has been transformed in Christ who makes all "one." The slave man has become the brother man and the slave-owner man has become the brother man. Paul, in his letter, has just announced in this church that meets in Philemon's home that this man, Onesimus, is a *brother*.

Which means what? Paul's next words in verse 17 say it all: "So if you consider me a partner, welcome him as you would welcome me." If there is any damage done to property, any theft of goods, Paul would repay for him. Wait, we must back up. Did Paul really say, "Welcome him *as you would welcome me*"? Paul just made Onesimus an equal to an apostle brother, and that means Philemon has been backed into a corner. How he responds to Onesimus in front of his entire church will show what he thinks of Paul. Paul now pulls out a clever move. Remember when he said in verse 7 that Philemon was known for "refreshing" others? Well, now Paul says, "Refresh my heart," and notice where he wants this refreshment: "refresh my heart *in Christ*." Right where there's to be oneness! Wow.

Paul signs off with, "I write to you, knowing that you will do even more than I ask" (v. 21).

"More than I ask." What might that mean?

Paul was not totally against slavery or he would have said that right here. He would have said, "Look, Philemon, I know how the Roman world works, and there are slaves everywhere. But we are Christians and we think it is morally wrong." But Paul didn't say that because he didn't think that. He was against selling slaves (1 Timothy 1:10), but he was not yet convinced that slavery was an immoral institution. The King and His Kingdom Story is on the move; there is innovation here; and more innovation would come later in the history of the world.

But in this moment in Paul's letter to Philemon, Paul curved history toward justice because Paul taught Philemon that Onesimus, his former slave, would no longer be a slave. He would be a "brother"—a sibling in a family where equality and love and forgiveness would be established. Where reconciliation would be a way of life.

Put differently, Philemon would learn to live in a way consistent with the King and His Kingdom Story.

CHAPTER 12

ATONEMENT IN THE KING AND HIS KINGDOM REDEMPTION STORY

For some people the heart of all Christian theology is a theology of the cross, how it works and what it accomplishes, which is usually called "atonement theory" by theologians. For some theologians, a specific theory of the atonement is not only right but the heart of Christian theology. What is more, many such theologians think most everyone else gets atonement theory wrong. I have learned in forty-plus years of reading and talking with theologians discussing the cross that every one of them has something valuable to say. I have also learned that those who are most shrill and defensive of their theory of the atonement have the most to learn from the others. Every theory of the atonement deserves a place in our minds, our hearts, and our praxes. The bigger the atonement, the better; the smaller, the worse. To keep the theme of *The Blue Parakeet* in front of us, this must be said: *no theme in the Bible deserves to find its precise location in the King and His Kingdom Story and its redemptive benefits more than the atonement.* Each theory only makes its most sense when it fits into the larger Story of the Bible.[1]

THEORIES OF THE ATONEMENT: In Brief

We enter here into some complex terms and theological discussions, but we need to have each of the main theories in mind before we can locate them in the Story.

The oldest approach to the atonement is *recapitulation*, and it means that Jesus the Son of God entered into our human existence and condition (our mortal, sinful realities) in every way so that he could redeem us in every way. One of the great summaries then is this: he became what we are so we could become what he is. Which is to say, he became human so we could become wholly redeemed, wholly human, and wholly present in God's presence. I have described this view in these terms: identification for the sake of incorporation. (He identified with us so we could be incorporated into God's redeemed family.) The celebratory note here is redemption in the sense of being rehumanized and reunited with God. This means we are *reconciled*.

Alongside recapitulation is what is called *the ransom theory*, or *Christus Victor*. Death is the enemy, sin propels us toward death, Satan and his cohort of fellow enemies seek and work for our death, death and Satan have captured us, and Jesus enters as a human into enemy territory. But his life of obedience and his death took our condition upon himself, and he died our death so death itself could die. Death, sin, and Satan and his enemy cohorts were defeated when Jesus entered death, was buried, and then was raised by the power of God. That defeat of death breaks the forces of sin, systemic evil, and Satan and unleashes victory for those who are in Christ. The celebratory note here is liberation and victory. This means we are *liberated and redeemed*.

With hints and glimpses in the Bible and in the history of church by various writers, a theory called *satisfaction* emerged with force among medieval theologians and the Reformers. The essential theory works like this: as sinners we are rebels, we are guilty, and we dishonor the glory of God. We have in effect ruined our chance for redemption because we can on our own never satisfy the glory and honor and law of God. As mortal flawed humans, we can never satisfy God's honor, so God sends someone who can be both fully human and fully divine. He becomes the God-Man who takes upon himself our humanity and satisfied the deity in his life, death, burial, resurrection, and ascension. The celebratory note here is that *God is satisfied himself and he is satisfied with Christ and therefore he is satisfied with us in Christ.* This means we are *justified.*

The most commonly used word since the Reformation for atonement is *substitution,* hence *substitutionary atonement.* There are, however, a few variants on substitutionary atonement, including these two primary ideas: representation and propitiation. The big idea of substitution is that Jesus died *instead of* us. Representation means much the same in that he "represents" us when he dies. Representation then is not as strong as *instead of.* Penal substitution clarifies the *nature* of Jesus's substitution and representation. The punishment, which is what "penal" means here, means Jesus died our death so we don't have to die our own eternal death. That is, he took upon himself our punishment. A yet more particular form of substitution is called *propitiation.* Once again Jesus both represents us and substitutes for us and so he dies *instead of* us. But the particular punishment he takes upon himself is not simply our death (penal substitution) but the wrath of God against us and against our sin (propitiatory penal substitution). The celebratory note here is *instead of* us. That is, Jesus shoulders the consequences of our sin so we don't have to, and his death ended the punishment. This means we are *justified and reconciled.*

Each of these theories tells us something true about the cross—how it works and what it accomplishes. Each of these theories, however, lacks elements that the others include, and hence choosing one minimizes the expansiveness of atonement. I don't believe we should ask, "Which of these is my favorite?" or answer, "I'll choose this one." Rather, what we most need is an encompassing theory that includes them all! That encompassing theory is the King and His Kingdom Story that brings all of the benefits mentioned at the end of each theory (and surely even more than those benefits).

The singular problem with atonement theories is this: each starts with a problem (our human condition, our enslavement to sin and Satan, our guilt and incapacity to honor God, our sin and guilt, and death and divine wrath) but *only resolves that problem.* Each theory is tied exclusively to the redemptive-benefits theory and not connected enough to the King and His Kingdom Story. Humans are in a complex problem, and so the solution requires a complex atonement. Forcing everything into one of these metaphors of atonement, or atonement theories, forces words to say things they can't say or do. So we need a more encompassing theory, and that theory is the King and His Kingdom Story. Before we show how the Story is sufficient for the complexity of the problem, I want to put on the table a few New Testament texts.

Vital Texts for Understanding Atonement in the Story

First, **Passover-Exodus-Covenant** texts. Three texts that speak of the atonement in terms of the Story of the Passover and the exodus appear in Mark 10:45, Matthew 26:26–29, and 1 Corinthians 5:7. These verses need to be quoted here and read carefully:

> For even the Son of Man did not come to be served, but to serve, and to give his life as *a ransom* for many." (Mark 10:45, emphasis added)

> While they were eating, Jesus took bread, and when he had given thanks, he broke it and gave it to his disciples, saying, "Take and eat; this is my body." Then he took a cup, and when he had given thanks, he gave it to them, saying, "Drink from it, all of you. *This is my blood of the covenant, which is poured out for many for the forgiveness of sins.* I tell you, I will not drink from this fruit of the vine from now on until that day when I drink it new with you in my Father's kingdom." (Matthew 26:26–29, emphasis added)

> Get rid of the old yeast, so that you may be a new unleavened batch—as you really are. For Christ, *our Passover lamb, has been sacrificed.* (1 Corinthians 5:7, emphasis added)

These texts do not begin where any theory of atonement begins because atonement theories abstract the problem from the human condition and from the divine nature rather than from the specific story from which these verses come. The Story out of which these passages come is the story of a community: that is, from Israel's enslavement in Egypt, God's merciful liberation of Israel through Passover, and the exodus and the covenant ceremony in the wilderness at Mount Sinai. Summaries of atonement theories don't emphasize these terms enough and sometimes ignore them altogether: Israel as community, enslavement, Passover, exodus, wandering, covenant.

Second, **Victory** texts. One of the great themes about the redemptive benefits of Jesus, which means his incarnation, his life, teachings, death, burial, resurrection, ascension, and second coming, is victory for the people of God. I cite Colossians 2:13–15 first.

> When you were dead in your sins and in the uncircumcision of your flesh, God made you alive with Christ. He forgave us all our sins, having canceled the charge of our legal indebtedness, which stood against us and condemned us; he has taken it away, nailing it to the cross. And having disarmed the powers and authorities, he made a public spectacle of them, triumphing over them by the cross. (Colossians 2:13–15)

In his death and resurrection, both of which are emphasized in Colossians 2 and 3, Jesus ended our death by dying instead of us and for us, and he was raised from the dead. His resurrection "made you alive," and through the death and resurrection God "forgave us all our sins" and "canceled the charge" against us that derived from the law. Not only that, in his death and resurrection, Jesus conquered "the powers and authorities," which are evil spiritual beings and their social-political grip in the world. At the cross he "triumphed" over them. We need to observe that an atonement theory that does not directly speak to the story of human enslavement, systemic evil and injustice, spiritual powers at work in this world, and conquering them and gaining victory over them is not a biblical atonement theory.

Now we turn to the book of Revelation. Fifteen times the word "conquer" appears—and that means victory over the principalities and powers was very important to John, and he knows that the atonement of Christ was a colossal triumph.

> Then one of the elders said to me, "Do not weep! See, the Lion of the tribe of Judah, the Root of David, has triumphed. He is able to open the scroll and its seven seals." (Revelation 5:5)

> They triumphed over him
> > by the blood of the Lamb
> > and by the word of their testimony;
> they did not love their lives so much
> > as to shrink from death. (12:11)

> They will wage war against the Lamb, but the Lamb will triumph over them because he is Lord of lords and King of kings—and with him will be his called, chosen and faithful followers. (17:14)

> Those who are victorious will inherit all this, and I will be their God and they will be my children. (21:7)

Jesus is in a battle with Satan and his cohorts; Jesus finally wins. In addition, the book of Revelation describes the people of God sharing in that victory by remaining faithful and by suffering and by obedience to the conquering Lamb. Again, one of the achievements of the cross is victory over the evil prince, Satan, and those who swear allegiance to Satan.

Third, **Forgiveness-Reconciliation** texts. At the heart of atonement is forgiveness, a term in the Bible that is wide-ranging enough to speak of God's forgiving a nation as well as a repentant sinner. Jesus rolls the first ball onto the court in the Lord's Prayer: "Forgive us our debts [transgressions, sins], as we also have forgiven our debtors [those who transgress or sin against us]" (Matthew 6:12). And then there's this famous comment that shows divine forgiveness of us and our forgiving of others are tied into a single knot: "For if you forgive other people when they sin against you, your heavenly Father will also forgive you. But if you do not forgive others their sins, your Father will not forgive your sins" (Matthew 6:14–15). When Peter summarized the redemptive benefits of Jesus, here are his words: "All the prophets testify about [Jesus] that everyone who believes in him receives forgiveness of sins" (Acts 10:43). Paul in Colossians summarizes Jesus's achievement at the cross with these words: "in whom we have redemption," which is "the forgiveness of sins" (Colossians 1:14). Any atonement theory that neglects sin and forgiveness fails to tell the Bible's King and His Kingdom Story.

I think too of Colossians 1:15–20, which many think is an early Christian hymn used in worship in early house churches. Here are some of its words about the redemptive benefits of the King and His Kingdom Story: "For God was pleased to have all his fullness dwell in him, and through him to reconcile to himself all things, whether things on earth or things in heaven, by making peace through his blood, shed on the cross" (Colossians 1:19–20). God's *reconciling* work concerns "all things" and that means "things on earth or things in heaven" and what the cross achieves is "making peace." This is why Paul earlier said "that God was reconciling *the world* to himself" (2 Corinthians 5:19, emphasis added), and he chased that one down with: "And he has committed to us the message of reconciliation" (5:19). At the heart of the cross is reconciliation of all things in all creation with God, who reveals himself fully in Christ, the King who summons you and me to be agents of reconciliation in the world.

We could pull out hundreds of verses, but all we need here is to illustrate the diversity of themes present when it comes to the cross: we have slavery and Passover with covenant and law, as well as evil and systemic evil connected to supernatural evil beings and victory, but also law and condemnation with erasure of debts or sin and forgiveness along with enmity and reconciliation and our need to become agents of reconciliation. There are others, like the Levitical sacrificial system and the Day of Atonement, and we could go on. Atonement theories, I am saying, are way too short for the tall order of comprehending the glory of the atonement in the Bible. Atonement needs to be removed from atonement theories and located in the King and His Kingdom Story if we want to locate the redemptive benefits of the cross properly.

The Atonement in the King and His Kingdom Story

The General Plot of the Bible, as explained earlier, is Theocracy, Monarchy, and then Christocracy. The central concern of the Bible is God's gracious and good rule over all creation and especially over God's people, Israel, and then the church. The Bible's Story under **Theocracy** reveals very quickly—Genesis 3—that Adam and Eve, who represent Israel and also all humans, slide over to live outside God's rule by choosing to listen to the words of the Evil One, the serpent (Satan), instead of to the words of God. They turn against one another; they are banned from Eden; they are in search of Eden from that moment on. Soon, to lead them back to Eden or toward the kingdom, God makes a covenant with Abraham to establish a community of the covenant who are to live obediently under God's rule and find forgiveness from God for their disobedience. In a sad imitation of Adam and Eve, however, Samuel tells God that Israel would rather have a human king instead of "just" a divine king, and God lets them have their way. Under a **Monarchy**, life is no better and at times it's worse: their kings can be corrupt, their institutions polluted, their morals defective, and their borders porous. Israel needs redemption; Israel needs the kingdom; Israelites need redemption; the world too needs redemption. Monarchy does not bring what is most needed. So the prophets announce God's will and predict the coming of a great king, the Messiah, who will forgive the people and teach them the full will of God and establish the kingdom and lead the community to that kingdom. When Jesus comes—and here we must say this means his incarnation, his life and teachings and ministry, his death, his burial, his resurrection, his ascension—**Christocracy** is formed. This means that God is once again ruling—Jesus speaks constantly of the Kingdom *of God* because it is no longer a Monarchy but a Theocracy in incarnate form. This also means that both national and personal redemption have come for God's people. This people is to live under a Christocracy as it worships God, as it obeys the King, as it witnesses to the world of the world's one true King Jesus, and as it waits for the fullness of the Kingdom of God (the new heaven and the new earth).

A biblical atonement theory has to fit into this Story of Theocracy, Monarchy, and Christocracy. Instead of arguing that one atonement theory is the best, it is better to show how the various themes at work in the various atonement theories appear and find their resolution in the King and His Kingdom Story. So, to this we must now proceed.

First, we need to know that the *goal* of God's plan for all creation is the kingdom, the new heaven and the new earth. That kingdom, as already stated, is made of a king (Father, Son, Spirit) who redeems a community (Israel, church) so they can enjoy God's gracious, peaceful, and just rule in God's special place for them (land, New Jerusalem) as that redeemed people know God, worship God, love God, and do God's good will through the gracious empowerment of the Spirit. In other words, the solution is the King and His Kingdom. The redemptive benefits of God's work in King Jesus are all designed to usher cracked *Eikons*, sinners, into this new people of God and participate in knowing, worshiping, loving, and obeying God. The King and His Kingdom Story is the Bible's one and only General Plot.

Second, *humans resist God's will, refuse allegiance to King Jesus*, and jeopardize their location in God's Kingdom. To discipline the resisters of God's will/law, God sometimes exiles them, and that is why enslavement is such an important theme in the Bible. The children of Israel were exiled into slavery three different times in the Bible: in Egypt, in Assyria, and in Babylon. New Testament sinners are also enslaved to the powers and principalities, structures and beings that turn God's good ways into evil's bad ways. These exiles are dramatic embodiments of the condition established for those who sin, for those who refuse to live under God's rule in the Theocracy, under God's or the king's rule in Monarchy, and King Jesus's rule in the Christocracy. Hence, the Bible explores a variety of words for "sin," words like rebellion, infidelity, disloyalty, ingratitude, pollution, wandering, trespass, transgress, and failure.[2] A capsule summary word in the New Testament is "sin," but this term folds into the mix all the above terms and more. Our problem then is not simply failure to obey God but a complex set of ways we find to evade God's will and resist God's Spirit and rebel against King Jesus. From this sin condition we need redemption.

Third, the atonement itself *is a death on the cross that was anticipated by millions of sacrifices in Israel's history.* If we explore the mechanics of atonement—how it happens—we do it through the central consequence of sin: death. Time and time again Israel's sacrificial system put animals to death as acts of atonement. The punishment for sin is death, so the enemy is death and the need is for death to be undone. To do this, Jesus must enter into death—this is what Romans 6 is all about—to look it in the face, absorb death itself by dying, but turning death inside out into eternal life by the resurrection. The death of an animal, the Passover blood smeared on a door, the Day of Atonement, the wrath and disciplinary exile of God against the rebellion of the people of God, the many sacrifices of blood in the Old Testament system of sacrifice and atonement . . . these and other indicators, like the suffering of the Son of Man and the suffering of the Servant of Isaiah, are the indicators and anticipators of the atonement of how God will deal death to death and turn death into life by the power of God's Spirit resurrecting Jesus and giving to us life in his resurrection.

Fourth, the atonement of God in Christ, which brings to completion the atoning acts of God throughout the entire Old Testament, aims to erase the above problems and create new people for the new heaven and the new earth. Once the problem (sin) is defined in a complex way, the atonement's solution—the redemptive benefits of the King and His Kingdom—becomes just as complex. I quote John Goldingay for getting this right and saying it better than I can (I reformat his words into an outline and put in bold the consequences of the sin).

God's act of atonement in Christ was designed to deal with the deep and incurable sinfulness of humanity which expresses itself in:

1. rebellion against God's authority,
2. infidelity which issues in **breakdown of the relationship**,
3. disloyalty which has **interrupted a friendship**,
4. ingratitude which has **imperiled love**,
5. stain which has **rendered humanity repulsive**,
6. perversity which has **landed us in exile**,
7. offensiveness which has **put us in debt**,
8. lawlessness which has **made us guilty**,
9. and failure which leaves us **far short of our destiny**.[3]

King Jesus addresses all this and more in his incarnation, his life, his death, his burial, his resurrection, and his ascension. As the one true King, he heals us of all these conditions, and through the Spirit—another element of the gospel ignored in many atonement theories—he re-creates us to be "new creations" who can live under his gracious, loving, peaceful, and just rule with unflinching, joyous allegiance. Atonement then is not just about erasing these sins but creating the true virtues on the far side of forgiveness:

1. Obedience
2. Faithfulness

3. Allegiance
4. Gratitude
5. Purity
6. Following Jesus into the Kingdom
7. Containment by the will of God
8. Law-abiding from the heart
9. Achieving our purpose

And if I summarize this, it means we are new creations who love God, love ourselves, love others, love the people of God, and love all of God's creation. Atonement is designed to create these kinds of new creations.

It will not do then to limit atonement theory to one problem—say "debt" or "guilt"—and then construct a mini-story that deals with that problem as if it is the whole problem. Nor will it do to stop with the elimination of the consequence of sin, be that God's judgment in its various forms including the sentence of guilty, enmity, wrath, or falling short. No, we need to see sin and its consequences being erased through the whole Christ for the whole world and the whole person so the whole world and the whole person can be what God designed each to be.

Finally, the atonement is about rescuing humans from one condition (sin) and relocating them in a new condition (the kingdom of God). The King and His Kingdom Story, if it does anything for our Bible reading, presents before our eyes a people of God living under the rule of God (Father, Son, Spirit) in a given location (our local church in our local community as it connects to the whole church in the whole world). This people swears allegiance alone to King Jesus and lives under his rule by following his teachings by the power of the Spirit. The new creation then is both personal/individual and corporate. New creation is as much about the body of Christ, the church in the world, as it is about you and me experiencing personal conversion.

The important consequence is that the King and His Kingdom Story is about God and humans, but those humans are narrowed by a covenant in Genesis 12, 15, and 22 to one man, one woman, one family and their descendants: Israel. God cares about a national-political entity (Israel of the Bible) and an ecclesial spiritual reality (the church that expands Israel to include gentiles) as the *primary location where God's redemptive benefits are taking root in the world.* Read the Bible, and what you will discover is a whole lot of Israel and a whole lot of church. The Bible is about the people of God far more than individual persons and their redemption, though the latter is vital for the flourishing of the former. No personal redemption, no redeemed people of God; but no people of God, no place for the redeemed to flourish in God's way.

These humans have a mission to the world: to be its light by pointing to the King and His Kingdom.

CHAPTER 13

JUSTICE IN THE KING AND HIS KINGDOM REDEMPTION STORY

J ustice is the new darling word for America's evangelical crowd. One generation back plus a decade, evangelicals were not tied into justice so much; what mattered was missions, gospel, evangelism, and church-planting. The new theme is justice. Justice spans the spectrum of evangelicals from progressives to conservatives.

This new enchantment with justice as social action for the common good and for the whole world has, however, a glaring weakness: the meaning of justice seems to come from the wrong place. What does justice mean? It all depends on whom you ask. If we ask the philosophers, this is what we get:

> Justice in one sense is identical with the ethics of who should receive benefits and burdens, good or bad things of many sorts, given that others might receive these things. [Many gulp after reading such an abstraction. Read on.] There are various contexts for talk about justice, including (at least) distributive, retributive, and "corrective" justice (which apparently overlap to some extent). Distributive justice concerns the ethical appropriateness of which recipients get which benefits and burdens. Retributive justice concerns the ethical appropriateness of punishment for

wrongdoing. Corrective justice concerns the ethical appropriateness of compensating with some good because of a loss or appropriating some good because of a gain.[1]

These are the ideas, or something quite like them, that are in the heads and hearts of many social activists: justice is about benefits and burdens, about things—like freedom and jobs and money and homes and health care provision. These senses of justice—distributive, retributive, corrective, as well as restorative—flow directly out of someone's beliefs about rights and wrongs as well as about protections of rights and mandating some corresponding duties.

Who Decides the Meaning of Justice?

Who decides the meaning of justice? This has been a major discussion in the history of Western thought with three strong approaches: some think justice is determined by God, others by intelligent people discerning natural law, while still others think justice is a social arrangement or contract shaped by a given community or nation with a history and tradition. This last one shakes out into discussions of justice as either Right Order or Right Action. This third approach, with its variety of understandings, is mostly at work in today's social activists, across the spectrum. It can be narrowed to a simpler answer: most people today derive their understanding of justice through our culture's educational and social influence. That is, they get it from the Constitution of the United States and its unfolding of laws. That Constitution—truth be told—is a product of the Enlightenment's strong affirmation and centralizing of human reason and human rights. Many today *think* they have a *right* to such things as jobs with adequate income for provisions and personal growth, health care, education, safety, solid roads, good neighbors, and reliable communities. These factors are in play when people say they are working for justice.

Three major ideas are included in this cultural understanding of the core values of democracy: equality, justice, and freedom. Or, as in the French expressions: equality, liberty, fraternity. The problem we see on every news page and in every news show on TV is that one person's equality infringes upon another person's liberty, and one person's view of fraternity or justice is another person's understanding of theft or invasion of privacy. Justice becomes a game of negotiation between action and standard, or behavior and ideal. Some say it is about balancing our rights with our duties. These terms are all very complex, and this is not the place nor am I the person to discuss these at length.

Justice is a *measurement*. It measures how a given action by a person or a society compares to a *standard*, which in the Western world means things like equality and liberty.

How then do we as Bible readers—readers who know the King and His Kingdom Story with its redemptive benefits—understand justice? It starts with this: in the Bible *God defines justice*. Neither Israel's legal scholars nor kings nor prophets got together and determined what justice was; nor did they have a constitutional congress of representative citizens who gathered to hammer out justice's major themes; nor was there a democratic vote on answers to the question, "What is justice?" In the Bible, God *reveals and declares what justice is.*

This is even more important: the cultural definition of justice at work in modern society may overlap in important ways with what the Bible says, but (1) they are not the same, and (2) the cultural understanding is *secular* and therefore neglects the most important element of justice in the Bible. The standards for secular justice and for the Bible's sense of justice *are radically different*. In our culture the standard is the US Constitution, but it is probably just as much how that Constitution is understood and presented in our specific world context. For Christians, the standard is the Bible. The Bible's standard determines what justice means and measures whether we are or are not just. So here's a set of lines that set up this whole chapter:

- In the **US**, a just person is a person who conforms to the *US Constitution* and to humanistic and secular ideals.

- In the **Old Testament**, a just person is a person who conforms to the *law of Moses*.
- In the **New Testament**, a just person is a person who conforms to the fulfillment of the law of Moses in *the teachings of Jesus and the apostles* as that person is empowered to do so by the Spirit.

Once again, locating justice in the King and His Kingdom Story will give us our North Star for understanding justice.

What Does the Bible Say?

There are just a few important terms at work in the Bible that help us understand justice, but the terms alone are not enough. The terms need to be soaked in the Bible's Story. Here are the principal terms: *mishpat, din, tzedek, dikaios, and dikaiosune,* as well as *krima* and *krino.* The first term, *mishpat,* can be translated as justice, judgment, rights, and redemption while *din* is translated judgment. The term *tzedek* can be translated as righteousness and justice while *dikaios* shows up in the New Testament translations as just and justice. And *dikaiosune* shows up as justification. Both *krima* and *krino* boil down to the idea of rendering judgment (both in favor of what is right and against what is wrong). Here in the span of four verses is an almost complete expression of the Bible's ideas about justice. I begin with an ideal vision of Israel's king, who is himself just, who renders just judgments and shows compassionate justice for the poor and prosperity to the obedient and renders punitive justice against oppressors.

> Endow the king with your justice, O God,
> the royal son with your righteousness (*tzedek*).
> May he judge (*din*) your people in righteousness (*tzedek*),
> your afflicted ones with justice (*mishpat*).
> May the mountains bring prosperity [or peace] (*shalom*) to
> the people,

> the hills the fruit of righteousness (*tzedek*).
> May he defend (*yishpat*) the afflicted among the people
> and save the children of the needy;
> may he crush the oppressor. (Psalm 72:1–4)

Since justice in the Bible is determined by one's relationship to God and the king ("the royal son" who has "your righteousness"), and since God expresses what is right in the Law (Torah), to be just (or righteous) is a description of a person who is in a right relation with God by conforming one's life to God's revealed will. Notice this: it is the *king's responsibility to ensure that justice* (and all the terms in its big family) are established and embodied.

Notice these two passages:

> For I, the LORD, love justice (*mishpat*);
> I hate robbery and wrongdoing.
> In my faithfulness I will reward my people
> and make an everlasting covenant with them. (Isaiah 61:8)

> Follow *justice* and *justice* [both are *tzedek*] alone, so that you may live and possess the land the LORD your God is giving you. (Deuteronomy 16:20)

And this text from the New Testament about being made right by God's judging us to be in the right on the basis of Christ's own redemptive work for us:

> Therefore, since we have been *justified* (*dikaioo*) through faith, we have peace with God through our Lord Jesus Christ, through whom we have gained access by faith into this grace in which we now stand. And we boast in the hope of the glory of God. Not only so, but we also glory in our sufferings, because we know that suffering produces perseverance; perseverance, character; and character, hope. And hope does not put us to shame, because

God's love has been poured out into our hearts through the Holy Spirit, who has been given to us.

You see, at just the right time, when we were still powerless, Christ died for the ungodly. Very rarely will anyone die for a *righteous* (*dikaios*) person, though for a good person someone might possibly dare to die. But God demonstrates his own love for us in this: While we were still sinners, Christ died for us. (Romans 5:1–8)

Those made right are to be righteous:

For I tell you that unless your *righteousness* (*dikaiosune*) surpasses that of the Pharisees and the teachers of the law, you will certainly not enter the kingdom of heaven. (Matthew 5:20)

> He has shown you, O mortal, what is good.
> And what does the LORD require of you?
> To act *justly* (*mishpat*) and to love mercy
> and to walk humbly with your God. (Micah 6:8)

If we tie this all together, what does justice look like when the Bible is the new standard? A just person is one who is a participant in God's covenant (justified), and God's redemptive covenant ushers that person into a life of hearing and following the will of God as taught in the law (justice). In the New Testament, of course, that covenant becomes the "new" covenant and that "law" becomes the "new law" as taught by Jesus (e.g., Matthew 5–7) and empowered by the Spirit (Galatians 5:22–23; 6:2). Thus, a just or righteous person in the New Testament is one whose life conforms to the new law as taught by Jesus and empowered by the Spirit. Justice then describes conditions in his world where that new law rules the new people. This challenges the secularized understanding of justice—equality, liberty, fraternity— even if at times there is clear overlap. Theft is contrary to the law of our land and to the law of Christ. Christian ethics, of which justice is a major theme, combines three streams: one from God, one from the people, and one pertaining to economics. That is, Christian ethics are theological, social, and economic.[2] What is lurking behind the doors of this disclosure is that a Christian sense of justice is thoroughly spiritual before it is social. Justice is covenant rooted. As Chris Wright puts it,

> For Israel, then, justice was no abstract concept or philosophical
> definition. Justice was essentially theological. It was rooted in
> the character of the Lord, their God; it flowed from his actions
> in history; it was demanded by his covenant relationship with
> Israel; it would ultimately be established on the earth only by
> his sovereign power.[3]

What then is justice? I believe God's first and foremost standard of measurement is love, the kind of love exhibited in God's own love (not in our American dictionaries). Love in the Bible is a rugged, affectional commitment to another person in offering presence, advocacy, and mutual progress in Christlikeness.[4] Justice is love, but justice is also peace and reconciliation and wisdom.[5] Those who live this way flourish—what we speak of as happiness is an echo of what "blessing" and "flourishing" mean in the Bible. But what needs to be observed before we take the next step in this chapter is that the standard has changed, so justice changes. When we shift from the US Constitution and Western values to the Bible's value of love, peace, and reconciliation, the very meaning of justice now shifts. If justice is comparing our actions with God's standard, and God's standard is love, then a just person is loving. That says it all.

Justice in the Bible's Story

The redemptive benefits in the King and His Kingdom Story in the Bible create a radically nuanced understanding of justice. What the Bible says about justice is radically different from what most activists today understand justice to mean. How so? The aim of all creation is the new heaven and the new earth where God will dwell with God's people (Israel, church), where God's people will live in loving fellowship with one another in just and peaceful and wise ways, and the entire world will be soaked with lives aimed at glorifying God. These are the major ideas of God's ultimate covenant with creation, but to participate in that kingdom one must be redeemed by that covenant and be transformed by the covenant God's Spirit to become a person who lives according to the covenant God's way of life among God's people, all of whom are living according to God's will. To say this in more New Testament language: one must be justified to live justly.

So justice in the Bible is shaped by God and God's creation, and by God's covenant with Abraham and the covenant, by Moses and the exodus and the law, and by David and the kingdom and the new covenant with Jesus. In Jesus, we get covenant, exodus, law, and kingdom. That covenant takes sinful people—cracked *Eikons*—and transforms them by God's Spirit so they can become loving and just *Eikons* who long for God's glory and who indwell fellowship with other redeemed *Eikons*. These themes are all tied together like a beautiful multicolored cord in Romans 5:1–8 cited above, and they are reminiscent of the new community, the church.

That fellowship, that love, that justice, that peace, that reconciliation, and that wisdom are God's will so that a "just" person is not only "justified" (declared and made right with God) but also lives according to the will of God through that redeemed relationship with God. A justified person then becomes a just person who is an agent of justice. God's covenant redemption makes possible God's covenant justice.

Justice, like so many other themes in the Bible, is more than an idea. Justice is a way of life.

What Does Justice Look Like?

Justice begins with evangelism because the redemptive benefit of the gospel is justification. It may well strike many as odd to connect justification with justice, but the Greek term for justification (*dikaiosune*) is a cognate to the term for justice (*dikaios*). That perhaps makes the point clear, that the first step in justice is redeeming cracked *Eikons* so they can become agents of redemption in the world, which is what justice is. Thus, those working for a biblical sense of justice will be committed to evangelism, to the gospel that justifies and transforms the justified into agents of justice in the world. One can say this stronger: there is no genuine work for justice that is not working for justification.

Justice is awakened in the life of a believer by the power of the Spirit. It follows then that justified people are indwelt by the Spirit, and it is the Spirit who awakens believers to love, to peace, to reconciliation, and to justice. That is, the Spirit empowers redeemed people to become agents of grace in the world. Justice is therefore Spirit-empowered, or it is not what the Bible means by justice.

Justice is embodied in a local church where justice is embodied among a people. Here is a critical moment in understanding the Bible's Story as it impacts justice. Justice is not the US Constitution, but the church's constitution. That is, what the Bible says about justice is for God's people (Israel, church) who are drawn into relation with God through the covenant. Justice is *embodied* by the people of God in fellowship with one another. What does this look like? Justice is when you and I act peacefully, justly, lovingly, and wisely toward one another in a local church in such a manner that *we as a body of Christ* embody justice as a group. Thus, we disestablish racism, classism, and sexism, and we establish love, peace, reconciliation, and wisdom as the way we live as a fellowshipping community in Christ.

Justice is expanded into the public sector by the believer on the basis of learning how to do justice in the fellowship of the church. One of the more remarkable features of the New Testament is that how Christians behave in the public sector, that is, what the New Testament calls the "world," is never called "justice" or "social justice." Rather, Israel practices justice amongst itself while the church practices justice in the body of Christ. Justice, then, *is learned among the people of God.* But this isn't a plea for isolationism. No, it means this: having learned justice in the body of Christ as we embody justice in our local church, *we are formed into agents of justice who are then to enter into the public sector.* In the New Testament, this is often called "doing good." I quote here some verses from Jesus and Peter to show where these references are found:

> In the same way, let your light shine before others, that they may see your *good deeds* and glorify your Father in heaven. (Matthew 5:16, emphasis added)

> Dear friends, I urge you, as foreigners and exiles, to abstain from sinful desires, which wage war against your soul. Live such *good lives* among the pagans that, though they accuse you of doing wrong, they may see your *good deeds* and glorify God on the day he visits us. (1 Peter 2:11–12, emphasis added)

> For it is God's will that by *doing good* you should silence the ignorant talk of foolish people. (1 Peter 2:15, emphasis added)

> But how is it to your credit if you receive a beating for doing wrong and endure it? But if you suffer for *doing good* and you endure it, this is commendable before God. (1 Peter 2:20, emphasis added)

> So then, those who suffer according to God's will should commit themselves to their faithful Creator and *continue to do good.* (1 Peter 4:19, emphasis added)

Over and over the apostle Peter, building on Jesus, says we are to be people noticeable for doing good. Which means what? In context, these terms referred to public acts of benevolence—caring for the poor, compassion following disasters, forming public policy for the common good, and the like. These in the Bible's Story are expansions, spillovers, inevitable consequences of the people of God having learned to be just with one another. In the Bible, learning justice in the people of God precedes practicing justice in the world, but the latter is *an inevitability for those who have learned to be just in the church.* Why? Because the church folks' character has been transformed by God's Spirit to become just, and being just means being just always. I believe that secular or social justice is an echo of redemptive-based justice among God's people.

PART 5

WOMEN IN CHURCH MINISTRIES TODAY

A Case Study in Rethinking How You Read the Bible

There is neither Jew nor Gentile, neither slave nor free, nor is there male and female, for you are all one in Christ Jesus.

The apostle Paul, according to Galatians 3:28

I have become all things to all people so that by all possible means I might save some. I do all this for the sake of the gospel, that I may share in its blessings.

The apostle Paul, according to 1 Corinthians 9:22–23

When I was a professor at Trinity Evangelical Divinity School (TEDS) from 1983 to 1995, the debate about women in church ministries was one of the hot topics. In writing here about "women in church ministries," I want to emphasize that I am not talking only about senior pastors and elders and preaching and teaching from pulpits on Sunday mornings, but about anything God calls women to do. Much of the debate about women in ministry, of course, revolves around the word "ordination" and senior pastors and public preaching. But we have a wider scope than that kind of ministry.

As a young professor, I made two decisions—one subtle and which I regret, and one enduring and about to be documented in the next few chapters. The subtle decision I regret is that, because the issues were so inflammatory and anyone who thought otherwise about women was held either as theologically liberal or intellectually suspect, I made the decision not to enter into the public debate at Trinity. Class preparation, some other writing projects, a young family, and an income that didn't make life anything other than a monthly chase did not give me the time to be proficient enough to enter the fray. (I now wish I had.) But I listened and learned.

The discussion itself led me into many hours of thinking and deliberating with students, but rarely with colleagues. What I concluded then was that I simply didn't read the Bible as did those who opposed women in church ministries, especially teaching and leading ministries. Some of the public debaters have the habit of calling anyone who moves in a different direction a liberal and of suggesting that those who differ must be denying inerrancy. Some announce that those who differ with the traditional view are on a slippery slope into theological liberalism. The facts are against this announcement. Many who do disagree with the traditional view are not in fact liberals. I could give you a list of them. Most of them are card-carrying evangelicals. I am one of them.

What I realized as I listened to the debates was that I read the Bible as Story (though that was not the term I was using at that time), and I thought (and still think) that many of the traditionalists read the Bible as a law book and a puzzle. Perhaps a gentler way of putting this is to suggest that I think traditionalists read the Bible about women in church ministries *through* tradition instead of reading the Bible *with* tradition. The latter challenges the tradition while the former does not. In this instance, the tradition got it wrong.

There are times for *conservation* and there are times for *innovation*.[1] When innovation is not organic to the tradition, it is called *revolution*, and there is no reason to consider revolution in this discussion. Of course, it deserves to be said: one person's conservation is another person's innovation, and one person's innovation is another person's revolution, while some of us think the revolution is actually a case of conservation! In my Anglican Church of North America context, I have seen two major innovations, both of which were wise. The first was the decision that continuing cooperation with The Episcopal Church of America (TEC) was causing too much pain for those who adhered to the Great Tradition of the church, that is, to classic orthodoxy in its many elements—inspiration of Scripture, the Bible's reliability to tell truth, the deity of Christ, the necessity of personal salvation, and a number of moral issues like homosexuality. The decision was to break from the TEC to form a separate North American "province" called the Anglican Church of North America. (I know, the debates between Christians of this magnitude too often have turned ugly—on both sides.) It is nothing short of an astounding innovation to break from one's province to form one's own province, and to do so not with the recognition of the central leaders (in Canterbury) but with recognition of other church leaders (in Africa).

A second innovation is seen in how Anglicans have defended

nonordination of women. The deep tradition was that women were ontologically subordinate and inferior to men. Any reading of church history will put you in touch with church theologians of the deep past who said nothing less than vile things about women.

But an innovation occurred in the middle of the twentieth century in the Western world: *women were seen as ontologically equal to men but were seen as having roles of subordination.* That, as one informed scholar has proven beyond doubt, is nothing less than an *innovation.*[2] I agree: Yes, it's an innovation among Anglicans and it had to be made. But it didn't go far enough.

This is where part 5 in this book is located. It will argue that innovation, organically connected to the Bible and to the church's tradition bringing those passages of the Bible into full view, is needed if we want to be faithful to the Bible. Women are not only ontologically equal to men but women are called to all ministries in the church. That's another innovation we need.

Now, before I get to this approach to women in ministry, a view I believe is more biblical and one that encourages us to expand the ministries of women, I want to sketch where I have come from.

How I Changed My Mind

Fundamentalism

I grew up in a fundamentalist Christian home and church in the Midwest. Our home was traditional in this sense: my father and mother lived their lives within what might be called traditional roles. My father was a public school teacher, and my mother was a housewife until my sisters and I were old enough for her to begin working to supplement the income. My mother was (and still is) an ambitious and talented woman who, had she been born thirty years later, would have become a successful businessperson or leader of some kind. My father called the shots but my mother ran the place, though I can't say I paid much attention to such things. I absorbed this way of living as natural.

Our church was traditionalist. We had no women in any kind of public ministry other than my mother, who was the choir director. I am reasonably certain no woman ever preached from our pulpit, though women did sing and give testimonies. The one exception was female missionaries who came through at times to report on their missionary efforts. They did not preach or teach; rather, they gave witness or reports and at times their stories were gripping. The difference between teaching and giving witness was important, even if mistaken.

However, the windows were slightly open in our fundamentalist church because one of our neighbors, Dorothy Libby, was a Sunday school teacher for young adults—post-high-school, college-age adults—even though she was a woman. She loved to study the Bible, had a mind of her own, read what was available in commentaries, books, and Bible dictionaries, and overall did something that technically was against the silent code—women were not to teach male adults.

Education

I went off to a fundamentalist Christian college, where the same ideas were present. I had a brilliant Western lit teacher named Diana Portfleet, who had a keen perception of theology and church history, but she did not teach Bible or theology. Dr. Portfleet at some level opened the window for me even more. I do not recall women in church ministries being an issue for me either when I was in college or when I was in seminary.

During my doctoral days in England, this issue came up in a variety of ways, and while my recollection is that I was a quiet and shifting traditionalist with more than a willingness to think about the problems, my intellectual interests were about other topics. I was focused on gospel studies and how Judaism worked. But one day riding my bicycle in Cambridge, England, I observed that the person riding a bicycle next to me was none other than Professor Morna Hooker, the great Methodist New Testament scholar at Cambridge University. In an odd sort of way, my heart was strangely warmed.

After exchanging pleasantries and fighting off the temptation to engage in nonstop prattle with her as we rode together across Cambridge, something occurred to me that opened the window more. I realized how much I had learned from Morna Hooker's exquisite and insightful scholarship. Most importantly, this moment of bicycle riding with her drove me to the conclusion that anyone who thinks it is wrong for a woman to teach in a church can be consistent with that point of view only if they refuse to read and learn from women scholars. This means not reading their books lest the women become their teachers.

Some people think it is pedantic to equate reading-to-learn with a teaching ministry. I don't, and I stand by it until someone can convince me that reading-to-learn is different from listening-to-learn. Right then and there, while riding a bicycle next to Professor Hooker, I realized that my own view was about to undergo a major change. I became convinced that teaching is teaching and learning is learning, and that reading her books is learning from her. If men could learn from a woman scholar's writings about theology and the Bible, if men could learn from a New Testament expert, a woman, who gave substance to their sermons and ideas and theology, then these men were being taught—call it what you want—by a woman.

Teaching

By the time I began teaching at Trinity Evangelical Divinity School, I cannot say that my mind was clear in all regards or that I had become consistent in my own head, but I can say that the genesis of change was in the past. I was a traditionalist at some level, but all I needed was an opportunity. Teaching students, especially women, became that opportunity. My change was gradual, and what most changed it was the study of the New Testament and the realization that I believed the New Testament—all of it—*emerged from and therefore was shaped by* the first-century Jewish and Greco-Roman culture, including what it said about women. Within a year or two I had become convinced that the traditionalist view was misreading and misusing the Bible. I taught at Trinity for more than a decade. Apart from classroom discussions, I did not get into these issues in public.

Writing this has led to some soul-searching. I read through what I wrote on Galatians 3:28 and 1 Peter 3:1–6 in my commentaries on those books—one passage about "neither male nor female" and the other about women submitting to their unbelieving spouse.[3] Those commentaries were written as I was making the transition from Trinity to North Park University in Chicago. They were the first time I went public with my views. In both commentaries I sketched how I thought we should read the Bible—as a culturally conditioned revelation of God's Word that needs to be worked out in a modern context. My views have developed since then, but the foundational argument was present in both commentaries. I regret that I did not engage traditionalists at that time, even though the views I was taking gave me a foundation to engage in the debate.

In the process of being interviewed to teach at North Park, two of my future colleagues, Sonia Bodi and Nancy Arnesen, took me to coffee. Nancy, a gentle, fair-minded woman and one firmly entrenched in a Christian feminist perspective, asked me my view of women in church ministries. I won't forget what I said: "I'm for women in ministry."

"But what about Paul?" she asked back.

"Paul's directions to his churches were culturally shaped," I replied. We spent time discussing that point of view. The window on women in ministry was open for me (and so was a teaching post I enjoyed for seventeen years).

I now teach at Northern Seminary in Lisle, Illinois, a seminary whose first graduate was a woman called to preach and teach. At Northern we are firmly committed to women in ministry, and I have a talented female colleague in systematic theology, Cherith Fee Nordling. She can teach, the students say, but she can preach even more! And she can. I am so proud of Northern's stance as one it has maintained for more than a century.

Before I go on, I must confess that I believe I (and my colleagues) failed our female students at Trinity, that we should have engaged this debate "tooth and claw," and that had we done so the Evangelical Free

Church as well as that seminary may have been a much more liberating institution than it is today. I want to confess to the many female students that we (and I) were wrong and I am asking you to forgive us (and me). I can only hope the recent hire of women like Dana Harris and Ingrid Faro will lead to more women on the Trinity faculty. I also hope such appointments come with an official confession and invited responses by former women students.

I have loads of respect for my friends and colleagues at Trinity, not the least of whom were my teachers, Walt Liefeld and Grant Osborne. Both Walt and Grant took a stand for women's ordination against the grain at Trinity and helped me in many ways to see the light on this issue, but none of us fought the battle as fiercely as was required for the time. I don't want to make it look as if I was simmering or seething under a tightly stopped-up lid of oppression. I could have done more; we could have done more. Walt and Grant did far more than I did.

Finally, I want to call attention to the many women students we had who endured traditionalist teachers. Unintentionally or intentionally, these women were suppressed from exercising their gifts and have been barred from ministries—some of whom, to my great delight, like Sarah Sumner and Alice Shirey, have found their way into careers of teaching, speaking, pastoring, and writing while others have had to pursue other careers in spite of a calling from God to teach and preach.

Since I've mentioned Sarah and Alice, I also want to mention two outstandingly gifted women who have never found a sacred space among evangelicals, Cheryl Hatch and Jane Goleman. These two women, and I could mention others, were some of the best students I have ever taught and some of the most gifted. But their own commitments to evangelicalism have kept them among evangelicals who, sadly, silence blue parakeets.

I want to tell more of Cheryl's story, but that will begin our next chapter.

CHAPTER 14

THE BIBLE AND WOMEN

Women in Church Ministries 1

In one of my early classes of teaching at Trinity Evangelical Divinity School, I had a fantastic student named Cheryl Hatch. She had already flourished for a decade as a campus minister with "Crusade" (her name for Campus Crusade for Christ, a ministry to college students). She had a firm grasp of both the Bible and Christian theology, she had exceptional interpersonal skills, and her mature faith was obvious. In my class of "exegeting" 1 Peter, each student was assigned to summarize how they would preach a given passage. Cheryl's "sermonette" stood head and shoulders above all the others. Not only was Cheryl mature in faith and competent theologically, she was also gifted to preach.

But when Cheryl graduated with her master of arts in religion with an emphasis in New Testament, she could find no church willing to call her as a preaching or teaching pastor. Why? She was a woman. She received offers to serve as a children's pastor or a youth pastor or a women's ministry pastor, but no church—zero—even considered her to stand behind a pulpit on Sunday morning to preach the gospel and expound the Bible *even though she was gifted and competent and willing* and felt God had called her to preach.

The irony of this haunts me. Cheryl is a gifted evangelist. One moment's reflection on the significance of evangelism, from which gift (to my knowledge) women have never been barred, should lead us to some about-face changes. If a woman is given the freedom to explain the gospel and persuade others to respond to the gospel, and if the message of evangelism shapes how a person will eventually live as a Christian, consistency would demand that we either bar women from evangelism or permit them to teach and preach as well. Anyone, so I would say, who permits women to evangelize ought to permit them to preach. After all, what is "preaching" in the New Testament if it does not include evangelism?

Cheryl returned to Washington, DC, where to this day she enjoys a full life of federal employment, participates actively in her local church, and perseveres in the ongoing development of her own theological studies. Kris and I remain friends with Cheryl. She appears to harbor no bitterness. I am willing to now say that the evangelical church missed out on someone who could have been a dynamic pastor.

Cheryl was a blue parakeet. Blue parakeets, the church was saying at the time she was "on the market," are to remain in their cages and keep silent. But are they? Let's look in the next few chapters how many people have discerned what we now are to do with blue parakeets, the women who believe they are called to sing and fly in the ministries of the church. I will argue that we should let the blue parakeets sing and fly, that in reading the Bible *with* tradition instead of *through* tradition, we are set free to respect and challenge that tradition. The direction of the Bible itself encourages us to face the future by expanding the place of women in church ministries.

We offer a positive argument for why we think the Bible affirms the ongoing presence of women in church ministries. We will look at a variety of topics, including a quick sweep through the Bible to show how the Bible as Story informs our reading of these passages. Any discussion that defends women in church ministries can be responsible only if it examines in more detail the so-called silencing of women passages in Paul (1 Corinthians 14:34–35 and 1 Timothy 2:8–15). We will examine those two passages in our final chapters.

However, I must ask for your sympathy about one point: in this book it is impossible to discuss all the issues and all the counterarguments about this debated issue of women in church ministries. I will not even try to do this, nor will I sketch the views of those who are traditionalists in these matters. There are other books that do that. Our book is merely illustrating how we read the Bible—story, listen, discern—by offering women in church ministries as a test case. Could more be said? Yes. I am deeply aware of the many, many issues I would like to bring up, and maybe at a later time I will develop this discussion at more length; but for now I offer the next few chapters as an example of how to read the Bible as Story, learn to listen, and discern how to live the Bible in our world.

Once again, we need to locate women in the King and His Kingdom Story. This is the big idea: In Christ, Paul says, there is not only no longer slave and free but neither is there "male and female." Paul does not erase embodied distinctions, but in Christ and in the church, gender no longer matters. In the final kingdom of God, one's gender will not be a mark of status or lack of status. All will be equal, yet radically unique. But if we focus too much on the redemptive benefits, we may well say, "Women like men are totally equal before God in that each can be saved. But there are roles assigned to men that women can't do." That contradicts what Paul says in Galatians 3:28 and clearly contradicts what women did in the early churches.

Similar but Shifting Contexts

It is customary for those who favor women in church ministries to begin with an infamous prayer of the rabbis and then to make it clear that neither Jesus nor the early Christians saw women this way. They suggest that Jesus and Christianity "liberated" women from an oppressive Jewish world, feeling a little bit morally superior for the progress we have made.

I will include this prayer, but I emphasize that this rabbinic statement tells only part of the story of women in Judaism and the biblical world. We should not forget the Song of Songs when it comes to what women thought of men and men of women! Still, the social conditions giving rise to this prayer are a real part of the ancient world—the part that reveals that women were considered unequal and in some cases inferior to men.

> R. Judah says, "A man must recite three benedictions every day:
> *Praised be Thou, O Lord, who did not make me a gentile;*
> *Praised be Thou, O Lord, who did not make me a boor;*
> *Praised be Thou, O Lord, who did not make me a woman.*"

Why did the rabbis say this of women? Because "women are not obligated [to perform all] the commandments."[1] The budding rabbi is to give thanks to God because, as a male, he gets to observe all the commandments, while a woman, for a variety of reasons—not the least being menstruation—is not so privileged. I don't believe this is what Jewish men thought of women in general. Some men? To be sure. All men? No. This prayer may have been a Jewish version of an ancient Greek saying. Thus, the Greek male is taught to be grateful "that I was born a human being and not a beast, next, a man and not a woman, thirdly, a Greek and not a barbarian."[2]

So, in general, what was it like for women in the Jewish world? Worse than today; sometimes much, much worse. Statements about women in the Bible, like the story of Jephthah and his daughter in Judges 11, may strike us today like a blue parakeet we'd like to tame, but we dare not. Instead, we must look these passages in the eye, let them be what they are, and embrace them as part of the Bible's story. Only then can we learn that reading the Bible as the redemption offered in the King and His Kingdom Story enables us to see how these texts fit in an ongoing story of "that was then, but this is now." So, a few points about the Bible and women.

He Who Writes the Story ...

We must say something not often admitted by Bible-reading, God-loving Christians: He who writes the story controls the glory.

What's the point? The Bible was written by men, and the Bible tells stories from the angle of men. We admit this because we admit that God spoke in those days in those ways, and those days and those ways were male days and male ways. Mary J. Evans, a professor of Old Testament at the evangelical London Bible College, wrote the essays on "Women" in the evangelical dictionaries from InterVarsity Press called *Dictionary of the Old Testament: Pentateuch* and the *Dictionary of the Old Testament: Historical Books*. After examining every reference about women in these books in the Old Testament, she admits that the Pentateuch's world is "patriarchal" and that the culture of Israel was a "strongly masculine-dominated one."[3]

Catherine Clark Kroeger, a widely accomplished and deeply respected evangelical, wrote the article on "Women" for the same publisher's *Dictionary of New Testament Background*, where she opens up with this statement: "In the main, history is written by, for and about men."[4] Our Bible is like this. We can pretend it is not, but pretending leads us to an ironic commitment to our faith and into hidden secrets and despair. Why not, I sometimes ask myself, just admit it? Will the Bible lose its power? No.

Does the Bible at times transcend that masculine-shaped story? It does, and for that we can be profoundly grateful. Our Bible is shaped by a male perspective because God, in his wisdom, chose to speak in those days in those ways. Our God is a living God; our God spoke within history and shaped that history to move us into the world in which we now live.

In General

One of the most knowledgeable scholars about women and the ancient world is David Scholer. In a dictionary article in the same series of dictionaries mentioned above on women in the ministry of Jesus, David writes this: "In very general terms Jesus lived in social-cultural contexts (the Jewish context and the larger Greco-Roman society) in which the male view of women was usually negative and the place of women was understood to be limited for the most part to the domestic roles of wife and mother."[5] Here is a famous statement made by the Jewish historian Josephus, a contemporary of Jesus and the apostle Paul: "The woman, says the Law, is in all things inferior to the man."[6]

In general, women were perceived as inferior. But there were plenty of exceptions, exceptions that reveal an undercurrent that would eventually alter the current itself. Let's look at one woman in that undercurrent. A wonderful fictional story of liberation is told of a Jewish woman named Judith in the Old Testament Apocrypha. The story transcends even the drama of the stories of Deborah and Esther, two Old Testament women—one a judge and the other a beautiful, wise, and clever woman. Judith uses her rhetorical and sexual charms to deliver Israel from the Assyrians by intrigue, and then she decapitates the king with his own sword and carries off his head in her kosher bag! No one suggests we should follow her example, but it is not without some significance that we find here a female hero in the Jewish world, even if it is fiction.

Again, in general women were seen as inferior to men. The church, for any number of reasons, fossilized this tradition into a rigid distinction between men and women when it came to ministries in the church. A good example of this teaching can be found in Augustine, one of the most powerful theologians in the history of the church.[7] Augustine thought women were companions for men in the sense that they were designed to be procreative partners. Though he believed women were human, he did not believe women *are* God's image. Males are the image of God. A woman "bears" God's image, but a man "is" God's image. By marriage, Augustine taught, a woman can become the image of God. What should be noted is that culture itself gave rise to this view of women, and there was little incentive for Augustine to challenge it. I have no desire to trash Augustine; we are deeply indebted to much good in his theology. But the culture surrounding him and the kind of theology that found its way in that culture were devastating to some passages in the Bible.

I am not saying the church had a uniformly negative view of

women; it did not.[8] But the widespread restriction of women from teaching and preaching ministries damaged the church's witness, because for centuries this became the tradition *through* which the church read its Bible. More could be said, and more deserves to be said, but this is not a book on the history of women in the church.[9] I use this example merely to illustrate the general view taken by the majority of the church. There were exceptions. The exceptions, however, were just that.

What Should We Do?

The question we need to ask today is this, and this question strikes to the heart of how we read the Bible: Do we seek to retrieve that cultural world and those cultural expressions, or do we live the same gospel in a different way in a different day? Is this a return and retrieve it all, a return and retrieve some, a reading of the Bible *through* tradition, or a reading of the Bible *with* tradition? Or, and I think this is the case, is this a tradition that needs to be challenged? How much *conservation* do we need and how much *innovation* do we need?

We could probably sketch out a dozen or so views of how Christians approach what the Bible says about women in church ministries, but many today are willing to eyeball it into three basic options.[10] Two views are connected to what might be called the tradition (hard patriarchy and soft patriarchy), while one is more connected to a renew-and-renewing mind-set: mutuality (sometimes called evangelical egalitarianism).[11]

The *hard patriarchy* view believes the biblical context and its teachings are more or less God's original and permanent design. A woman's responsibility is to glorify God, to love God, to love others, and to love her husband and her children. That is, if she is married and has children (exceptions duly noted). More narrowly now, she must submit to her husband in all things, she must submit to male leadership in the church in all things, and she should also not find her way into leadership in society. For whatever reason, God ordained males to be leaders. The hard patriarchy view shapes life by a perception of the divine order in gender and roles; it believes these roles will create peace. Chrysostom wrote, "God's purpose in ordering marriage is peace. One takes the husband's role, one takes the wife's role, one in guiding, one in supporting. If both had the very same roles, there would be no peace."[12]

The *soft patriarchy* view believes the biblical context is cultural but the principles are permanent. We are called to find a living analogy in our twenty-first-century Western context to the teachings of the Bible, including the teaching of gender roles. A woman's responsibility is to glorify God, to love God, to love others, and—if married—to love her husband and her children (if there are any). More narrowly now, while affirming the importance of submission and gender and roles, this view frees the woman to do more than the hard patriarchy view. She can work outside the home in any manner for which she is qualified and competent, always with her primary role being wife and mother. She can participate in an appropriate female manner at church, but this would not include being senior pastor or teaching men or leading men in any way.

I believe that both of the above views, to one degree or another, are stuck in the fall of humankind. We must remind ourselves over and over again that the Bible's story is a story about the establishing of the Kingdom of God under King Jesus.

That story is a theocracy that unfolds into a monarchy that eventually becomes a Christocracy. In that kingdom of Christ, there is neither male nor female, for they are equal in Christ in all ways. In the kingdom of God women will not be in submission to men nor will men be hierarchically above women. In light of that we turn to the redemption that we discover in the King and His Kingdom Story that moves from:

God's Trinitarian oneness, to
the Adam, who was one and alone, to
Adam and Eve, who were one and together, to

Adam and Eve and others, who through sin become others, to
Jesus Christ, who was the one God incarnate, to
becoming one (as in Eden) all over again in Christ, to
the consummation, when we will be one with God and others.

Whatever we say about women in church ministries, about women
in marriages, or about women who are single must be connected to
this story. I believe the next view, *mutuality*, makes the most sense of
how women fit into the Bible's story.

The *mutuality* view, which taps deeply into this redemptive
"oneness-otherness-oneness" theme, also believes a woman's responsibility is to glorify God, to love God, to love others, and—again if
married and if with children—to love her husband and her children.
More narrowly, a mutuality view liberates women from the tradition
because it believes the biblical context is cultural and that even the
biblical teachings reflect that culture. Even more importantly, it knows
that reading the Bible *through* a long-established church tradition
needs to be challenged. Why? Because tradition does not reflect the
original innovation in the message about and practice of women in the
Bible, most especially in the churches of the apostle Paul.

Instead of seeking to impose that outside culture and those culturally shaped teachings on women in a completely different world
and culture, the mutuality view summons Christians to the Bible. It
knows the story of the Bible is one in which Jesus Christ makes men
and women one again, in Christ and in marriage. And, in conscious
dependence on the Spirit in the context of a community of faith that
seeks to live out that oneness, it gives women the freedom to discern
what God has called them to do—whatever it might be, including
preaching, teaching, and leading in the church. The conclusions
are that women are encouraged by the so-called "exceptions" of the
Bible—and there are more than most realize. These passages are not
exceptions; they are common. Moreover, the ongoing guidance of the
Spirit may lead women into ministries that break down the tradition
with deeper innovations.

Jesus told us the Spirit would guide us. This book is an attempt to sketch how that guidance works itself out for many of us. Here are Jesus's words, which I will quote before we look at the biblical exceptions that provide a map for our guidance: "But when he, the Spirit of truth, comes, he will guide you into all the truth. He will not speak on his own; he will speak only what he hears, and he will tell you what is yet to come" (John 16:13).

Do we believe this? I do. Do you? Believing this verse, we must have the confidence to strike out in conscious dependence on the Spirit and in organic ways bring the Bible's kingdom vision into our world. We do so by mastering the plot and the redemption at work in the King and His Kingdom Story so that the path we take is the natural Spirit-led waterslide that will guide us to the waters in our world in our way. The intent of the next two chapters is to put the tradition in its (biblical) place.

CHAPTER 15

WHAT DID WOMEN DO IN THE OLD TESTAMENT?

Women in Church Ministries 2

Many of my friends, when a discussion arises about women in church ministries, gravitate to Paul's two famous statements—that women should be silent in the churches:

> Women should remain *silent* in the churches. They are *not allowed to speak*, but must be in submission, as the law says. If they want to inquire about something, they should ask their own husbands at home; for it is disgraceful for a woman to speak in the church. (1 Corinthians 14:34–35, emphasis added)

> A woman should learn *in quietness and full submission*. I do not permit a woman to teach or to assume authority over a man; *she must be quiet.* (1 Timothy 2:11–12, emphasis added)

Some of my friends are for and some are against women in leadership ministries. Both kinds of friends gravitate to these texts. For me, gravitating to these passages for this discussion is like asking about marriage in the Bible and gravitating toward the divorce texts. Talking marriage through the divorce texts is beyond short-sighted, if not distorting. The same applies to women in ministry texts. Yes, I say, these statements by Paul about silence are important, and we will look at them in due time, but there is something else we should do first.

Know the Story of the Bible

The story of the Bible, that is the King and His Kingdom Story that is fulfilled in the elimination of gender hierarchies once and for all, tells us stories about women that I call stories of "WDWD." Many of you know about the bracelet that some have worn since the mid-1990s with these letters on it: WWJD. Those letters stand for "**W**hat **W**ould **J**esus **D**o?" and they are a moral reminder of our renew-and-renewing approach to the Bible to live as Jesus would have us live in our day and in our way. My WDWD acronym is one we should consider when we think about women in church ministries: **W**hat **D**id **W**omen **D**o? in Bible times. In classes I teach that deal with this topic I ask students to chart what many of the women in the Bible did, and as the class progresses, the charts get longer and the activities of women more obvious. You might try it on your own.

To name some of the more obvious women, think of Miriam, Deborah, and Huldah; think of Esther and Ruth and the woman in the Song of Songs; think of Priscilla, Junia, and Phoebe. Think (and this is hard to do for Protestants) of Mary, mother of Jesus, whose influence on Jesus, James, and some early Christians is largely ignored.[1] Many more names could be added. Our point is that those of us who claim the Bible as the foundation of our faith need to ponder exactly what *these women* did.

What did they do? They led, they prophesied, they taught, they were apostles, they were deacons, they were co-workers in Paul's mission, and they were local church mentors. At this point, all we need to grant is that there are—at a minimum—women who were *exceptions* to the dominant cultural perception of women as inferior. They were exceptions whom God raised above the norm to accomplish his will.

I will go beyond the word "exception" in what follows, but for now we can ask if we are permitting women these same (supposed) exceptions in our churches. I know many who believe there should be no exceptions—they are caging and silencing even the exceptional blue parakeet. That is contrary to the Bible itself and I will contend also that making women exceptions is also contrary to the Bible.

In my conversations with friends after we have discussed both the WDWD passages and the "**W**omen **K**eep **S**ilence **P**assages" (WKSP), I always conclude with this question: Do you permit women to do in your churches what women did in the Bible and in the early churches?

No matter how seriously you take the WKSPs, it is profoundly unbiblical to let those passages overcome the WDWDs so that all we have left is silenced and caged blue parakeets! Whatever Paul meant by silence, he did not mean that the WDWD passages were false. The man who spoke of silence did not, in fact, totally silence women in his churches.

So now we ask: What did women do in the Bible?[2] If we want to be biblical, this question needs to be asked and answered. I believe reading the Bible *through* a fossilized tradition has prevented us even from asking the question, let alone answering it. The place to begin is with an all-encompassing text—the creation narrative—that establishes how the Bible's story is to be read.

Creation and New Creation

If we read the Bible as Story, we begin all questions at the beginning, with Genesis 1–3. And if we begin here, the entire story is reshaped. We learn from these chapters that *God created male and female as mutuals—made for each other—and they were at one with each other. They were made for an Eden-like world, which in the Bible's Story will be the Kingdom of God, but they preferred another world.* The fall[3] distorted mutuality by turning women against men and men against women; oneness became otherness and rivalry for power. Here are the climactic, tragic words from Genesis 3:16: "Your desire will be for your husband, and he will rule over you." We read here a prediction of what life will be like for those living in otherness instead of oneness.

The sin of Adam and Eve, or better yet, Eve and Adam, created tension in relationship. The woman's desire is for the man but the man's desire is corrupted to rule over her. Her sin turned the woman to seek dominance over the man, and the man's sin turned the man to seek dominance over the woman.[4] A life of struggling for control is the way of life for sinners. This war of wills was not God's design, but God has granted to both males and females a freedom to exercise the will, and the Bible's description and prediction (not prescription) is that men and women will not always get along! But the good news story of the Bible is that the broken creation eventually gives way to new creation; the dead can be reborn and re-created; instead of a war of wills there can be a unity of wills. Sadly, the church has far too often *perpetuated what is described in Genesis 3:16 as a permanent condition designed by God until the new creation.* Perpetuating Genesis 3:16 and the war of wills with the male ruling the female entails failing to *restore creation conditions* when it comes to male and female relationships. This is against both Jesus and Paul, who each read the Bible as a story that moves from creation (oneness) to new creation (oneness). Reading Genesis 3:16 as divine prescription (God's will until the new creation but partly undone with redemption) rather than prediction and description means God has willed women to be contrarians and men as dominators. This is far from the way of God in the Bible's Story: God's redemption means oneness and mutuality, not hierarchy and a war of wills.

Jesus informed his disciples that although Moses permitted divorce, which annihilates the Creator's designed union in marriage, divorce was *not God's original intention.* Permanence, love, oneness, and mutuality were God's intent in the original creation. Jesus, then, appeals to the first chapter in the King and His Kingdom Story, to the original creation, to show how God's people are supposed to live in the new creation. Moses's permission for divorce pertains, so it seems to me, to a life too deeply marred by the fall. A Jesus community undoes the distortions of the fall because it seeks to live out the fullness of the Story.

The apostle Paul twice appeals to original creation to explain God's redemption. In 2 Corinthians 5:17 Paul says: "If anyone is in Christ, *the new creation* has come: The old [the fall] has gone, the new [creation] is here!" (emphasis added). What can this mean but that the implications of Genesis 3:16 are being undone for those who are in Christ? This draws us directly back to Genesis 3:16 to see that the otherness struggle for control between the sexes has ended because we are now in the new creation. New creation means we are being restored to the equality and mutuality of Genesis 1–2.

Paul does much the same in Galatians 3:28: "There is neither Jew nor Gentile, neither slave nor free, *nor is there male and female*, for you are all *one* in Christ Jesus" (emphasis added). The words Paul uses for "male … female" are quoted from Genesis 1:27, the original creation story. The word "one" evokes God's oneness and God's design for oneness among his created beings. What is Paul claiming here? He is—and notice this carefully—contending that in Christ we return to Eden's mutuality. He is contending that life in Christ creates unity, equality, and oneness.

What we learn from Genesis 1–2, then, is that God originally made Adam and Eve as mutuals, that their sin distorted that relationship, and that the story of the Bible's plot leads us to see redemption in Christ as new creation. Both Jesus and Paul see in Genesis 1–2 the original design for what Christ's redemption brings to men and women in this world. If there is any place in the world where this mutuality should be restored, it should be in the church. Ironically, it can be the least redemptive place of the week!

We now move to some specific women in the Old Testament. That these three women are not household names concerns me, not just because it means that we don't read our Bibles thoroughly enough. No, what concerns me more is that we can discuss women in church ministries without taking into consideration concrete examples of what women did in the Bible. The principle of WDWD brings them to the table.

Miriam, Deborah, and Huldah

That God could raise up into leadership women who exercised considerable authority can be seen in three women who come alive in the pages of the Old Testament. They are part of Israel's story, and no storytelling is fair that does not include them. Miriam was one of Israel's spiritual leaders, Deborah was a presidential leader of God's people, and Huldah was a prophet above (mostly male) prophets.

Miriam: Spiritual Leader

Miriam was one-third of Israel's triumvirate of leadership: Moses as lawgiver, Aaron as priest, and Miriam as prophetess. When the children of Israel escaped the clutches of Pharaoh, it was Miriam who led the Israelites into worship with these inspired words:

> Sing to the LORD,
>   for he is highly exalted.
> Both horse and driver
>   he has hurled into the sea. (Exodus 15:21)

The Song of Moses, found now at Exodus 15:1–18, may well have been composed under inspiration by Miriam. Other women are found singing within the pages of the Bible's story—women like Deborah (Judges 5:1–31) and Mary (Luke 1:46–55). Singing was connected to the gift of prophecy in the Bible (1 Chronicles 25:1–7). When a later prophet, Micah, spoke of Israel's deliverance, he quoted the Lord, saying: "I brought you up out of Egypt. . . . I sent Moses to lead you, also Aaron and Miriam" (Micah 6:4).

Miriam was the one who fetched Moses from the Nile; as Moses's older sister she no doubt participated in Moses's own family celebrations of Passover in Egypt; and as older sister she sang alongside Moses and Aaron about God's deliverance. In Numbers 12 she sticks her neck out: Miriam thought Moses's choice of wife inappropriate and summarily gives him the business and gossips with Aaron about him

(Numbers 12:1). "Hasn't he [the LORD] also spoken through us?" she asks, knowing full well the answer (yes) and the silliness of her stance. God hears and summons them both, but clearly Miriam is the problem here, for she is envious and jealous of Moses's expanding power. The Lord reveals to Miriam and Aaron that prophets (as she is) hear from God in dreams and visions, but God speaks with Moses "face to face." God is not happy with Aaron and Miriam and departs, and when the cloud of glory lifts, Miriam has a defiling skin disease. Her skin became "white as snow." Aaron calls for a family prayer meeting in which Moses petitions God and Miriam is healed.

It takes some *chutzpah* to speak against Moses, and we should not condone what Miriam (or Aaron) did. But what we should see is the strength, power, and authority Miriam possessed that led her to think that she, even she, could call Moses into question. She made a mistake, a serious one, but it was not because she was a woman. It was because she envied Moses—her sin was envy, not being a woman. Other leaders sin in the Old Testament, including Moses (who does not get to enter the promised land) or David (whose sins shook the kingdom). Miriam was a blue parakeet who was permitted to sing because God had given her his voice.

Deborah: Presidential Leader

Deborah was, to use modern analogies, the president, the pope, and Rambo all bundled up in one female body! Judges 4–5 reveals that God called women—it is not mentioned that she is an "exception"—to lead his people. Every reading of her story reveals she was exceptional.

Like Miriam, Deborah was a *prophet*: "Now Deborah, a prophet, the wife of Lappidoth, was leading [*shapat*] Israel at that time" (Judges 4:4). When the Bible says she was "leading" Israel, it uses the term for the *judge* of Israel. She was to her generation what Moses was to his. The word translated "judged" (*shapat*) combines the ideas of "national leadership," "judicial decisions," and "political, military savior." If we ask what did women do, and we ask this question of Deborah, we learn that women could speak for God as a prophet, render decisions in a law court as a judge, exercise leadership over the entire spiritual-social Israel, and be a military commander who brought Israel to victory. To use other terms, she led the nation spiritually, musically, legally, politically, and militarily. Let us not pretend her tasks were social and secular; Deborah was a leader of the entire people of God.

Deborah's theology flows gloriously out of the Song of Deborah in Judges 5. I include her words here and ask you to read this song, saying it aloud, and then jot down some ideas about her theology. I will offer minimal commentary as we read this text together. Barak, under the leadership of Deborah, defeated Jabin, king of Canaan, and they sang together this masterpiece victory song, which clearly is Deborah's own Spirit-led song:

On that day Deborah and Barak son of Abinoam sang this song:

> *"When the princes in Israel take the lead,*
> *when the people willingly offer themselves—*
> *praise the* Lord!

> *"Hear this, you kings! Listen, you rulers!*
> *I, even I, will sing to the* Lord;
> *I will praise the* Lord, *the God of Israel, in song.*

[Notice that God's victory over the Canaanites reaches back into the victory of God through the Exodus, the giving of the Torah, the forming of the covenant, and entry into the land:]

> *"When you,* Lord, *went out from Seir,*
> *when you marched from the land of Edom,*
> *the earth shook, the heavens poured,*
> *the clouds poured down water.*
> *The mountains quaked before the* Lord, *the One of Sinai,*
> *before the* Lord, *the God of Israel.*

[Israel began to fade in its commitment until Deborah, "a mother in Israel," arose to stir the nation to action:]

"In the days of Shamgar son of Anath,
in the days of Jael, the highways were abandoned;
travelers took to winding paths.
Villagers in Israel would not fight;
they held back until I, Deborah, arose,
until I arose, a mother in Israel.
God chose new leaders
when war came to the city gates,
but not a shield or spear was seen
among forty thousand in Israel.

[Those who mustered the courage to act in good faith are now praised by Deborah:]

My heart is with Israel's princes,
with the willing volunteers among the people.
Praise the Lord!

"You who ride on white donkeys,
sitting on your saddle blankets,
and you who walk along the road,
consider the voice of the singers at the watering places.
They recite the victories of the Lord,
the victories of his villagers in Israel.

"Then the people of the Lord
went down to the city gates.
'Wake up, wake up, Deborah!
Wake up, wake up, break out in song!
Arise, Barak!
Take captive your captives, son of Abinoam.'

[The roll call of participants in the battle:]

"*The remnant of the nobles came down;*
    the people of the LORD *came down to me against the mighty.*
Some came from Ephraim, whose roots were in Amalek;
    Benjamin was with the people who followed you.
From Makir captains came down,
    from Zebulun those who bear a commander's staff.
The princes of Issachar were with Deborah;
    yes, Issachar was with Barak,
    sent under his command into the valley.
In the districts of Reuben
    there was much searching of heart.
Why did you stay among the sheep pens
    to hear the whistling for the flocks?
In the districts of Reuben
    there was much searching of heart.
Gilead stayed beyond the Jordan.
    And Dan, why did he linger by the ships?
Asher remained on the coast
    and stayed in his coves.
The people of Zebulun risked their very lives;
    so did Naphtali on the terraced fields.

[The battle is fought against Canaan and its leader, Sisera. God's people win, and Deborah's triumph becomes clear as she sums up what was recounted one chapter earlier in Judges:]

"*Kings came, they fought,*
    the kings of Canaan fought.
At Taanach, by the waters of Megiddo,
    they took no plunder of silver.
From the heavens the stars fought,
    from their courses they fought against Sisera.

The river Kishon swept them away,
the age-old river, the river Kishon.
March on, my soul; be strong!
Then thundered the horses' hooves—
galloping, galloping go his mighty steeds.

[Meroz, a village that acts faithlessly, is cursed by Deborah
because they are not loyal to God:]

'Curse Meroz,' said the angel of the LORD.
'Curse its people bitterly,
because they did not come to help the LORD,
to help the LORD against the mighty.'

[Barak, because he sought help, did not finish off the victory;
instead, Jael, a woman, kills Sisera. Yes, the battle is gruesome and
the victory bloody and the language graphic:]

"Most blessed of women be Jael,
the wife of Heber the Kenite,
most blessed of tent-dwelling women.
He asked for water, and she gave him milk;
in a bowl fit for nobles she brought him curdled milk.
Her hand reached for the tent peg,
her right hand for the workman's hammer.
She struck Sisera, she crushed his head,
she shattered and pierced his temple.
At her feet he sank,
he fell; there he lay.
At her feet he sank, he fell;
where he sank, there he fell—dead.

[Deborah turns to recount the experience of military victory through the eyes of another woman, the mother of Sisera,

the fallen Canaanite king, who thinks the delay of her son is because he's mopping up Israel. Deborah has the last word, and it strikes the modern reader as a combination of bitter contempt and exultant satire:]

> *"Through the window peered Sisera's mother;*
>   *behind the lattice she cried out,*
> *'Why is his chariot so long in coming?*
>   *Why is the clatter of his chariots delayed?'*
> *The wisest of her ladies answer her;*
>   *indeed, she keeps saying to herself,*
> *'Are they not finding and dividing the spoils:*
>   *a woman or two for each man,*
> *colorful garments as plunder for Sisera,*

[I interrupt; the singer and reader know that Sisera's mother, who is depicted as staring through the lattice in anticipation of victory, is living a dream. The reality is that the "highly embroidered garments for my neck" she is about to mention turned out to be sackcloth and ashes.]

> *colorful garments embroidered,*
> *highly embroidered garments for my neck—*
>   *all this as plunder?'*

[In a final flourish Deborah seeks the glory of God for those who love God and sure defeat for those who do not:]

> *"So may all your enemies perish, LORD!*
>   *But may all who love you be like the sun*
>   *when it rises in its strength."*

Then the land had peace forty years.

The courage of this woman is remarkable. Her theology is bathed in zeal for the Lord, her exhortations capable of drawing all to the battle plain, and her hopes inspiring to this day. I shudder at her *Schadenfreude,* her "joy over the defeat of her enemies," but I trust our zeal for God's glory is as resolute as hers. If there is any single line that captures the spiritual vision of Deborah it is verse 21c: "March on, my soul; be strong!" This too is part of our story.

Deborah is a blue parakeet who was permitted to sing and fly.

Huldah: Prophet above the Prophets

When King Josiah is informed of the discovery of the long-lost Torah in the temple, a certain Shaphan reads the text to Josiah. The king, who has "the most responsive royal heart since the hearing heart of Solomon,"[5] realizes the nation has failed to live according to God's covenant. He falls apart in godly repentance and needs discernment. What should he do? To which of God's prophets shall he send word to consult? Here are his options: he can consult Jeremiah, Zephaniah, Nahum, Habakkuk, or Huldah. The first four have books in Israel's collection of prophets. But he chooses Huldah above the rest. Huldah is not chosen because no men were available; she is chosen because she is truly exceptional among the prophets.

She confirms that the scroll is indeed God's Torah and this, in some sense, authorizes this text as Israel's Scriptures from this time on. Furthermore, the prophet Huldah, unafraid to tell the truth, informs Josiah that indeed God's wrath is against the disobedience of this nation. But, she adds, because the king has humbled himself before God, he will be gathered to his ancestors in peace. All of this is found in 2 Kings 22.

Huldah is a female blue parakeet who sang more beautifully than a company of males.

Conclusion

From this brief sketch, we can repeat the question: What did women do?

They spoke for God;
they led the nation in every department;
they sanctioned Scripture; and
they guided nations back to the path of righteousness.

These women were blue parakeets who were allowed to fly and to sing.

But that was then, and this is now. What about in the New Testament? Did women's roles decrease or increase? If one takes into consideration the King and His Kingdom Story and considers that Jesus ushers in the beginning of the new creation, one should not be surprised to learn that women begin where the Old Testament leaves off and take on new responsibilities. That is exactly what happens.

CHAPTER 16

WHAT DID WOMEN DO IN THE NEW TESTAMENT?

Women in Church Ministries 3

A young woman came to me at the end of class and said, "I'm so upset." I asked her why. "Because I've never heard about any of these women we have been studying."

"Which women?" you might ask.

Junia, Priscilla, and Phoebe.

Let me ask you (the reader): Do you know about these women? If your experience is like this student's, you have every right to ask why not. My experience is that more don't know these women than do.

You are also entitled to ask why so many Protestants ignore the most significant woman in the entire Bible, Mary, mother of Jesus. We begin with her and we ask again, WDWD (in the New Testament). As we ask this question of Mary and other New Testament women, the entire theme of oneness—of God's restoring men and women to be one in Christ—begins to take on concrete realities.

MARY: A Woman of Influence

Mary makes some Protestants break out in an emotional rash and rant; I've seen it happen. Once when I told an older woman that I was studying what the Bible says about Mary, she said to me, "Why? She's so Catholic!"

Ah, I thought, that's reading the Bible *through* the (anti-Catholic) tradition! We believe in the Bible, and it reveals that Mary was a woman of influence, and some of that influence, if you weigh the verses carefully, had to be at the level of teaching.

To begin with, Mary was the mother of the Messiah, and it was no small vocation to be part of forming Jesus the Messiah as he matured. Furthermore, if the early tradition is accurate, Mary became a widow, so when we look at her influence in the early church, we are looking at a widow. I see her influence in the New Testament in three ways. Mary's influence emerges in her training of Jesus and of his brother James, and she was critical in the formation of our Gospels.

Mary had a powerful influence on her sons—including Jesus. Themes from Mary's majestic Magnificat show up so centrally both in the teachings of Jesus and in the letter of James, I believe it is clear that Mary *taught* and was involved in the *spiritual formation* of Jesus and James.[1] I would not want to claim that Jesus learned only from Mary; of course he learned from Joseph and from others. But can we expect that God would give Mary to Jesus as a mother and not qualify her to be a singular and godly influence on him? I think not.

Perhaps turning to another of Mary's sons, James, is a safer way to make this point. Here are the words of Mary's Spirit-prompted Magnificat (Luke 1:46–55):

And Mary said:

> *"My soul glorifies the Lord*
> *and my spirit rejoices in God my Savior,*
> *for he has been mindful*
> *of the humble state of his servant.*
> *From now on all generations will call me blessed,*
> *for the Mighty One has done great things for me—*
> *holy is his name.*

His mercy extends to those who fear him,
from generation to generation.
He has performed mighty deeds with his arm;
he has scattered those who are proud in their inmost thoughts.
He has brought down rulers from their thrones
but has lifted up the humble.
He has filled the hungry with good things
but has sent the rich away empty.
He has helped his servant Israel,
remembering to be merciful
to Abraham and his descendants forever,
just as he promised our ancestors."

The themes of Mary's song are clear: justice for the poor and marginalized, judgment on the oppressors, holiness, and God's faithfulness to his covenant promises. James writes in his letter these words:

Believers in humble circumstances [the "poor"] ought to take pride in their high position. But the rich should take pride in their humiliation—since they will pass away like a wild flower. For the sun rises with scorching heat and withers the plant; its blossom falls and its beauty is destroyed. In the same way, the rich will fade away even while they go about their business. (James 1:9–11)

This prediction of a reversal of fortunes is a central theme to the Magnificat and a central theme in Jesus's own teachings. It punctuates nearly every chapter of James's book.

But what strikes me when I read James are these words from James 1:27: "Religion that God our Father accepts as pure and faultless is this: to look after orphans and widows in their distress and to keep oneself from being polluted by the world." James and Jesus and their other brothers and sisters were, in terms of first-century Jews, "orphans" because they did not have a living father. An orphan in that society was anyone who had lost one parent. James states that showing compassion for orphans and widows—like his mother—reveals the presence of genuine "religion" or "piety."

I cannot prove that either James or Jesus got these ideas from their mother. But this Spirit-inspired woman was their mother—the one who uttered potent warnings about rich oppressors and promised comfort to the oppressed poor, rocked their cradles, taught them to sing, and explained to them their "family history" (how does one explain the plan of God to bring the Messiah when one is the mother of the Messiah?)—and she had a nurturing impact on the boys that unquestionably showed up in what they believed, how they acted, and what they taught. The things that show up are her godliness, her compassion, her intelligence, and her devotion.

One more point makes sense to me and I hope to you. Where did you think Luke acquired the stories he tells us in Luke 1–2? There are only a few possible sources: God, Mary, Joseph, Zechariah, Elizabeth, Simeon, Anna, Jesus, and his brothers and sisters. The only person who knew the story of Mary's words with the angel Gabriel was Mary; Luke may have not spoken with Mary (though I think Luke easily could have since he was in and around Jerusalem collecting information for his gospel), but somehow what he learned about those early days of impregnation and song somehow came from Mary. However you look at it, *the first two chapters of our gospel of Luke derive somehow from Mary.*

What did Mary do? Mary *influenced* her messianic Son, her New Testament–writing son James,[2] and *provided information* to Luke as seeds for stories that got his gospel off to a great start. Are you aware that not a few interpreters see Mary, mother of Jesus, in Revelation 12? Read the chapter and think about it.

JUNIA: An Apostle above Other Apostles

Do you know who Junia is?[3] Here's all we know: "Greet Andronicus and *Junia*, my fellow Jews who have been in prison with me. They are *outstanding among the apostles*, and they were in Christ before I was" (Romans 16:7, emphasis added). Here are words of utter profundity, words that have been silenced like a blue parakeet perhaps more than any other words in the Bible about women: "outstanding among the apostles." Junia is an outstanding apostle, though to be sure, being a woman had little to do with it. What mattered were her intelligence, her giftedness, and her calling.

Junia is a woman's name. But because women aren't supposed to be "apostles," someone copying the letter to the Romans changed the spelling so that Junia (female) became Junias (male). The RSV of 1946 has "Andronicus and Junias" and adds "men of note among the apostles." Recent exhaustive study has uncovered this mistake, and we now are virtually certain "Junia" was a woman.[4] And she was an "apostle"! Junia and her husband-apostle Andronicus were relatives of Paul or fellow Jews like Paul, they came to faith in Christ prior to Paul's own conversion, and they were imprisoned with Paul (no doubt because they were believers and leaders among the Christians).

But more importantly, Andronicus and Junia are "outstanding" or "prominent" (NRSV) among apostles. This could mean they were recognized as leaders *by* the apostles, but the evidence in the early church is that everyone translated this expression as "prominent apostles" among the first generation of Christians. Perhaps we should take a deep breath and get our bearings before we go any further. A statement by St. Chrysostom, a famous preacher and theologian who read and preached in Greek, seals the deal; I put in italics the most significant words:

> "Greet Andronicus and Junia ... who are outstanding among the apostles": *To be an apostle* is something great. *But to be outstanding among the apostles*—just think what a wonderful song of praise that is! They were outstanding on the basis of their works and virtuous actions. *Indeed, how great the wisdom of this woman must have been that she was even deemed worthy of the title of apostle.*[5]

We draw two conclusions: Junia was a woman and Junia was an apostle. A third: not "an apostle" but a "prominent" apostle.

But what kind of apostle? Some forget to ask this question. She clearly was not one of the twelve apostles chosen and sent out by Jesus. So what kind was she? The answer is in the Bible. As the story of the Bible unfolds, not only were there the twelve apostles but there were other apostles. Some have called them missionaries. While this is in the right direction, the term "apostle" can only mean they were specially sent because of special giftedness, and they would have been church-planting, teaching, theology-forming leaders in the churches they planted. They were both like modern-day missionaries (called, gifted, sent, church-planting) but they were also quite unlike our missionaries. How so? It is exceedingly rare for anyone to call our missionaries "apostles." Why? That title belongs to a special giftedness. There were others in the New Testament called "apostle" in this sense, including Barnabas (Acts 14:14), James (Galatians 1:19), Epaphroditus (Philippians 2:25), and other "brothers" (2 Corinthians 8:23). (Sometimes the Greek term *apostolos*, our "apostle," is translated as "messenger" or "representative" in these passages.) Even if we rank Junia among the missionary apostles, she is still an apostle and is considered top drawer for her work.

Leading us to this question about what women did: What kind of work did an apostle like Junia get involved in? Or what did women do? We cannot be sure but probably these kinds of things: Junia, along with her husband, Andronicus, were commissioned or recognized as having gifts from God. Those gifts involved such things as evangelizing, teaching, preaching, establishing, and leading churches. Underneath it all would have been an exemplary character of godliness and love that provided a template for others to observe and imitate.

PRISCILLA:
A Teacher of Scripture and Theology

We know much more about Priscilla, the wife of Aquila, than we do of Junia. Aquila and Priscilla were from Rome (Acts 18:2); they were kicked out of Rome when Claudius ordered all "Jews" to evacuate. They became acquainted with Paul in Corinth and began to make tents together (18:3). This friendship led to their traveling with Paul to Ephesus, where—and here we are offered another glimpse into what women did in the early churches—Priscilla and Aquila "explained to [Apollos] the way of God more adequately" (18:26). This husband and wife, instead of fighting for power with each other (cf. Genesis 3:16), worked together for the gospel. The mutuality theme is obvious here. Their availability to God for an itinerant life is also obvious.

There are some details here that deserve a careful look. First, Priscilla's name is often given first (Acts 18:18, 26; Romans 16:3; 2 Timothy 4:19). Listing a woman's name first was not impossible in the ancient world, but it was unusual. More significantly, she is almost always named before her husband, leading many to think she was the leading light when it came to this ministry and also probably more socially prominent. The only exceptions are Acts 18:2 and 1 Corinthians 16:19. We should not make too much of her name being first since she may have had more social status in the Roman world.

More importantly, "they"—and again her name is first—"explained" to the scholar Apollos "the way of God more adequately." Priscilla knew her theology and her Bible, and she knew it so well she could lead Apollos from a John-the-Baptist faith to a Jesus-faith. This husband-wife team taught Apollos so well he was able—two verses later—to refute nonmessianic Jews in public debate by opening up the Scriptures for them (Acts 18:28). Clearly Priscilla was a theological teacher. This is why Priscilla and Aquila are called Paul's "co-workers" in Romans 16:3.[6] "Co-worker" was Paul's special term for his associates *in church ministries*. What did they do? They—including Priscilla—shared with Paul in being called by God, in preaching the gospel, in carrying on pastoral work with churches, and in risking their lives for their faith.

So what did women do in the New Testament church? We have one woman who was an apostle and another who was a fellow worker and teacher. We must look at one more—a woman who was at a minimum the official interpreter of Paul's letter to the Romans!

PHOEBE: Deacon and Benefactor

> I commend to you our sister Phoebe, a *deacon* of the church in
> Cenchreae. I ask you to receive her in the Lord in a way worthy
> of his people and to give her any help she may need from you,
> for she has been the *benefactor* of many people, including me.
> (Romans 16:1–2, emphasis added)

One of the most noticeable features of women in the earliest
churches was that they directed their own households. So when the
churches moved into the homes, these household-directing women
became de facto directors and leaders of local household churches.
A good example is Phoebe; another is Nympha (Colossians 4:15).
Unlike Priscilla and Junia, who were both married, Phoebe's husband
is not mentioned. This could indicate that she was single. Perhaps she
was a widow. Perhaps her husband was not a believer. We cannot be
sure. She stands in this text alone as a single woman. What matters
is her calling from God and her giftedness. Paul tells us that she was
from Cenchreae, a city just outside of Corinth in Greece, and that she
had traveled to Rome. Many today think Paul wrote Romans from
Cenchreae and that he may well have written from her home. What
did Phoebe do?

To begin with, Phoebe is called a "deacon." This word "deacon"
is the same word in the New Testament, whether the person is a man
or a woman, for a leader in the church. When Paul calls her "deacon,"
he is not thinking of the "deaconesses" in our churches who clean up
communion cups in the church kitchen. Phoebe is called "deacon"
because she exercised a ministry, or service, in the church.

What kind of ministry? Deacons are often connected to "ministry/
service of the word" in Paul's letters—see, for example, 1 Corinthians
3:5–9.[7] But since Phoebe is called "a deacon *of the church* in Cenchreae,"
we should think of her "ministry" in terms of the list of qualifications
and ministries we find in 1 Timothy 3:8–12. Doug Moo describes a
safe conclusion: "It is likely that deacons were charged with visitation

of the sick, poor relief, and perhaps financial oversight."[8] Others think more is involved, that is, that "deacon" describes an official ministry of God's Word. I think the latter view may be closer to the facts, though it is unwise to stretch the evidence to fit what we'd like to be true.

At some level Phoebe was a "minister." She was also significant. When Paul asks the church at Rome to "receive her," he surely has in mind that they are to roll out a red carpet of hospitality—the way they do for "saints." But it is also possible that Phoebe, a benefactor or wealthy patron of Paul's ministry of bringing the gospel to the Roman Empire, was responsible for getting this letter to the right people. Most today think Phoebe was Paul's courier for the letter to the Romans. Since couriers were charged with taking responsibility for their letters, Phoebe probably read (performed is a better word) the letter aloud and answered questions the Roman Christians may have had. (If today's Christians, who struggle to make sense of this dense treatise called Romans, are any indication, then Phoebe may have spent days explaining this letter to the Roman churches.) Phoebe, to put this graphically, can be seen as the first "commentator" on the letter to the Romans.[9] We can say this too: there are probably six or so house churches in Rome (see Romans 16:1–16), which means Phoebe almost certainly read that letter aloud at least six times! One more point. A recent exhaustive commentary on Romans by Robert Jewett contends that Phoebe is not just a "benefactor" in an ordinary sense but that she is the patron for Paul's strategic plan to preach the gospel from Rome to Spain.[10] We cannot be sure that Phoebe's role is that defined, but there are enough hints here to suggest that Phoebe was an important part of Paul's letter to the Romans as well as his missionary strategy. One of her most important contributions was providing funds. It is worth noting that in the fourth century, in an inscription found on Jerusalem's Mount of Olives, a woman named Sophia was called the "new Phoebe" or the "second Phoebe" because of her financial support for Christian ministries.[11]

What Did Women Do?

What did women do? Another way of asking this question is this: What did women do if we read the New Testament as Story? How do we see the King and His Kingdom Story with its redemptive oneness theme begin to take shape in the story of the New Testament?

Mary was influential with Jesus and James and gave to Luke crucial information for writing his gospel. *Junia* was an apostle who was involved in missionary work. *Priscilla* taught Bible and theology alongside her husband. *Phoebe* financially supported the apostle Paul in his ministry, carried the letter to Rome, and helped to explain its contents as Paul prepared for his Spanish mission. What did women do (WDWD)? They were influential, they were a source for stories about Jesus, they were church planters, they were teachers, they were benefactors and interpreters of Paul's letters.

We learn a little more about each: Junia and Priscilla were married, Mary became a widow, and Phoebe may well have been single. There is no indication that women could teach and lead only if they were connected to a man who was also a leader. And to tie these four women into the story of the Bible, each of these women exhibits the mutuality (or oneness) theme that begins in creation, is threatened by the fall, and begins to become more and more a reality in Christ.

If women did all this, why does Paul speak of silencing women in public assemblies? How does such silencing fit within the theme of oneness—of God's work of redemption, restoring men and women into unity in Christ? This is where reading the Bible as Story, asking WDWD, becomes important. Though we may read the Bible *through* tradition (where women are silenced), we are at times called to challenge the tradition, which we will do in the next chapter.

CHAPTER 17

SILENCING THE BLUE PARAKEET (1)

Women in Church Ministries 4

In one of my classes I asked students to read 1 Timothy 2:8–15 and isolate the commands. (I list the seven basic commands below.) Then I asked them to discern whether they thought we should or should not practice that command today. Finally, I asked them to state why they thought the way they did. Here is the passage; you can do the same assignment with us:

> Therefore I want the men everywhere to pray, lifting up holy hands without anger or disputing. I also want the women to dress modestly, with decency and propriety, adorning themselves, not with elaborate hairstyles or gold or pearls or expensive clothes, but with good deeds, appropriate for women who profess to worship God.
>
> A woman should learn in quietness and full submission. I do not permit a woman to teach or to assume authority over a man; she must be quiet. For Adam was formed first, then Eve. And Adam was not the one deceived; it was the woman who was deceived and became a sinner. But women will be saved through childbearing—if they continue in faith, love and holiness with propriety.

We break the passage into seven basic commands. You can tick off the ones you think are "for today" as stated by Paul.

1. Males should pray with their hands lifted up (2:8).

No students thought men had to lift their hands when they prayed.

2. Males should pray without anger or disputing (2:8).

Every student in the class thought men should pray without getting themselves into angry moods and arguments.

3. Women should dress modestly (2:9).

Two students balked at what "modestly" means in verse 9. They didn't think braiding hair, wearing gold and pearls, or dressing up in expensive clothes is how we define modesty today. But both students thought modesty was a good thing. In short, they had a "that was then, but this is now" approach to this passage, and they thought modesty's meaning differs from culture to culture. I asked the females to comment on what "immodest" means today. One commented that a low top was immodest while another said that a top baring one's belly was immodest. Most seemed to agree. I asked males to comment on "immodest" for males. A one-word comment from the back of the class said it all: "Spandex!" We moved to the next point. Since those days clothing has in some cases become more immodest and so modesty perceptions have changed accordingly.

4. Women should not have elaborate hairstyles or wear gold or pearls or expensive clothing (2:9).

The class was divided: twenty-five thought these commands were for today but nineteen thought they were not. Most students thought women should not overdress, but not all were convinced Paul's specific commands were transferable to our world.

5. Women should have good deeds (2:10).

Every student agreed with Paul.

6. Women should be silent and quiet (2:11–12).

Not one student in the class stated that he or she agreed with Paul on this command. I suspect a few students did agree with this command of Paul's but did not want to endure stares and glares. The same result and observation applies for the last one.

7. Women should not teach or have authority (2:12).

Whether these numbers of no-silence-for-women are precise or not, the overwhelming majority of the students in this class thought there should be no such restrictions on women today. We could get into a number of issues here, including whether or not this class is typical, but we are not striving for a scientific poll or for accurate numbers. What these students reveal is not at all unusual today; many don't think some of these inspired words of Paul are for today.

But many others do. They think women should be silent. We enter now into a minefield of debate. It is impossible for me to discuss each issue, so I will streamline this discussion as a positive explanation of why I think this passage teaches silence *only for women who have not yet been taught*. Once these untaught women are taught, they can sing like the other blue parakeets in the Bible.

A Troubling Irony

We have already sketched some passages in the story of the Bible where we discover the presence of women in leadership and public ministries. I have called these passages the WDWD passages. Now for a theoretical point with enormous significance for women in ministry: some believe the silencing passages should control the WDWD passages. Such persons give any number of reasons, but the point needs to be made clear: such persons believe the silencing passages are permanent and there is no place in the local church today for women prophets, apostles, or leaders or for women to perform any kind of teaching ministry.

There is a troubling irony in this approach, and it concerns whether we Christians are to live under the conditions of the fall or under the conditions of the new creation, whether we are to emphasize otherness or oneness. To explain this, I want to remind you again of the words in Genesis 3:16: "Your desire will be for your husband, and he will rule over you." These words are not an ironclad rule for the rest of history.

Sadly, some think Genesis 3:16 is a *prescription* for the relationship of women and men for all time. Instead of a prescription, these two lines are a *prediction* of the fallen desire of fallen women and fallen men in a fallen condition in a fallen world. Fallen women yearn to dominate men, and fallen men yearn to dominate women.[1] The desire to dominate is a broken desire. The redeemed desire is to love in mutuality. This verse in Genesis 3, in other words, predicts a struggle of fallen wills; they don't prescribe how we are *supposed* to live.

Genesis 3:16 speaks of fallen humans seeking to control other people. But the fall is not the last word in the Bible, and surely the Song of Songs is a profound example of Israelites finding a better way than what is found in Genesis 3:16. For the Christian we have to factor in new creation, the day God began to renew all things in Jesus Christ, and in the gift of the Holy Spirit.

Here is the most important verse in the Bible about new creation: "Therefore, if anyone is in Christ, the new creation has come: The old has gone, the new is here!" (2 Corinthians 5:17). Christian men and women are to live a life that moves beyond the fall, beyond the battle of wills. If new creation does anything, it unleashes the power to undo the fall in our world. I cannot emphasize this enough: the story of the Bible is the story of new creation in Christ. The words of Genesis 3:16, to put the matter directly, are overcome in new creation. These words in Genesis 3:16 are not words for anyone other than unredeemed, fallen women and men. Newly created followers of Christ can find a better way in mutuality. Paul teaches that we are all "one in Christ" and that in Christ "nor is there male and female" (Galatians 3:28).

Now for the troubling irony: seeking to control or limit the applicability of the WDWD passages by appealing to the silencing passages illustrates the fall, not the new creation. When men seek to control women by silencing them permanently in the church, we stand face-to-face with a contradiction of the very thing the new creation is designed to accomplish: to undo the fall. What we see in this desire to silence women is the desire to rule over women, a desire that pertains to the fall, not to the new creation. What the Spirit does when the Spirit is present is to release and liberate humans from their fallen condition so that God's will can be completely done. The Spirit creates mutuality. Always.

A Brief Reminder

So, when we come upon the two silencing passages, we need to learn to read them out of the story of the Bible. We need to remind ourselves of this:

- Women in the Old Testament exercised leadership.
- Women in the Old Testament spoke for God as prophets.
- Women in the New Testament era were gifted by God's Spirit for such things as teaching and leading.
- New creation begins to undo the fall, which means that men and women are drawn back into being "one" in Christ.

Even if the Bible's WDWD actions by women were exceptional instead of the norm, God has always raised up women with such gifts. I do think someone could explain the Old Testament WDWD passage as exceptions to the norm, but there's more going on than exceptions in the New Testament. Something new is happening with women in the New Testament.

Another Silenced Blue Parakeet Passage

One of the most significant passages about women in church ministries is often completely ignored, and I'm asking you to drink in what this text says. The plot in the Bible's story reveals that the messianic era would release the Spirit so that *women would also be gifted to exercise prophecy and leadership in the churches*. Just pick up your Bible and open it to Acts 2. When the Spirit fell upon the Pentecostal assembly, including Mary and other women, Peter said:

> This is what was spoken by the prophet Joel:
>
> > In the last days, God says,
> >   I will pour out my Spirit on all people.
> > Your sons and *daughters* will prophesy,
> >   your young men will see visions,
> >   your old men will dream dreams.
> > Even on my servants, both men and *women*,
> >   I will pour out my Spirit in those days,
> >   and they will prophesy. (Acts 2:16–18, emphasis added)

Pentecost was the day the music of the cracked *Eikons* died and the day new creation music began to be sung. It doesn't take but a lazy reading of Acts 2 to see that something big and something new was happening, and that bigness and that newness included women. Pentecost, so the Bible tells us, leads us to think of an *increase* in women's capacities to minister, not a decrease. Women's ministries *expand* as the Bible's plot moves forward; they do not shrink. Many today have shrunk the role of women in ministries; this flat-out contradicts the direction of the Bible's plot.

We must return to the point made in the previous chapters. We must ask WDWD, what did women do? We must ask about how the Story moves forward in the Bible. This kind of Bible reading means that when we read about women being silenced in Paul, you and I are drawn into a decision. Either we see Paul contradicting the way God has used women in the Story or we are being asked to see the silence as a special kind of silence. That is the point we will sketch out for both 1 Corinthians 14:34–35 and 1 Timothy 2:8–15.

Silencing Women at Corinth

The reason some believe in silencing women begins with 1 Corinthians 14:34–35.[2] Here are the words as recorded in 1 Corinthians. That might sound a bit odd so let me say up front that there is much discussion among the experts on whether Paul even wrote these words, and Appendix 3 sketches that discussion. There are, one must say now, good reasons not to think Paul wrote these words. One observation before I quote the words: if one concludes (as I do) that Paul did not write these words, what they say is said more forcefully in 1 Timothy 2 than here so nothing is gained for any side in this debate. Again, see Appendix 3. Now to 1 Corinthians 14:34–35:

> Women should remain silent in the churches. They are not allowed
> to speak, but must be in submission, as the law says. If they want
> to inquire about something, they should ask their own husbands
> at home; for it is disgraceful for a woman to speak in the church.

Knowing what we know from our WDWD reading about the role of women in the early churches, we are surprised that Paul would say, "Women should remain silent in the churches." Paul himself gives instructions on women prophesying in the churches in this same letter to the Corinthians. One can't prophesy (or pray) in public and remain completely silent; prophesying means talking in public!

In 1 Corinthians 11:5, Paul says this about women in public church gatherings: "But every woman who *prays or prophesies* with her head uncovered dishonors her head—it is the same as having her head shaved" (emphasis added). And we know from the book of Acts that women exercised the gift of prophecy in the churches. Peter saw this as a fulfillment of the prophet Joel (Acts 2:17–18; 21:9).

So, yes, we are surprised by the sudden appearance of a command for silence for women. Many of us, when reading these words about silence after we have absorbed the King and His Kingdom Story and have learned that redemption includes "nor is there male and female" in Galatians 3:28, ask this: If women did what we have already seen they did (WDWDs) and if Paul offers clear directions on how women should exercise their gift of prophecy in public gatherings, how can he suddenly say women should "remain silent"? Has he not contradicted himself? A shallow reading of the Story points a long finger at Paul's inconsistency. Reading the Bible as Story, however, discerns what Paul was saying in a very specific circumstance. So how do we explain 1 Corinthians 14:34–35?

Many today believe that Paul's silencing of women is a *special kind of silencing*. Paul is not totally silencing women; that would contradict his own teaching and the WDWDs of the Bible. We are not sure what kind of special silence he has in mind, so let me sketch three options. Some think Paul prohibits women from *evaluating prophesies*. Others think Paul is asking women to be silent when it comes to *speaking in or interpreting tongues*, another special concern in this passage. The third option comes from Craig Keener, an expert scholar on the historical background to the New Testament, who keenly observes that Paul's own words clarify this best. Paul silences women in regard to *asking questions*: "If they want *to inquire about something*, they should ask their own husbands [if they are married] at home; for it is disgraceful for a woman to speak [inquire about something they don't yet under-stand] in the church."[3] I think Keener gets this one right, and even more can be said that clarifies what is being said in 1 Corinthians 14 (again, to back up, if Paul wrote these words).

Why would Paul restrict the asking of questions? The best answer is because these women were not yet educated theologically or biblically as well as the men. (We will learn more about this in our next section on 1 Timothy 2.) When these women heard what was being said, they had questions. Paul thinks those sorts of questions should be asked elsewhere, probably because questions interrupted the service. This conclusion has significant implications. Paul's silencing of women at Corinth is then only a *temporary* silencing. Once the women with questions had been educated, they would be permitted to ask questions in the gatherings of Christians or, better yet, would have no need to ask questions.

An implication of Paul's statements is the responsibility of Christian men and leaders to educate women, and this would have stood out in the ancient world as a progressive ideal. As Keener states it, Paul "supports learning before speaking."[4] He adds that such an educational process would not "prohibit women in very different cultural settings from speaking God's word."[5] Furthermore, we must pay special attention to the fact that women today are not uneducated—in fact, some male pastors are! This passage testifies to the importance of education—of knowing the Bible and theology and having pastoral gifts and skills—and once those basics are met, anyone with gifts should be encouraged to use their gifts.

This message in 1 Corinthians 14 is completely explored in 1 Timothy 2. So, let's look at this most famous of silencing passages.

Silencing the Women at Ephesus

Because Paul's instruction for the elders in Ephesus (note that Timothy was in Ephesus when Paul wrote this letter to him; see 1 Timothy 1:3) to silence women is a blue parakeet passage used by some to silence women, and because many think such a view is politically incorrect, the passage itself has become a blue parakeet and has been silenced by both sides!

A Brief Sketch

I begin with a brief summary of 1 Timothy 2:9–15. In this sketch I will anticipate some points I will clarify a little later.[6] Before doing so, let me call attention to the significance of this passage in the history of the church—in particular, to its significance in the shaping of how the Great Tradition has understood the role of women in church ministries. This passage is number one in restricting women's ministries from public teaching and preaching. In this and the next chapter, I will push against that Tradition. But because this passage has had such an enormous impact, I am asking you to plow through it with me. In the next chapter we will explore some of these verses in more detail.

Modesty (1 Timothy 2:9–10)

I also want the women to dress modestly, with decency and propriety, adorning themselves, not with elaborate hairstyles or gold or pearls or expensive clothes, but with good deeds, appropriate for women who profess to worship God.

First, Paul expects the women to whom he is speaking to dress modestly; by that he means they are not to dress elaborately or to demonstrate their high status by their clothing nor are they to dress seductively but instead are to focus their attention on "good deeds." The reason for this has to do with the respectability of the gospel and the church, and as we will explain in the next chapter, Paul is concerned with the influence of the new Roman women who threatened the reputation of the gospel by using public worship as an opportunity for finding a husband (more in the next chapter on this).

Learning before Teaching (1 Timothy 2:11–12)

A woman should learn in quietness and full submission. I do not permit a woman to teach or to assume authority over a man; she must be quiet.

Second, and I highlight these verses because they are our concern here, Paul expects women first to learn in quietness and full submission to those who know, and only then does he say they are not to teach or exercise authority. *Learning* women—and this now sounds like 1 Corinthians 14—are to "be quiet." Paul does not say that women are always to sit in the learning posture and never to be teachers; he does not say they are forever to remain silent, for that would contradict the WDWD passages and practices in the early churches. The main idea in this verse is that women are to become *learners*.

Adam and Eve (1 Timothy 2:13–14)

For Adam was formed first, then Eve. And Adam was not the one deceived; it was the woman who was deceived and became a sinner.

Third, in these two verses Paul anchors the silencing of unlearned women in two points: (1) Adam was "formed first," and (2) Eve was first to be deceived. These two statements surprise the reader. It is entirely possible Paul is responding to the new Roman women, whom we will describe in the next chapter. These new Roman women could have been claiming that the gender order should be reversed, with women subordinating men, and that the original creation was first females and then males.

We cannot be sure why Paul says what he says here. However one interprets these verses—and let's be honest enough to say they are difficult—if we make them an inflexible rule that women should always be silent, we have a flat-out contradiction to the Story of the Bible, to the practices of Priscilla and Junia and Phoebe, and to Paul himself. My personal opinion is that Paul is responding to the claims of new Roman women that women were superior to men because they were prior to men in creation.

Childbearing and Salvation (1 Timothy 2:15)

But women will be saved through childbearing—if they continue in faith, love and holiness with propriety.

Fourth, Paul continues to say that if women—and here he is speaking to married women—continue in the faith, they will be "saved through childbearing." Once again, no one knows for certain what this verse means. Many today think the verse has something to do with the new Roman women's avoidance of marriage while others also suggest that he is responding to the growing attraction on the part of the new Roman women to terminate their pregnancies because motherhood was unworthy of them. Yes, if this is so, we may have an allusion to abortion in the New Testament. Paul discerns that these Christian (and married) women need to know that being married and being mothers are worthy vocations for women. (By the way, Paul is not here advocating that all women must be married.)

We must now examine the cultural context of Paul so we can discern both what he was saying in his day and in his way and how we can live this out in our day and in our way.

CHAPTER 18

SILENCING THE BLUE PARAKEET (2)

Women in Church Ministries 5

Kris and I once participated in a church where some women wore "head coverings" whenever we assembled for worship and teaching. These women (and their husbands) believed they were following Paul's instructions in 1 Corinthians 11:6, which reads: "For if a woman does not cover her head, she might as well have her hair cut off; but if it is a disgrace for a woman to have her hair cut off or her head shaved, then she should cover her head."

There was some discussion, because of a book in the 1980s, about whether Paul meant a cloth head covering or just long hair drawn up over the head. More importantly, many of us had discerned a more historical intent to Paul's words. We knew the research that suggested that the women at Corinth were "letting their hair hang down." We knew that unkempt hair was how prostitutes dressed. So we discerned that Paul was concerned about how this appearance by women would impact the reputation of the gospel. These loose-haired women, in Paul's opinion, gave off the suggestion that the Christian gatherings were sexual in nature.

One of my closest friends, a brilliant scholar of the New Testament, made this observation about the situation at our church in light of the context of Paul's words: "Scot, some at your church don't seem willing to ask if insisting on head coverings might do *the opposite* of what Paul was actually doing." In other words, insisting on head coverings does as much (if not more) damage to the gospel today as *not* wearing head coverings did in the first century. How so? If we demand women do something so totally contrary to culture that non-Christians are offended or turned off, we should reconsider what we are doing. Paul didn't want the dress of Christian women to bring a bad name to the gospel, so he asked them to wear head coverings; by contrast, demanding women to wear head coverings in our world may do the very same damage to the gospel. (In fact, I'm quite sure it would.)

My friend was right. Context is everything. Knowing context permits deeper and wiser discernment. So what was the historical context to Paul's words in 1 Timothy 2:9–15?

NEW ROMAN WOMEN IN EPHESUS: Dress, Public Discourse, Anti-Marriage

When Paul wrote his letters to the Christians in Corinth and to Timothy in Ephesus, *a gender and sexual revolution was observable in many of the major cities of the Roman Empire.* What some today are calling the "new Roman woman"—whether this description is the most accurate isn't as important as knowing what was "in the air" when Paul was writing—describes an aggressive, confrontational public presence on the part of women during the very time Paul was writing these letters. The following paragraphs discuss its characteristics, and you can look at Appendix 4 for a specific text that illustrates the sort of thing Paul probably was referring to. Three features of the new Roman woman set our passage in its historical context.

First, the new Roman woman was expressing her newfound freedoms in *immodest, sexually provocative, and extravagant dress.* Rome was not terribly conservative, but these women were flouting even the limits of the Romans. A text I had not seen until a couple years back is a first-century Roman novel called *Anthia and Habrocomes* (sometimes called *Ephesiaca*). For some reason this text is nearly totally ignored or unknown to many New Testament readers. It describes a love affair, a glorious one, between Anthia and Habrocomes, two social elites of Ephesus. Some recent scholars date this novel to about AD 50, in other words, at about the time Paul is in Ephesus. Besides the love affair's winding and twisting through the Mediterranean cities, there are two text features in *Anthia and Habrocomes* that demonstrate that Paul was worried about the influence of women connected to the Artemis cult in the church at Ephesus. Recall Paul's words about modesty: "Not with elaborate hairstyles or gold or pearls." In *Anthia and Habrocomes* the young folks are in a procession through Ephesus and down to the Temple of Artemis, and this is what is said of Anthia's appearance: "Her hair was golden—a little of it plaited" (1.2). Nearly exact words as one finds in 1 Timothy 2. But this is what matters even more. The young folks get to the temple itself and during the worship service, this is what the author (Xenophon of Ephesus) writes:

> And so when the procession was over, the whole crowd went into the temple for the sacrifice, and the files broke up; men and women and girls and boys came together. Then they saw each other, and Anthia was captivated by Habrocomes, while Love got the better of Habrocomes. He kept looking at the girl and in spite of himself could not take his eyes off her. Love held him fast and pressed home his attack. And Anthia too was in a bad way, as she let his appearance sink in, with rapt attention and eyes wide open; and already she paid no attention to modesty: what she said was for Habrocomes to hear, and she revealed what she could of her body for Habrocomes to see. And he was captivated at the sight and was a prisoner of the god (1.3).[1]

Seduction in the middle of a worship service, that's what Xenophon described in this novel, and that is why Paul says what he says about women in the church services at Ephesus.

Second, the new Roman woman was noted for *snatching the podium for public addresses and teaching.* Here are words that describe something like what Paul was concerned about:

> But most intolerable of all is the woman who as soon as she has sat down to dinner commends Virgil, pardons the dying Dido, and pits the poets against each other, putting Virgil in the one scale and Homer in the other. The grammarians make way before her; the rhetoricians give in; the whole crowd is silenced: no lawyer, no auctioneer will get a word in, no, nor any other woman; so torrential is her speech that you would think that all the pots and bells were being clashed together.... She lays down definitions, and discourses on morals, like a philosopher.[2]

(See Appendix 5 for more of the text from Juvenal's *Satire 6* where men complain about educated women.)

Third, especially in Ephesus, alongside the presence of the new Roman woman was *the Artemis religious fertility cult.* This worship cult not only favored the freedom of women in public religion but it also surrounded these worshipers with eunuch (castrated male) priests. Part of their worship was the elimination of normal sexual relations; these women despised marriage and childbearing and child-rearing. Furthermore, this fertility cult extended their sexual and gender freedoms into open practices of abortion and contraception.[3]

The Roman Empire was hardly prudish when it came to dress codes, but this new Roman woman movement alarmed the establishment. Caesar Augustus, for instance, passed laws legislating what respectable women were to wear and how prostitutes and adulteresses were to dress. Naturally, these laws were debated and they were flouted by the new Roman woman.[4] But our concern is with Paul and the women in Ephesus, who were under Timothy's leadership. Paul was all for Spirit-led gifts on the part of women—a liberating impulse on his part. But he had deep concerns over the influence of certain Roman women and their behavior. They were beginning to jeopardize the holiness of the Christian church. Some critics of the church were apparently suggesting that the church was little more than a fertility cult.

This is the context for Paul's statements in 1 Timothy 2:9–15. The big point Paul makes is not to "keep the women silent" but to "teach the women." His principle was "learning before teaching." If I am asked how this text "applies" to our modern world, I would discern that we need "learning before teaching." I would also discern something Paul didn't think he needed to say: men too need learning before teaching. Why? Because in that day men were more privileged in education than women. It's that simple. Any reading of the Bible, especially a passage like this, that doesn't recognize male privilege will not come to terms with the social codes in the text.

Now let's make a connection that readers of 1 Timothy 2 do not make often enough. A major clue to reading 1 Timothy 2 is found in the very same letter—in 1 Timothy 5.

Problems in the Churches at Ephesus

Paul's letter to Timothy is laced together with two strings—the danger of false teaching and the need for orthodox teaching. Of particular concern to Paul was a group of young widows whom we meet directly in 1 Timothy 5:11–14. Paul's words there, which can strike the modern reader as terribly simplistic, are directed to a specific group of young widows who had behavior issues. When Paul silences women in 1 Timothy 2, he is almost certainly silencing especially the widows we find in chapter 5, and I would encourage you to read 1 Timothy 2 and 5 in comparison. Below are the words of Paul from 1 Timothy 5 about some young widows, and we need to read each word carefully because themes we have just touched appear over and over.

Sensuality among the Younger Widows (1 Timothy 5:11–12)

As for younger widows, do not put them on such a [widow] list. For when their *sensual desires* overcome their dedication to Christ, they want to marry. Thus they bring judgment on themselves, because they have broken their first pledge [of faith in Christ]. (emphasis added)

The language Paul uses for these women is noteworthy: he is describing a widow who has developed a promiscuous, sexual lifestyle and who is thus abandoning the faith. These are not ordinary Christian young widows; these widows are a group of young women with a well-known reputation of public sexuality. This sounds very much like the new Roman woman. Their sexual lifestyle is not the whole point, and it is the next verse that shows us that the women of chapter 2 are in view.

Busybody Teachers (1 Timothy 5:13)

Besides, they get into the habit of being idle and going about from house to house. And not only do they become idlers, but also busybodies who talk nonsense, saying things they ought not to.

If we set these words in the new Roman woman context, and if we remember what we read in 1 Timothy 2:9–15, we will see that 1 Timothy 5 is referring to young widows who, because they are not yet theologically formed, are being accused by Paul of idling and busybodying. *What* they were doing—visiting friends—is not Paul's concern. What they were *saying and teaching* was Paul's concern.

The Virtue of Marriage (1 Timothy 5:14)

So I counsel younger widows to marry, to have children, to manage their homes and to give the enemy no opportunity for slander.

This verse sounds yet again like 1 Timothy 2:15: "But women will be saved through childbearing—if they continue in faith, love and holiness with propriety." I doubt very much that Paul is demanding that all women everywhere marry, have children, and manage their homes. But if we factor in the new Roman woman's desire to end marriage and childbearing and to pursue instead a sexually promis-cuous life, Paul is countering those ideas with the virtue of marriage and managing a home.

Summary

Let me now sum all this up, for it is this context that gives rise to the silencing of women. Women in the Roman Empire and in particular in Ephesus were advocating counter-Christian ideas and practices. Paul was concerned about the reputation of the gospel and the respectability of Christian women for fear they might be associated with the offensive side of such behaviors. So Paul turns to the women in Ephesus—in particular, to a group of young widows. He urges them to live a life of holiness and to learn before they start teaching.

We are thus led to the conclusion that when Paul asks women to be silent in 1 Timothy 2, he is not talking about ordinary Christian women; rather, he has a specific group of women in mind. His concern is with some untrained, morally loose, young widows who, because they are theologically unformed, are teaching unorthodox ideas. Paul does not advocate, then, that women should not teach but that they should learn sound theology before they teach.

Context is everything, and in this case a little knowledge of the Roman world and a glance at 1 Timothy 5 provides all we need. Even if we lacked knowledge about the new Roman woman, what Paul says about widows in 1 Timothy 5 tells us about all we need to know to make clear sense of 1 Timothy 2.

It's All in Our Passage!

First Timothy 2:9–15 is aimed directly at women, especially the young widows, who are following the new Roman woman in public behaviors and who don't know enough theology to teach sound doctrine.

Paul, ever vigilant about the reputation of the gospel, urges these women to wear modest clothing, to exercise sexual restraint, and to do good deeds. Yet *more than that*—and often ignored—Paul utters something that should completely shift the focus of this passage: "A woman should *learn* in quietness and full submission" (1 Timothy 2:11, emphasis added). Paul's focus here is not on what women *cannot* do, which unfortunately is how the silencers of blue parakeets read this passage, but on what these women must do: *learn*. He is not concerned with silence in general but with *silence in order to learn*. In light of the Story and of how we have answered WDWD, we conclude that the silence Paul talks about in both 1 Corinthians 14 and 1 Timothy 2 is a temporary silence—temporary until these women have learned.

The teaching that Paul prohibits, then, is unorthodox theology. Until these young women are informed and until they are formed in character, they need to be learners. (The same can be said for men who, in Paul's world, had more opportunities to learn.) So when Paul says they need to "*learn* in quietness and full submission," he is speaking here of deference to the wise teachers, the elders, who are orthodox and godly, not to a permanent condition of utter silence. Once they learn, they will be ready to teach and to travel from house church to house church to impart wisdom and demonstrate godliness.

Paul's two comments about silence are actually consistent, then, with the story and plot of the Bible. Women, who have always been gifted by God to speak for God and to lead God's people, were doing just those things in Paul's churches. But women who had not yet learned Bible and theology or who had not yet learned how to live a Christian life were not to become teachers until they had learned orthodox theology.

What drives 1 Corinthians 14 and 1 Timothy 2 is a principle that much of the church tradition has nearly smothered when it comes to women: "Learning precedes teaching." When churches today ask leaders questions about the Bible and theology and when pastoral search committees ask about the education of candidates, they are living out what Paul was saying in these two passages.

What about Scripture?
What about Today?

Some are surprised by what they learn when they read explanations like this. Some want to throw away their Bibles and say, "Only the experts can do this!" Some find liberation. Some say they almost threw away their Bible until they learned the Bible too emerged out of a context. They say, "Show me how to do this on my own!"

Both of these groups believe in the Bible.

Perhaps you disagree with my reading of these silencing passages. Let me then put it another way. We can at least begin with two basic options: *either* we have a general prohibition of women teaching and leading *with some exceptions* (the hierarchical view, *through* the many layers of church tradition), *or* we have the possibility of women teaching and leading *with some restrictions* (the mutuality view, *with* [and perhaps *against*] tradition). There is no ground, however, for total silencing of women in the church. Total silence makes Paul a total contradiction between what he teaches and what women were doing in his churches—about which he says nothing when they pray or prophesy, or are deacons or apostles, or when they are more or less the leaders of house churches.

When we consider these two options, does it not strike you that, at the very least, women can *sometimes* teach and lead? *In the Bible, women did lead and women did teach.* Some today want to take back what women did, while others (I include myself here) want to expand what women can do today because we live in a different world. Those who are taking back the teaching and leading ministries of women are fighting the Bible, not embracing it. They are silencing blue parakeets. They are saying, "We know what women did in the Bible, but that's not for today!" Let me ask you a question: Is this being biblical? Is this following the clear expansion of ministries from Pentecost on? I believe a post-Pentecost reading of the Bible encourages us to give the blue parakeets a chance to sing!

You might ask me, "Why do you think we can expand the ministries of women?" Very simply: the plot of the Bible, the redemptive world created by the King and His Kingdom Story, and the behaviors of women in that Plot and Story reveal to me an increasing expansion of women in church ministries. Some of the restrictions were based on respectability and culture. If those restrictions have changed, then I see no reason to limit the ministries of women to the sensibilities and cultures of that time. God spoke in those days in those ways, and I believe he is speaking in our days in our ways.

But I have no desire here to suggest this expansion of the role of women is for all in all places. I return to Phil Towner's observations—and here he brings in the unique combination of not only an expertise on our text but also decades of experience on the mission field. Phil and I generally agree on how to read this passage. But he offers us this caution: "What this means for Christianity in traditional Asian or Muslim contexts is that too much too fast could endanger the church's witness and credibility. But in much of the Western world, too little too slow could neutralize the church's impact in society just as effectively."[5]

What we need is discernment.

The Pauline Principle of Discernment

If any words in the Bible capture the essence of this book, they can be found in the first letter Paul sent to the Corinthians. What I'm not sure we always ponder, perhaps because it will attract a yard full of blue parakeets, is just how creative, liberating, and forward-looking this passage is. Here are Paul's words from 1 Corinthians 9:19–23:

> Though I am free and belong to no one, I have made myself a slave to everyone, to win as many as possible. To the Jews I became like a Jew, to win the Jews. To those under the law I became like one under the law (though I myself am not under the law), so as to win those under the law. To those not having

the law I became like one not having the law (though I am not free from God's law but am under Christ's law), so as to win those not having the law. To the weak I became weak, to win the weak. I have become all things to all people so that by all possible means I might save some. I do all this for the sake of the gospel, that I may share in its blessings.

Here's a question I hope you can toss around with your friends: Do you think Paul would have put women "behind the pulpit" if it would have been advantageous "for the sake of gospel"? I believe Paul would exhort us to open the cages and let the blue parakeets fly and let them sing.

What Paul states in 1 Corinthians 9 forms the core of how we have to learn to read the Bible. Paul himself adapted the gospel to every situation he encountered: a Jewish expression for Jews, a gentile expression for gentiles, and a philosopher's approach when on the Areopagus (Acts 17). What Paul did is simple: he knew the Story and the Plot, he listened to God and was open to the Spirit, and he discerned how to live out that gospel and speak that gospel into each cultural setting. Paul's mode was renewing and always renewing.

Recently in a class session of college students, I sketched three options we have in reading the Bible (the three views I sketched in chapter 2): read and retrieve it all, read the Bible *through* tradition, and read the Bible *with* tradition (including challenging the tradition). After class, a fine student pressed me, with intellectual articulation and heartfelt passion, that if we choose the third option we are led to hundreds of views with no real unity. How can we let everyone read the Bible for themselves? Won't that lead to millions of readings?

My response? No, it won't lead to millions of readings, but it will lead to many readings. Culturally shaped readings of the Bible and culturally shaped expressions of the gospel are exactly what Paul did and wanted and practiced: what occurred in Jerusalem was not what happened in Corinth, and what happened in Corinth was not what happened in Rome. That's exactly what Peter and the author of

Hebrews and John and James and the others were doing. Culturally shaped readings and expressions of the gospel are the way it has been, is, and always will be. In fact, I believe that gospel adaptation for every culture, for every church, and for every Christian is precisely why God gave us the Bible. The Bible shows us how.

The Waterslide Again

God has given us his Word, the Bible. That Word provides for us the gospel. That gospel is the waterslide, banked on one side by the Bible's canon and banked on the other side by the wisdom of the church, the Great Tradition. The water running down the slide is the Holy Spirit. We are called to enter the slide at the top (Genesis) and ride it all the way down—safely protected by canon and conversation with Tradition—to the end (Revelation). If we ride it properly, wetted down as we are by the Holy Spirit and cheered on by the communion of saints, we will land in the water where we need to be—in our day and in our way.

F. F. Bruce

In the spring of 1981, as a doctoral student in Nottingham, England, I piled Kris and our two kids, Laura and Lukas, into our small car and drove to Buxton. Professor F. F. Bruce, perhaps the most widely known evangelical scholar of the previous generation and a specialist on Paul, had invited our family to his home for late-afternoon tea. When we arrived, we were welcomed into the home by Professor Bruce, and we sat in the living room for about two hours. During that time our son managed to spill a glass of orange squash on the Bruce's rug, which Professor Bruce dismissed with a "whatever can be spilled has been spilled on that rug."

During a break, as Kris was talking to Mrs. Bruce, I asked Professor Bruce a question that I had stored up for him (and I repeat our conversation from my memory): "Professor Bruce, what do you think of women's ordination?"

"I don't think the New Testament talks about ordination," he replied.

"What about the silencing passages of Paul on women?" I asked.

"I think Paul would roll over in his grave if he knew we were turning his letters into *torah*."

Wow! I thought. *That's a good point to think about.* Thereupon I asked a question that he answered in such a way that it reshaped my thinking: "What do you think, then, about women in church ministries?"

Professor Bruce's answer was as Pauline as Paul was: "I'm for whatever God's Spirit grants women gifts to do."

So am I. Let the blue parakeets sing!

CHAPTER 19

NOW WHAT?

We've covered lots of ground in *The Blue Parakeet*, but that is only because the question—"How, then, do we read the Bible?"—deserves our attention. There are enough passages in the Bible—and I began to sense this when I was a young Christian—that, when we read them, make us think all over again about how we are reading the Bible. I call these passages the "blue parakeet passages."

Blue parakeet passages are oddities in the Bible that we prefer to cage and silence rather than to permit into our sacred mental gardens. If we are honest, blue parakeet passages often threaten us, call into question our traditional way of reading the Bible, and summon us back to the Bible to rethink how we read the Bible. Though we could have chosen other themes or ideas, the issue of women in church ministries was our test case for how we both read the Bible and how we bring it into our world.

So, how then do we read the Bible? I'd like to sum up what this book has said.

The Big Temptation

Many of us will be tempted to take the shortcuts when we read the Bible and especially when we encounter a blue parakeet passage. Instead of reading each passage in its storied context, we will zoom in on getting out of the Bible what we want. Once again, the shortcuts we have all learned in reading the Bible are:

- to treat the Bible as a collection of laws;
- to treat the Bible as a collection of blessings and promises;
- to treat the Bible as a Rorschach inkblot onto which we can project our own ideas;
- to treat the Bible as a giant puzzle that we are to puzzle together; and
- to treat one of the Bible's authors as a maestro.

We have only one other genuine option, to read the Bible from front to back as a redemptive message shaped by the King and His Kingdom Story. Before we summarize what we said about the Story, let's see what's wrong with each of these shortcuts. Yes, strategy will guide us to something true about the Bible: there are laws, there are blessings and promises, there are moments when we see in the Bible something about our own lives, there are parts of the Bible that we are challenged to puzzle together, and there are maestros—many of them. But there are problems with each of these:

- The Bible is more than laws, and each law is connected to its context.
- The Bible is more than blessings and promises; there are some warnings and threats as well.
- The Bible is something that comes to us from God and not something onto which we can impose our wishes and desires.
- The Bible is a story to be read, not a divinely scattered puzzle to be pieced together into a system that makes sense of it all.
- The Bible is a collection of wiki-stories of the Story, and each author, each maestro, is but one voice at the table.

It is tempting to return to the safety of our former reading habits. But if we listen to the blue parakeet passages in the Bible, which are there at God's discretion, and if we think about how we are reading them, the Bible somehow unfolds before our eyes as a brilliant Story.

The Story

God chose to give us a collection of books, what I call wiki-stories of the Story, and together these books form into God's story with us and God's story for us. Acts 7 is a good example of how to read the Bible as Story even though Stephen's speech in Acts 7 is only one wiki-story of the Story. Again, each author in the Bible is a wiki-storyteller and each book is then a wiki-story, one story in the ongoing development of the big story. These are the major elements of that story:

Theocracy
1. God and creation
2. Adam and Eve as *Eikon*s who crack the *Eikon*
3. God's covenant community, Israel, where humans are restored to God, self, others, and the world

Monarchy
1. Israel as God's covenant people who desire a king; God grants them a king but this does not solve Israel's problems; God uses the kings and the prophets and the sages to anticipate the one true king, prophet, and sage.

Christocracy
1. Jesus Christ, who is the King of the Story and in whose story we are to live
2. The church as Jesus's covenant community
3. The consummation, when all the designs of our Creator God will finally be realized forever and ever

What we discover in reading the Bible is that each telling of the Story, each wiki-story, was a Spirit-inspired telling of the Story in each person's day in each person's way. God spoke through Moses in Moses's ways for Moses's days, through David in David's ways for David's days, through Jesus in Jesus's ways for Jesus's days, and through John in John's ways for John's days. God always speaks a "contemporary" word. The genius of the Bible is the continuity of the Story as each generation learns to speak it afresh in its days and in its ways.

Furthermore, each wiki-storyteller, each author in the Bible, tells a story that will lead us to the person of the Story: Jesus Christ. As Moses and Isaiah look forward to that person, so Paul and Peter and the author of Hebrews look back to that person. Jesus Christ, then, is the goal and the center of each wiki-story. The Theocracy worked through a Monarchy, but the whole Story was aimed at the Christocracy, the rule of the Messiah as the world's one true Lord.

This leads me to a major strategy in reading the Bible. Every author in the Bible was divinely directed through God's Spirit to tell a true story of the one Story. This means that our task in reading the Bible is to "map" the elements of the Story in each wiki-story. If we keep our eyes on the seven elements of the Story as outlined above, we will have all we need for reading the Bible. These seven elements govern the story of the Bible and each book focuses on one or more of these elements.

Living Out the Story Today

We must never make the mistake of exalting the paper on which the Bible is written over the person who puts the words on that paper. Our relationship to the Bible is actually, if we are properly engaged, a relationship with the God of the Bible. God gave us the Bible as a person who speaks to you and me as persons through words. God gave us the Bible so we could be transformed and bring glory to him by living out a life in this world that God designs for us. How do we do this?

We are summoned by the God who speaks to us in the Bible to *listen* to God speak, to *live out* what God directs us to live out, and to *discern how* to live out the Story in our own day. One way of saying all of this can be found in Moses's original words and in what I call the Jesus Creed version of Moses's words: we are to love God and to love others. If we love God and love others, we will listen to God in the Bible, live out what God calls us to live out, and discern how to live out the Story in our world today. Discernment, of course, calls for some special attention.

I used the image of the waterslide in this book for how we discern how to live today. Graced by the watery gift of the Spirit, we sit on the gospel and are constrained by the Bible and guided by the wise mentors of the church (reading the Bible *with* tradition), and we ride this all so we can land in our world with a gospel for our day shaped in our way. What we need are two things if we are to do this well.

First, we need to be mastered by the *Story* by reading the Bible so deeply that its story becomes our story. If we let that story become our story, we will inhabit the Bible's very own story. Let me remind us that it is not simply this story that masters us, but the God of that story. By indwelling the story of the Bible, we indwell the God who tells that story.

Second, together as God's people we are to so inhabit the Story that we can *discern* how to live in our world. Our calling is to live out the ageless Story in our world. To do this we have to bring back the Spirit of God into our interpretation of the Bible. We read the Bible with all the tools of history and language that we can muster, but a proper reading of the Bible is attended by the Spirit, who will transform us, guide us, and give us discernment to know how to live in our world.

What Now?

Reading the Bible as Story teaches us to look forward by looking to our past. It teaches us to go back to that story so we know how to go forward in our world. We must not be afraid of where God will lead us as we live out this story today, just as David and Isaiah and Jesus and Paul and Peter were unafraid where God might lead them. We cannot think that we will find security by going back and staying in the past. We cannot think that our task is complete once we've figured what Paul or Peter meant when they spoke the gospel in their world. Instead, we are given a pattern of discernment in the Bible, a pattern that flows directly out of the Story, to listen to what God said in that world so we can know what God is saying to us through our world. So we can know what God wants us to say about that story to our world—in our world's ways.

If the Bible does anything for us as we read it as Story, it gives us the confidence to face the future with the good news about Jesus Christ in the power of the Spirit. God's Spirit, the Story tells us, is with us to guide us and to give us discernment.

The story of the Bible is not only the story of our past, it is the story for our future.

AFTER WORDS

I teach the Bible, and as my friend and former colleague Brad Nassif and I often remind ourselves, not only do we teach the Bible but this is our job. I could not have dreamed of a better job or of a better opportunity than having former colleagues like Brad—such as Boaz Johnson, Joel Willitts, Ginny Olson, and Jim Dekker. Now that I'm at Northern Seminary, I get to add new colleagues' names who have discussed this topic with me: David Fitch, Cherith Fee Nordling, Geoff Hosclaw, Jason Gile, and Bill Shiel. I give thanks for my former graduate assistant, Tara Beth Leach, for modeling the new voice of Junia in her teaching and preaching in Pasadena.

This teaching kind of life has given me many good friends, fellow Bible readers who teach me and probe me. Those who have read parts of this book or who have listened to me talk about it, besides the wonderful crowd we had at the National Pastors Convention in San Diego in February 2008, include my longtime friend Joe Modica and his colleague Dwight Peterson at Eastern University, where I was invited one evening for a public conversation about the contents of this book. Their questions pushed me to reshape parts of this book.

I wish to mention others who, through conversation or reading some or all of this manuscript, have helped me shape my thoughts more accurately: Norton Herbst and Jason Malec, both at North Point in Atlanta; J. R. Briggs, Roseanne Sension, Nancy Beach at Willow Creek Community Church; Nancy Ortberg, Cheryl Hatch, Doreen and Mark Olson, Julie Clawson, Kent and Phyllis Palmer, Peter Chang and Kathy Khang, Greg Clark, and Alice Shirey.

John Raymond of Zondervan is not only my editor, but his father was my college basketball coach; John himself was our "manager" as a teenager, and he has been a friend to me and Kris and our kids for decades. I am grateful for John. In a strange turn of fate, I have ceased reading his papers and he is now reading mine! I am grateful to my agent, Greg Daniel of the Daniel Literary Group, for his wisdom and advice on this manuscript. Both John and Greg made this a much better book. An earlier version of the appendix on Junia was edited and improved by Patton Dodd.

Kris refers to books like this one as my "readable" books. She doesn't read my "unreadable" ones, but books like this one are important to her. She read every chapter, made detailed comments at times, and urged me time and time again to make the book better. She began to refer to one of the chapters in this book as "The Boring Chapter," and so we gave that chapter her words. Without her you might not be holding this book in your hand. Kris has been my best friend and loving wife for more than thirty years. Proverbs 31 doesn't even come close to describing her.

Kris and I chose to dedicate this book to our friend and my former student Cheryl Hatch. Let me put it this way: even if you try to clip the wings or silence the voice of a blue parakeet, somehow her glory and her gifts find a way.

SCOT MCKNIGHT

BIBLE VERSIONS

In addition to the NIV, these Bible versions are quoted in this book:

Scripture quotations marked CEB are taken from the Common English Bible. Copyright © 2011 Common English Bible Committee.

Scripture quotations marked ESV are taken from the ESV® (The Holy Bible, English Standard Version®). Copyright © 2001 by Crossway, a publishing ministry of Good News Publishers. Used by permission. All rights reserved.

Scripture quotations marked HCSB are taken from the Holman Christian Standard Bible®. Copyright © 1999, 2000, 2002, 2003, 2009 by Holman Bible Publishers. Used by permission. HCSB® is a federally registered trademark of Holman Bible Publishers.

The Scripture quotations marked NRSV are taken from the New Revised Standard Version Bible. Copyright © 1989 National Council of the Churches of Christ in the United States of America. Used by permission. All rights reserved.

Scripture quotations marked RSV are taken from the Revised Standard Version of the Bible. Copyright © 1946, 1952, and 1971 National Council of the Churches of Christ in the United States of America. Used by permission. All rights reserved.

Scripture quotations marked TNIV are taken from the Holy Bible, Today's New International® Version TNIV®. Copyright © 2001, 2005 by International Bible Society.® Used by permission of International Bible Society®. All rights reserved worldwide. "TNIV" and "Today's New International Version" are trademarks registered in the United States Patent and Trademark Office by International Bible Society®.

A DISCERNMENT QUIZ[1]

This quiz was an assignment asked of me by Skye Jethani, the editor of *Leadership Journal*. Our initial conversation at a coffee shop generated so many ideas, we could not contain them all in one quiz. So we drafted a quiz to see if we could get a conversation going about how we read the Bible and how we "apply" the Bible. For most questions we sensed we could have had ten or more different answers, and scaling our answers proved especially difficult. That quiz also gave some labels connected to scores that generated more controversy than was intended.

I have one desire with this quiz: we need to talk more about how we are reading the Bible. Instruments like this are one way of getting us to rethink how we read the Bible. I've eliminated the labels in this edition of the quiz.

On a scale of 1–5, mark the answer that best fits your approach to reading the Bible. If, for example, you fall between response 1 and response 3, give yourself a 2; or between 3 and 5, give yourself a 4. Place your score in the space after the colon. Maybe you want to rewrite the whole question; go ahead. Choose, in other words, the answer that is closest to your own view. What interests me most is getting you and others into a conversation about how we read and apply the Bible.

A. The Bible is: _____
   1. God's inspired words in confluence with the authors (genuine dual authorship).

3. God's inspired words that arise out of a community and then are written down by an author (less author, more community).

5. Words of an author who speaks out of a community's tradition, but which sacramentally lead us to God.

B. The Bible is: _____
   1. God's exact words for all time.
   3. God's message (instead of exact words) for all time.
   5. God's words and message for that time but need interpretation and contextualization to be lived today.

C. The Bible's words are: _____
   1. Inerrant on everything.
   3. Inerrant only on matters of faith and practice.
   5. Not defined by inerrancy or errancy, which are modernistic categories.

D. The commands in the Old Testament to destroy a village, including women and children, are: _____
   1. Justifiable judgment against sinful, pagan, immoral peoples.
   3. God's ways in the days of the judges (etc.); they are primitive words but people's understanding as divine words for that day.
   5. A barbaric form of war in a primitive society and I wish they weren't in the Bible.

E. The story of Hosea (the prophet) and Gomer (his wife) is: _____
   1. A graphic reality that speaks of God's faithfulness and Israel's infidelity.
   3. A parable (since, for example, God would never ask a prophet to marry a prostitute).
   5. An unfortunate image of an ancient prophet that stereotypes women and too easily justifies violence against women.

F. The command of Jesus to wash feet is: _____
    1. To be taken literally, despite near universal neglect in the church.
    3. A first-century observance to be practiced today in other ways.
    5. An ancient custom with no real implication for our world.

G. The gift of prophecy is: _____
    1. Timeless, despite lack of attention in the church today.
    3. An ancient form of communication that is seen today in proclaiming scriptural truths.
    5. No longer needed and dramatically different from today's preaching.

H. Prohibitions of homosexuality in the Bible are: _____
    1. Permanent prohibitions reflecting God's will.
    3. Culturally shaped, still normative, but demanding greater sensitivity today.
    5. A purity-code violation that has been eliminated by Christ.

I. The unity of the Bible is: _____
    1. God's systematic truth that can be discerned by careful study of the Bible.
    3. The gospel call to living by faith that is expressed in a variety of ways by different authors in the Bible.
    5. Not found by imposing on the integrity of each author in the Bible to conform to overarching systems; the unity is in the God who speaks to us today through the Word.

J. The Holy Spirit's role in interpretation is: _____
    1. To guide the individual regardless of what others say.
    3. To guide the individual in tandem/conversation with the church.
    5. To guide the community that can instruct the individual.

K. The injunctions on women in 1 Timothy 2:9–15 are: _____
1. Timeless truths and normative for today.
3. Culturally shaped but, with proper interpretation and transfer, for today; e.g., we can learn from how Paul addressed a situation with uninstructed women in Ephesus.
5. Needed for early Christians, bound in the first century, but not for today.

L. Careful interpretation of the Bible is: _____
1. Objective, rational, universal, timeless.
3. Dialectical, relational, culturally shaped, timely.
5. Subjective, personal, culturally bound, time specific.

M. The context for reading the Bible is: _____
1. The individual's sole responsibility.
3. The individual in conversation with, and respect for, church traditions.
5. The confessional statement of one's community of faith.

N. Discerning the historical context of a passage is: _____
1. Unimportant since God speaks to me directly.
3. Often or sometimes significant in order to grasp meaning.
5. Necessary and dangerous to avoid in reading the Bible.

O. The Bible: _____
1. Can be examined and understood without bias.
3. Can be understood but with bias.
5. Can be only partially understood by a reader with bias.

P. Capital punishment: _____
1. Should be practiced today because the Bible teaches it.
3. Should be examined carefully to determine if it is the best option today; some instances of capital punishment in the Bible are no longer advisable.

5. As delineated in the Bible pertains to ancient Israel; such practices are no longer useful and should be universally banned.

Q. Tattoos: _____
   1. Are forbidden because of Leviticus 19:28.
   3. Are forbidden in Leviticus as idolatrous marks, which we know from study of the ancient Near East.
   5. Are permissible, because the purity codes are not for Christians today.

R. The requirement of the Jerusalem Council (Acts 15:29) not to eat any meat improperly killed (strangled instead of having the blood drained properly): _____
   1. Is a permanent commandment for all Christians today.
   3. Is for Jewish Christians only.
   5. Is a temporary custom for first-century Jewish Christians and is no longer a concern for Christians.

S. Adultery: _____
   1. Deserves the death penalty, as stated in the Old Testament.
   3. Was not punished by death when Jesus confronted it, and therefore death is not a Christian punishment.
   5. Adultery and divorce were governed by Old Testament laws from a primitive culture, very different from our own; just as these concepts developed within Bible times, our understanding of proper punishment has been improved.

T. Sabbath: _____
   1. Was never eliminated by New Testament writers and should be practiced by Christians (on Saturday).
   3. Developed into a Sunday worship observance for Christians, and Christians should not work on that day.
   5. Turned into Sunday for Christians, who need to worship together (on the weekend, at least) and can work if they think they need to.

IMAGES OF JESUS[1]

This test is not produced by or for North Park University, and its questions should not be taken to imply any views of North Park University. Obviously, in a test of this type there are no "correct" answers. This test should be taken at the beginning of a semester and again at the end of the semester to assess change in image of Jesus and image of self.

Note: Your professor will never know who answered what on this test.

Part 1: What Do You Think of Jesus?

Please answer each question with a "yes" (Y) or "no" (N). Work quickly and do not think too long about the exact meaning of the questions. Please answer this part 1 for what *you* think about Jesus.

1. Does his mood often go up and down?	Y	N
2. Is he a talkative person?	Y	N
3. Would being in debt worry him?	Y	N
4. Is he rather lively?	Y	N
5. Was he ever greedy by helping himself to more than his share of anything?	Y	N
6. Would he take drugs that may have strange or dangerous effects?	Y	N

7. Has he ever blamed someone for doing something he knew was really his fault?   Y   N

8. Does he prefer to go his own way rather than act by the rules?   Y   N

9. Does he often feel "fed-up"?   Y   N

10. Has he ever taken anything (even a pin or button) that belonged to someone else?   Y   N

11. Would he call himself a nervous person?   Y   N

12. Does he think marriage is old-fashioned and should be done away with?   Y   N

13. Can he easily get some life into a rather dull party?   Y   N

14. Is he a worrier?   Y   N

15. Does he tend to keep in the background on social occasions?   Y   N

16. Does it worry him if he knows there are mistakes in his work?   Y   N

17. Has he ever cheated at a game?   Y   N

18. Does he suffer from "nerves"?   Y   N

19. Has he ever taken advantage of someone?   Y   N

20. Is he mostly quiet when he is with other people?   Y   N

21. Does he often feel lonely?   Y   N

22. Does he think it is better to follow society's rules than go his own way?   Y   N

23. Do other people think of him as being very lively?   Y   N

24. Does he always practice what he preaches?   Y   N

Part 2: Who Are You?

25. Which sex are you?
    ☐ Female   ☐ Male
26. What is your age?
    ☐ 18–19   ☐ 20–21   ☐ 22–23   ☐ 24–25   ☐ older than 25

27. Which school year are you in?
    ☐ Freshman   ☐ Sophomore   ☐ Junior   ☐ Senior
28. Are you taking this BTS course to fulfill General Education requirements?
    ☐ Yes   ☐ No
29. Which denomination do you belong to?
    ☐ Covenant   ☐ Roman Catholic   ☐ Evangelical
    ☐ Pentecostal-Charismatic   ☐ Mainline Protestant
30. Do you go to church ...
    ☐ weekly   ☐ at least once a month   ☐ sometimes
    ☐ once or twice per year   ☐ never

PART 3: What Do *You* Think About *Yourself?*

[Do not look at your answers to questions 1–24.]

31. Does your mood often go up and down?	Y	N
32. Are you a talkative person?	Y	N
33. Would being in debt worry you?	Y	N
34. Are you rather lively?	Y	N
35. Were you ever greedy by helping yourself to more than your share of anything?	Y	N
36. Would you take drugs which may have strange or dangerous effects?	Y	N
37. Have you ever blamed someone for doing something you knew was really your fault?	Y	N
38. Do you prefer to go your own way rather than act by the rules?	Y	N
39. Do you often feel "fed-up"?	Y	N
40. Have you ever taken anything (even a pin or button) that belonged to someone else?	Y	N
41. Would you call yourself a nervous person?	Y	N

42. Do you think marriage is old-fashioned and
should be done away with?   Y   N
43. Can you easily get some life into a rather dull party? Y   N
44. Are you a worrier?   Y   N
45. Do you tend to keep in the background on social
occasions?   Y   N
46. Does it worry you if you know there are mistakes
in your work?   Y   N
47. Have you ever cheated at a game?   Y   N
48. Do you suffer from "nerves"?   Y   N
49. Have you ever taken advantage of someone?   Y   N
50. Are you mostly quiet when you are with other people? Y   N
51. Do you often feel lonely?   Y   N
52. Do you think it is better to follow society's rules
than go your own way?   Y   N
53. Do other people think of you as being very lively? Y   N
54. Do you always practice what you preach?   Y   N

1 CORINTHIANS 14:34–35

One solution that ends every problem for the silencing of women in 1 Corinthians 14:34–35 is to argue that Paul did not even write these words. If you look carefully at your Bible (and I'm using the NIV), you may observe a small footnote letter at the end of 1 Corinthians 14:35. At the bottom of this page in my Bible a footnote reads: "*34, 35* In a few manuscripts these verses come after verse 40." (The TNIV had "some" so the NIV 2011 has shrunk the number of witnesses to this reading.) In my copy of *The Harper Collins Study Bible* on the NRSV, verses 34 and 35 are enclosed in parentheses and a note similar to the NIV is found as a footnote. Most modern Bibles inform the reader that there is a problem about where these verses were originally located, and some experts conclude that they were not in Paul's original letter at all.

Why do they conclude this? Three reasons:

1. All attentive readers will feel the seeming contradiction between Paul's words here and what Paul said earlier in this very letter about women praying and prophesying in public. Something unusual is going on here.
2. Furthermore, verses 34 and 35 at face value overtly contradict the actual ministry conduct of women in the earliest churches. Women weren't completely silent in churches.
3. Some early manuscripts put these verses in another location, probably because they did not seem to fit between verses 33 and

36. Gordon Fee is one of evangelicalism's finest scholars. He is also a world-class expert on textual matters, and he is a leading scholar on 1 Corinthians itself. Fee, bringing all of his expertise to bear on these verses, came to the conclusion that *Paul did not write these verses,* that someone added them to a margin of an early manuscript, and that from there they found their way into 1 Corinthians in two different locations.[1] Recently, P. B. Payne wrote a technical article showing that one of the earliest manuscripts of the New Testament uses marginal signs to indicate that these verses were not in some manuscripts.[2] This article makes it probable that 1 Corinthians 14:34–35 were not written by the apostle Paul. If Fee and others like him are right, these verses, and not women, need to be silenced! Yet many are not so sure Fee is right.

4. The singular problem Gordon Fee faces is that there is no manuscript evidence that these verses were ever omitted from any of the copies we have of 1 Corinthians. The statement about silence always shows up, either after verse 33 or after verse 40. So the majority think these two verses should be included.[3] For that reason, I chose to ignore this problem and explain the text as if it where authentic to Paul.

APPENDIX 4

PETRONIUS ON THE NEW ROMAN WOMAN

I want to quote a section from one of Rome's famous contemporaries of the apostle Paul, a man named Petronius, who describes what many today are calling the new Roman woman.[1] Who was Petronius? He was Emperor Nero's adviser in luxury and extravagance! Petronius describes the new Roman woman by speaking of the woman Fortunata at a dinner banquet where she and another woman, Scintilla, fall into admiration of themselves.

Fortunata greets Scintilla:

> At this [Fortunata] entered at last, her frock kilted up with a yellow girdle, so as to show a cherry-colored tunic underneath, and corded anklets and gold-embroidered slippers. Then wiping her hands on a handkerchief she wore at her neck, she placed herself on the same couch beside Habinnas' wife, Scintilla, kissing her while the other claps her hands, and exclaiming, "Have I really the pleasure of seeing you?"

Fortunata displays gold jewelry:

> Before long it came to Fortunata's taking off the bracelets from her great fat arms to show them to her admiring companion. Finally she even undid her anklets and her hairnet, which she assured Scintilla was of the very finest gold.

Trimalchio speaks of the women's extravagances:

Trimalchio, observing this, ordered all the things to be brought to him. "You see this woman's fetters," he cried; "that's the way we poor devils are robbed! Six pound and a half, if it's an ounce; and yet I've got one myself of ten pound weight, all made out of Mercury's thousandths." Eventually to prove he was not telling a lie, he ordered a pair of scales to be brought, and had the articles carried round and the weight tested by each in turn.

Scintilla shows a jewelry box:

And Scintilla was just as bad, for she drew from her bosom a little gold casket she called her Lucky Box. From it she produced a pair of ear-pendants and handed them one after the other to Fortunata to admire, saying, "Thanks to my husband's goodness, no wife has finer."

Tipsy women:

Meanwhile the two women, though a trifle piqued, laughed good humoredly together and interchanged some tipsy kisses, the one praising the thrifty management of the lady of the house, the other enlarging on the minions her husband kept and his unthrifty ways. While they were thus engaged in close confabulation, Habinnas got up stealthily and catching hold of Fortunata's legs, upset her on the couch. "Ah! ah!" she screeched, as her tunic slipped up above her knees. Then falling on Scintilla's bosom, she hid in her handkerchief a face all afire with blushes.

APPENDIX 5

JUVENAL ON FIRST-CENTURY WOMEN

To give an example of Roman women being educated, quite well in some cases, I want to quote from Juvenal,[1] another first-century Roman contemporary of Paul, who writes satirically about women. What is so interesting about this text is what it reveals about what women could do when it came to public teaching and discourse. Also, this text shows that Paul's strategy of educating women was in sharp contrast with some public opinions of women.

On women asserting authority:

> But most intolerable of all is the woman who as soon as she has sat down to dinner commends Virgil, pardons the dying Dido, and pits the poets against each other, putting Virgil in the one scale and Homer in the other. The grammarians make way before her; the rhetoricians give in; the whole crowd is silenced: no lawyer, no auctioneer will get a word in, no, nor any other woman; so torrential is her speech that you would think that all the pots and bells were being clashed together.... She lays down definitions, and discourses on morals, like a philosopher; thirsting to be deemed both wise and eloquent, she ought to tuck up her skirts knee-high, sacrifice a pig to Silvanus, take a penny bath.

On limiting women's education:

Let not the wife of your bosom possess a special style of her own; let her not hurl at you in whirling speech the crooked enthymeme! Let her not know all history; let there be some things in her reading which she does not understand. I hate a woman who is for ever consulting and poring over the "Grammar" of Palaemon, who observes all the rules and laws of language, who like an antiquary quotes verses that I never heard of, and corrects her unlettered female friends for slips of speech that no man need trouble about: let husbands at least be permitted to make slips in grammar!

Appendix 6

JUNIA IS NOT ALONE

In one of my classes of forty-five students, I asked if anyone had ever heard of Huldah, that famous prophet whom the young King Josiah sent a messenger to after the book of the Torah was found in the temple. None of my students had ever heard of Huldah, so I asked them to Google her name. Then we found 2 Kings 22 and read it. Huldah was the singular prophet who helped provoke Israel's greatest revival.

Why the silence?

Moving toward the middle of my third decade of teaching students in seminaries and a university, more than half of whom grew up in a church, of this I am certain: churches don't talk about the women of the Bible. Of Mary, mother of Jesus, they have heard, and even then not all of what they have heard is accurate. But of the other women saints of the Bible, including Miriam, the prophetic national music director, or Esther, the dancing queen, or Phoebe, the benefactor of Paul's missions, or Priscilla, the teacher, they've heard almost nothing.

Why the silence?

Why do we consider the mother/wife of Proverbs 31 an ideal female image but *shush* the language of the romantic Shulammite woman of the Song of Songs? Why are we so obsessed with studying the "subordination" of women to men but not a woman like Deborah, who subordinated men and enemies? Why do we believe that we are called to live out Pentecost's vision of Spirit-shaped life but ignore what Peter predicted would happen? That "in the last days ... your sons *and daughters* will prophesy …" and that "even on my servants, *both men and women*, I will pour out my Spirit."

Why the silence?

When I told someone about the subject of this study, I was asked: "Who is Junia?" Maybe we should all open our Twitter or Facebook accounts and ask that very question: "Who is Junia?" Why doesn't everyone already know?

Why is there so much silence in the church about the women in the Bible?

This appendix is dedicated to ending the church's deafening silence on women in the Bible. It is dedicated to giving voice to women, and it comes with the prayer that we will become more faithful to the Bible's Story, a Story that clearly involves women who were not silenced by the Bible or the earliest followers of God, but are being silenced by us.

In this appendix I will tell the story of Junia. Alongside her story, we will encounter others like her—women who had a wonderful voice, and then no voice, and who are experiencing a re-voicing.

Now to the story of Junia.

Junia

Junia, who had no idea she would someday be the subject of endless discussions, appears innocently enough in Romans 16:7 alongside her husband, Andronicus. Innocence has a way of ending—in some translations her name is changed to a male name (Junias), and in some translations her status as an apostle is called into question (suggesting she was well known *to* apostles).

One way to make this clear is to read a few translations of that verse. So I want to open a few different Bibles to Romans 16, a chapter that, along with 1 Chronicles 1–9, is among the least preached chapters in the Bible.

In some Bibles, like the New International Version 2011, Junia is a woman, but it is not entirely clear if the apostles like her or if she is actually an apostle:

Greet Andronicus and Junia, my fellow Jews who have been in prison with me. They are outstanding among the apostles, and they were in Christ before I was. [A footnote in the NIV reads "Or *are esteemed by*" in place of "are outstanding among."]

But in other Bibles, like the English Standard Version, Junia may be a woman or may be a man. While she (or he) is not an apostle, the apostles liked her (or him). Furthermore, in the ESV, Junia, or Junias, may only be a "messenger" anyway:

Greet Andronicus and Junia, my kinsmen and my fellow prisoners. They are well known to the apostles, and they were in Christ before me. [Two footnotes appear: One has "Or Junias" instead of "Junia," while another note says "Or messengers" instead of "apostles."]

And then in the Common English Bible, Junia is a woman and she is an apostle:

Say hello to Andronicus and Junia, my relatives and my fellow prisoners. They are prominent among the apostles, and they were in Christ before me. [No notes are included.]

Other translations, like the New Revised Standard Version and the Holman Christian Standard Bible, mix the options.

NRSV: Greet Andronicus and Junia, my relatives who were in prison with me; they are prominent among the apostles, and they were in Christ before I was. [A note reads: Or *Junias*; other ancient authorities read *Julia*.]

HCSB: Greet Andronicus and Junia, my fellow countrymen and fellow prisoners. They are noteworthy in the eyes of the apostles, and they were also in Christ before me. [A note reads: Either a feminine name or "Junias," a masculine name.]

And who says translations are not political documents?

We don't have time to dwell over each issue at length. Instead, the conclusions of Eldon J. Epp, in his outstanding little book *Junia: The First Woman Apostle*, will be sketched as my own because I agree with him.[1] His conclusions are:

1. Junia was a woman.
2. There is no evidence that any man had the name "Junias."
3. Junias is not a contracted name of Junianus.[2]
4. "Among the apostles" means Junia herself was an apostle and not simply that the apostles thought she was a good companion.

So we conclude that there was a first-century relative of the apostle Paul named Junia; she entered into Christ before Paul did; and this Junia was an *apostle*. Which means (because this is what apostles did) she was in essence a Christ-experiencing, Christ-representing, church-establishing, probably miracle-working, missionizing woman who preached the gospel and taught the church.[3]

What surprises some folks in the church today is that when Paul wrote those words about Junia the apostle in Romans 16:7, he was not snickering with a mischievous look in his eye because he had just pulled off the incredible act of calling a woman an apostle. He didn't wonder, after he dictated those words, "OMG, what will they say about me next? That I'll want the high priest to be a priestess? #apostlegonewild." Paul didn't give those words about Junia a moment's afterthought.

Why? Because Junia was not alone. Paul knew that she fit comfortably into the Bible's storied history about women.

Junia is with *Rebekah*, who had the chutzpah to make sure that her favorite son, Jacob, got the inheritance and that God went along with her plans.

Junia is with *Ruth*, whose persistence kept her in the family of Israel and who became an ancestor of King David—and Jesus.

Junia stands with *Esther*, who was the beauty queen in ancient Israel's story and who saved the whole nation.

Junia is with the inspired prophet[4] *Miriam*, whose words gave to Israel an interpretive stance on the Exodus when she taught the ransomed to sing.[5]

No, Junia is not alone.

She's with *Deborah*, whose *Schadenfreude* exceeded that of Miriam as she exulted in the defeat of Israel's enemies. Deborah was Ms. Everyone in those days: she was president, pope, and Rambo bundled in one female body.[6]

Alongside Junia also stands *Huldah*. Josiah passed over Jeremiah, Zephaniah, Nahum, and Habakkuk when he consulted Huldah. Why? Like Junia, we could say, she was "outstanding among the prophets." When it came to prophets in Josiah's day, Huldah may well have been ranked at the top.[7]

Junia was flanked in her own day by *Mary*, mother of Jesus, who had an enormous influence on Jesus and James and the early church.[8]

Alongside Mary stood *Priscilla*, who taught Apollos, and next to Priscilla and Mary was *Phoebe*, a "deacon," which meant she was a church leader.[9] Paul also calls her a "benefactor," and this probably—it is disputed—means she financially provided funds and wisdom for Paul's missionary trips.

But there's more here: as Reta Finger has contended,[10] Phoebe was probably the first person to read Romans aloud in public. If so, she was the first to utter Junia's name from an apostolic letter in a church, and she was responsible (as the letter courier) to answer questions from the Romans who heard Paul's letter. Thus, the first commentator on Romans, so Reta Finger argues, was a woman.

Which brings me to my next question: Why the silence of women commentators on Romans? Though Princeton seminary professor Bev Gaventa is writing a commentary on Romans these days, there haven't been many commentaries on Romans by women.

The sad truth about Junia is that in the Bible and in the New Testament era, she was not the only woman who had a distinct Christian ministry.

But that story was about to change. And it changed dramatically.

Junia Gets a Sex Change

In the subsequent history of the church, a new kind of logic about women began to dominate. The logic was simple: the person in Romans 16:7 is an apostle, and apostles can't be women, so Junia cannot have been a woman. Junia was a man named Junias. This was a sex-change operation by way of redaction.

It happened, or can be illustrated, in Greek by changing the accent in an originally unaccented text from Jun-I-an to JuniAn. This change in accent led to the male name, Junias, the Anglicized form. But as Epp and others have shown, *Junias is a man who didn't exist with a name that didn't exist in the ancient world.*

Here are some of the developments in the twisted history of silencing Junia by turning her into Junias.

First, all early translations of the New Testament into other languages listed Junia as a woman. Epp, a master of the history of our New Testament in all its various translations, says that Junia was a woman in the Old Latin, the Vulgate, and Sahidic and Bohairic Coptic and Syriac. What about English? It's simple: from Tyndale to the last quarter of the nineteenth century in English translations, Junia was a woman. But Junia-the-woman wasn't the only view known to the church: there lurked the unknown Junias in some people's minds.

So, a second part of this twisted history: Martin Luther played a decisive role in turning Junia into a man. Clearly dependent on Jacobus Faber Stapulensis (or Jacques LeFèvre d'Étaples), Luther gave to the German name Juniam a masculine article (*den Juniam* [today, *den Junias*]). Then he said, "Andronicus and Junias were famous apostles" and were "*men* of note among the apostles."[11] Luther's influence is inestimable, and some have suggested that he might be the one on whom to pin the blame for the sex change from Junia to Junias. We are aware, however, that prior to him by two centuries, back in the thirteenth or early fourteenth century, Aegidius or Giles of Rome called Junia a male. Luther didn't invent the change, but his influence gave the nonexistent male Junias a new life.

Just as important as Luther, though, is the history of official Greek New Testaments. It's important to recognize that the Greek New Testaments that Christians have used and pastors have studied and students are told to master are composite texts. They are not the "original" New Testament. They are "composite" texts, in which one word was taken from one manuscript and another word from another manuscript to compile what the best of scholarship thinks was the original text or, better yet, as close to the original text as we can now get.

Don't get me wrong—we are reasonably confident that we have the original words in about 98 percent of the New Testament (and none of the rest matters to our faith). But here is how it works: Scholars examine ancient manuscripts and translations and liturgical texts and quotations from the Bible in ancient sermons and books and scrolls and papyri and then say, "This is what we think is most likely the earliest text we can reconstruct from all this evidence." Then they publish a "Greek New Testament," and these composite texts are what people use to translate the New Testament today.

And in Greek New Testament composite texts—*now hear this*—from Erasmus in the Reformation era to the famous German scholar Erwin Nestle's edition of the Greek New Testament in 1927, *Junia was a woman*. Apart from one lesser known publication of the Greek New Testament, which had Junias in a footnote but not in the text, *no Greek New Testament had anything but Junia, a woman's name, until Nestle's edition in 1927.*

Then it happened. In 1927, in the thirteenth edition of his composite Greek New Testament, Eberhard Nestle silenced Junia and gave birth to a new Christian man named Junias.[12] How did Nestle do this? In 1927, Nestle *put Junias in the text* with a hat tip in the footnotes to other Greek New Testaments that had the female Junia. That is, Junia was but a footnote for Nestle. (And who reads footnotes?) We need to remind ourselves of this: Pastors and students study these composite Greek New Testaments, and translators rely on these composite Greek New Testaments, and by and large they don't worry about the footnotes. They trust the editors to get the text right.

In changing her name and creating a new male name, Nestle buried Junia alive.

When Kurt Aland, the twentieth century's most famous New Testament textual scholar, became the new editor of that famous Greek New Testament established by Nestle, he carried on Nestle's text—until 1979, when Junia died in her footnote tomb. "Died?" you ask. Yes. In the 1979 edition of Aland's text, Junia was simply erased from the footnote. And so she ceased to exist. In 1979!

The United Bible Society's edition of the New Testament, one that many seminary students learned to use instead of Nestle-Aland, grades its decisions. The UBS New Testament rated the male *Junias* reading with an "A," and that meant "virtually certain." So from 1927 until the 1990s we had the two principal Greek (composite) texts, Nestle-Aland and UBS, which all pastors, students, and translators use, providing us with a man named Junias.

Let me be clear once more: The editors of Greek New Testaments killed Junia. They killed her by silencing her into nonexistence. They murdered that innocent woman by erasing her from the footnotes.

And Junia is far from alone in suffering from that silence.

Junia Is Not Alone in Her Silence

How many sermons about the women of the Bible did you hear when you were being nurtured into the faith? How many sermons about Miriam or Deborah or Huldah? Or Ruth or Esther? How many sermons about Mary or Priscilla or Phoebe or Junia? Or Philip's daughters?

This struck me hard after class one day when a woman approached me and said, "I'm so pissed." She had been reared in a good church and was very serious about her faith—indeed, she graduated from a seminary. She explained, "I grew up in the church, and I have never ever heard of Phoebe or Priscilla or Junia. And my church ordains women."

Junia is not alone in her enforced silence. She's not alone, because the silencers and erasers are still at work, and sometimes it takes extra energy to get a silenced voice back into performance shape.

Consider a few of those who have been silenced with Junia.

One certain woman played a significant role in the reforms in Geneva. As a devoted young Roman Catholic woman, she entered in 1521 into an Augustinian convent, where she quickly became a leader. Three years later, she converted to Luther's gospel and left the convent. By 1526, she had stirred her hometown church in Strasbourg enough that she was chased from her home and church.

Two years later, she married a former priest, and before long, she and her husband followed William Farel to Valais, where they became—in the words of no less than the Lutheran Reformer Martin Bucer—"the first French married couple to accept a pastoral assignment for the Reformed church." When Simon, her husband, died, her status in society as a widow with five children was jeopardized—until she married Antoine (Froment). They all moved to Geneva in 1535, where they entered into Calvin's complex world of the Reformation woman.

While the priesthood of believers seemingly promised a restoration of the Juniases of this world, and while equality in Christ did the same, the Reformation's evident emphasis on *sola scriptura* curtailed liberation for women. Most notably, both the silence of women passages as well as subordination of women to men played their part in Calvin's Geneva. The situation for women was complex, and Kirsi Stjerna argues that subordination was dialectically related to an egalitarian spirit, so that early on, even Calvin supported some women preaching. But Calvin's support didn't last long.

In Calvin's Geneva our woman in question had caught only the egalitarian spirit and began a vigorous effort to convert nuns out of the convents into Calvin's churches and into liberation. And into conflict. One of her biographers put it this way: "Forced as a woman to find non-institutional ways to promote reform through writing and public preaching in taverns and on street corners, she incurred the wrath of

Calvin, who publicly discredited her by calling her a heretic." Her tone was preachy, her mood was argumentative, her hermeneutic was clearly liberationist, and her biblical knowledge was vast. She used Scripture to pounce on the Catholics, the Lutherans, the Calvinists, and the Anabaptists. Even the Poor Clares went to war with her.

Which Scriptures did our unnamed woman use? Those about the women who were biblical friends of Junia and the priesthood of all believers and the Christology of Galatians 3:28. Her aim was to liberate women to use the gifts God had given to them. She wrote a history of the reforms in Geneva, a remarkable eyewitness and biased account. They tried to destroy all copies of her book. Her actions led to restrictions on printers in Geneva. They tried to silence her, and Farel denounced her husband Antoine for "complicity" and for his wife's "domineering" behaviors. Calvin had already denounced her—but then, in a stroke of irony and worse, asked her to write the Preface to a sermon on female attire. (The irony only got more pronounced when she accepted the invitation.)

She disappeared from the scene; no one suspects foul play. More importantly, her memory all but disappeared, and most of what remained was distorted into calumny. "As a woman," one of her biographers observes, "she was criticized for achievements and fortitude for which a man would have been praised." Not until 2002 was her name added to the Wall of Reformers in Geneva.

Junia is not alone in her silence because most people don't know this woman's name. We know Luther and Calvin and Zwingli and Bucer and Cranmer, but we don't know this woman's name. Why? Because of the silencers and erasers.

Or take another woman, and this time just a brief mention before I move on to a fuller example. She hoped her life would display the symmetry of holiness in a balanced influence of theology, revivalism, feminism, and humanitarianism. Her Luther-like life-changing experience of "entire sanctification" propelled her into a life of profound influence, and she was perhaps the most influential woman of the nineteenth century. It has been said that she led more than 17,000

Britons to Christ and thousands more in the United States. She traveled the country in a passionate fire for Christ; she wrote eighteen books, edited one of the most popular magazines of her day, wrote a 400-pager on women in ministry, and pushed against male chauvinism on the basis of the Bible and theology.

Again, Junia is not alone in her silence, because most of us don't know this woman's name. We know Charles Finney, D. L. Moody, and Billy Sunday, but we don't know this woman's name. Why? Because of the silencers.

One more example. This woman was the first African-American woman to establish a four-year institution of higher learning and the first African-American woman to hold a high-level government directorship. She advised three American presidents and, between 1933 and 1945, according to one of her biographers, she was "arguably the most powerful African-American person in the United States."

Her parents were slaves; her mother's and father's faith and piety were extraordinary. She grew up loved, and before she could read, she was given a little New Testament to hold in church in order to instill a sense of yearning for the book. But because she was black, education was not in the offing.

Still, the Presbyterian Board for Freedmen opened a school for children in Maysville, South Carolina. She attended that school, and it led to her being confirmed in the Presbyterian church. She was in school until she was about twelve, when she had to return to the cotton fields. Miracle of miracles, someone far off in Denver sensed a whisper from God to give money to a child with potential, and our unknown woman was selected to attend Scotia Seminary in Concord, North Carolina. Her response? "I pulled my cotton sack off, got down on my knees, clasped my hands, and turned my eyes upward and thanked God for the chance that had come." Many neighbors saw her off to Scotia.

At Scotia, she entered a brick building for the first time, climbed into an upstairs the first time, and had teachers who were black and white for the first time. When she finished, she attended a school that later became Moody Bible Institute, where she experienced both a mighty baptism of the Holy Spirit and a calling to be a missionary to Africa. But the Presbyterians turned her down because they had no place for an African-American female missionary.

So she went south and famously taught young African-Americans and at one point had over a thousand local children in her Sunday school program. This work expanded her horizons, and when she had the opportunity to go to Daytona Beach, Florida, to establish a college, she jumped on it. Her part began in 1904, and her school was called the Daytona Educational and Industrial School for Negro Girls. Her focus was evangelistic, educational, and social reform. When her school expanded into Bethune College, her curriculum was Bible, industry, and English. Today it is called Bethune-Cookman.

In 1936, she reflected on her life and her situation and on the way Christianity worked in the US:

> The Negro must go to a separate church even though he claims to be of the same denomination as whites. He is not allowed to sing, in unison with the white man, the grand old hymns of Calvin, the Wesleys—the triumphant songs of Christ and eternal glory. When at last he is called to his final resting place on earth even his ashes are not allowed to mingle with those of his white brother, but are borne away to some remote place where the white man is not even reminded that this Negro ever lived. Judging from all that has preceded the Negro in death, it looks as if he has been prepared for a heaven, separate from the one to which the white man feels he alone is fit to inhabit.

She experienced the utter violation of dignity that white folks used against African-Americans, but that didn't stop her. She reversed the thunder of racism by conquering her enemies with love, with industry, with strategy, and with an educational system designed for the "uplift" of women and African-Americans.

And we—and I say this bitterly—returned the favor by not even knowing who this woman is.

Junia is not alone in her silence. We know the stories of Martin Luther King Jr., but this woman is all but forgotten today. Why? Because of the silencers.

Remember, Junia was a woman, *and* she was an apostle. But since a woman couldn't be an apostle, Junia became the male Junias. You don't have to dig deep to know why this happened. Bernadette Brooten has put it memorably: "Because a woman could not have been an apostle, the woman who is here called an apostle could not have been a woman."[13] There was no evidence in ancient manuscripts that anyone understood Junia as a male, no evidence in translations she was a male, and there was no ancient evidence that Junias was a man's name. But still the church got into a rut and rode it out until some courageous folks said, "Oh, yes, Junia was a woman and she was an apostle, and we've been wrong, and we're going to do something about it."

Eldon Epp sums this all up well:

What may be more difficult to understand now is that such a sociocultural environment, one imbued with a view of a limited role for women in the church, *still could influence some editors of the Greek New Testament in the mid-1990s to the extent that they could impose the masculine form upon an unaccented name ... when all the church writers of the first millennium of Christianity took the name as feminine ... when ... the name was a very common female name ... and ... that the alleged masculine forms are nowhere attested.*[14]

But there is some good news here. Like Aslan's Stone Table that cracked with new life, Junia has been raised from the dead. She's back in the text, in all the texts. As if to compensate for their past sins, the editors of those composite Greek New Testaments have killed off the nonexistent Junias.

In 1998 the Jubilee Edition of Nestle-Aland and the UBS printed the same text. Junia is there, and Junias has disappeared. Junias was erased the way Junia had been erased. Murdering nonexistent males is a Christian thing to do and can even be done by pacifists. Junia has come back to life, and she is now in the text. Junias has disappeared (except in some translations), and we have again an "A" rating.

How odd it was to have an "A" rating for someone who didn't exist and who had a name that didn't exist. And now, how odd it is to have an "A" rating for a woman who had been erased from the apparatus. *Who says New Testament texts and translations are not political?*

In Having a Voice, Junia Is Not Alone

Today, in being present in the text as a powerful woman with a mighty voice, Junia is not alone anymore. In a sense, she never was, because there have always been voices who affirmed Junia as woman and an apostle. It began in the fourth century with John Chrysostom, and it is regrettable—that's too soft a word—that the church both ignored him and then let others have the louder voice. Chrysostom, probably in about 344 AD, said:

> To be an apostle is something great. But to be outstanding among the apostles—just think what a wonderful song of praise that is! They were outstanding on the basis of their works and virtuous actions. Indeed, how great the wisdom of this woman must have been that she was even deemed worthy of the title of apostle.[15]

His words were echoed by Theodoret, bishop of Cyrrhus, and John of Damascus. Other than the original commendation by Paul himself in Romans 16:7, Chrysostom's comment gave the church a statue-like memorial to Junia, and it was that memorial that gave an anchor to the contemporary feminine reading of Romans 16:7.

Junia, my friends, is not alone. Many women today are active in ministry and are continuing with confidence and power the storied history of women in the Bible and the silenced history of women in the church. They are not silenced as they once were, and so we look around and sing to the women among us who are embodying the gifts God has given to them.

Unlike Marie Dentière[16] and Phoebe Palmer[17] and Mary McLeod Bethune,[18] whose stories I sketched above but who were silenced for too long, a woman I know named Alice can be known and broadcast even as she does her work today.

Alice was a student of mine at Trinity Evangelical Divinity School way back in the days when people were wearing leisure suits and not really even wondering what to do with women in the church. She landed on her feet in the middle of America, in Iowa, an heir to Calvin's Reformed churches.

Some stereotypes about America's heartland are true in Alice's case, or were for a time. She had a Northwestern undergraduate degree with a master's from Trinity in counseling and psychology, a Harvard husband, and a Campus Crusade set of beliefs that included some traditional views of marriage and women in ministry. Alice had three kids and was running a medical research business when she up and got the idea that she should run for the school board. She didn't win, but the experience of speaking publicly energized her because people were moved by her words.

She got to thinking God might want to use her teaching gift in the church, and when her husband Chuck's investment work flew away with the rest of the American economy, Alice decided to teach an adult church class on money. "People came," she told me, "and the next time even more people came." Then she realized she liked it, so she taught another subject. An elder, after observing and sitting in her class, said to her, "Alice, you've got the gift. And we've been praying for a woman teacher in our church."

Because of the stereotypes at work in cases like these, she and her husband spent some time renegotiating their relationship. Chuck has an MDiv from Fuller Theological Seminary but isn't called to be a teaching pastor; Alice doesn't have the MDiv, but she has the gift. Chuck has become Alice's biggest supporter.

Alice thought she might also face stereotypes with her pastor, so she summoned up the pluck to speak to him. Alice now knew she had the gift of teaching, so she said, "I think I have the gift to teach and preach, and I'd like to know if it will be safe for me here." The pastor's response: "Do you want to find out? How about July 6? No one is scheduled to preach." She spent six weeks preparing that sermon.

In America's heartland, Alice was a "lay teacher" for seven years. Her church battled gender stereotypes by using them: they explained that Alice was a "mom" and a "wife" and even a "stay-at-home mom," and she kept on teaching.

A few years ago, Alice approached the pastor with these evocative words: "I've been wearing this JV uniform for seven years now. Don't you think it's about time I get a varsity uniform?" Sure enough, Alice can be seen wearing a varsity preacher's uniform three out of four weeks in a church with multisite campuses, including a little rural church that in 120 years had never had a woman preach. Recently, one of the pastors on staff caught wind of what the good folks in that rural church thought. His report: "Alice, they like you."

Junia is not alone. She's accompanied by a host of women who have been gifted by God to teach and preach and lead.

And now it's time for you to do something about it.

How to Help Junia Gain Her Voice

First, if you're a pastor, I want you to take to the pulpit someday and get folks to open their Bibles to Romans 16:7, and I want you to ask them to do something that may make them feel sacrilegious if not abominating. I want you to ask them to strike out Junias from their Bibles. The man never existed, the name never existed, and it is an embarrassment to the church to have that name in a Bible.

If you want to do this emphatically, above the place where they strike out "Junias," have them write "Alice" or some woman who went through the struggle to gain the recognition for what God had gifted her to do. Of course, I'm aware of how this may make some people feel, but with all due respect for the authority of God's Word, we need people to see that what is not original is not God's Word.

Second, women's stories must be told. We must end the silence of Junia and give Junia her voice again. So I am urging you to tell stories of women from the Bible and from the history of the church. If you are a writer, tell stories of women in what you write.

Not long after I wrote *The Jesus Creed*, a reader and leader wrote me a note. He said something to this effect: "Scot, thanks so much for *The Jesus Creed*. I've gained so much from it. Can I ask a question: Why are there only women's stories in your chapter on Mary?" I asked him to call me, and as we talked, he uttered words that I need to repeat here. He asked, "We need to strive for balance in our storytelling, don't we?" I thought (but didn't say aloud), "Balance. The balance, my brother, is so out of balance we don't even know what balance looks like. If we want real historical balance, it would mean we would be telling nothing but women's stories for the next two millennia."

I opened my book quickly as I was talking to him, and I saw names of three women: Roberta Bondi, Frederica Mathewes-Green, and Dorothy Sayers. His last words were not meant to be deconstruction, but they were: "I don't identify with women as much as I do with men." And who gets deconstructed by those words? The man who thinks he doesn't identify *with* women needs to see that this is what men have done *to* women for the better part of two millennia!

Junia was a woman. Junia was an apostle. Junia was an outstanding apostle. And Junia is alive and well today. There are many like her—like Alice—in our churches today. It is our calling to let freedom ring, to let the Spirit use people whom God chooses, to let the gospel's inclusiveness have its way with us. It is our calling to hold one another accountable to Junia's noble example.

Junia is not alone.

Do you hear her voice?

APPENDIX 7

GENESIS AND SCIENCE

Readers of the Bible encounter the creation narrative of Genesis 1–3 with a variety of responses: Some think it's flat-out wrong because of what they have learned in science classes. Some think these chapters are a myth on the order of the ancient Near East's creation stories like *The Gilgamesh Epic*. Yet others simply wish they weren't in the Bible in the way they are because when they read these chapters, their science and their faith clash.

Bible-reading Christians have discussed the opening chapters of Genesis for two thousand years, but it was the rise of evolutionary science that provoked the biggest discussions, though historians of science are quick to point out that Darwin's famous *The Origin of the Species* was not nearly the controversy then as it is today in some circles. Christians want their Bible to sustain itself as God's Word while also respecting science, so they have thought through various models for relating science to the question of origins as we learn about it in Genesis.[1] Here in general terms are six models:

Models of Origins

First, *naturalistic evolution* is a non-Christian, mostly agnostic or atheistic, and purposeless theory of origins that affirms what scientists call "common descent" (gradual descent from a common ancestor through natural selection) and a universe that is 13.5 billion years old. The key term is that this process of evolution is spontaneous and entirely *natural*. There never was any divine intervention.

Second, *nonteleological evolution* believes in a non-interventionist Creator who formed through the evolutionary processes a *purposeless* creation, and this view affirms common descent, a 13.5-billion-year-old universe, but that the Creator formed the conditions that were needed for life to become what it is today. The parameters for evolution then were established by the Creator at creation.

Third, *planned evolution* believes in a non-interventionist Creator who formed through the evolutionary process a creation with *purpose*, and this view too affirms common descent, a 13.5-billion-year-old universe, and that the Creator's creation was perfectly formed to become what the world now is as it fulfills the Creator's purposes.

Fourth, *directed evolution* believes in an *interventionist* Creator who created the world with purpose some 13.5 billion years ago and who established the realities of common descent but who *directs* evolution itself. The operative words here are "directed" and "interventionist."

Fifth, *old-earth creationism* substantively shifts the conversation from directed evolution to a more direct form of intervention. While those affirming old-earth creationism differ on the age of the universe, some do not affirm the universe as old as 13.5 billion years, while others do. Once again, this view affirms an interventionist Creator of a purposeful creation but also affirms *de novo creation*, that is, a creating mechanism that is sometimes sudden rather than pervasively gradual (as in evolutionist approaches). Old-earth creationists affirm that creation itself is a witness to the Creator God. This approach is "concordist" (see our next section) in that it finds scientific information in Genesis and challenges science with the Bible's (prescient) scientific information. For example, the order of the days in Genesis 1 will correspond with the scientific theories of their ordering, even if the Bible's order corrects what nearly all science concludes.

Sixth, *young-earth creationism*'s distinct belief is that the earth is 10,000 years old or less. Again, it affirms the classic Christian conviction that God is the Creator of all, that God created this universe with purpose and that this purpose is made manifest in creation itself. This God, again, is interventionist, an emphasis is given to divine *de novo* creation and that the earth is not as old as science thinks. Each "day" combines to witness to God's creating the earth and its inhabitants in one seven-day week (as we know seven days).

Concordism

While two of the models above are unafraid to challenge some of science's most important conclusions, a specific idea emerges in the conversation of faith and science that is now called "concordism." The basic idea at work in concordism, though this is sometimes misunderstood, is that concordists think the Bible teaches some science, and the Bible's science is therefore infallible and at times teaches that scientific theories (which is not the same as a mere "theory" or simply a "hypothesis" but instead a proven and as yet non-contradicted conclusion) are false. The noticeable element here is that concordists find science in the Bible. In the recent *Dictionary of Christianity and Science*, concordism is defined and it is worth recording the substance of the entry because it matters for Bible readers who are conversant with science:

> CONCORDISM. Concordism refers to the position that the teaching of the Bible on the natural world, properly interpreted, will agree with the teaching of science (when it properly understands the data), and may in fact supplement science. The concordist not only believes that nature and Scripture will harmonize, but sees specific references in the Bible to current scientific understanding of the universe. The concordist, then, looks for those close parallels in order to show that Scripture concords or agrees with scientific conclusions.
>
> Because the concordist holds Scripture as entirely truthful, there cannot be any ultimate contradiction between Scripture

rightly interpreted and nature rightly interpreted. In both Scripture and nature, of course, there is the potential for error in the interpretation. Concordism, however, assumes that correlations can be made, believing in a degree of accuracy of interpretation (though not infallibility) in current science and in showing the Scripture supports clear scientific conclusions....

An alternative view in the origins debate agrees that in the end science and Scripture will accord in what they affirm. However, this position believes that we are missing the point when we try to read Genesis in light of modern science or to interpret scientific data in light of Genesis. Instead, we need to read the text in light of its ancient context for its original intent. In this view, the Genesis creation account does not affirm a position on modern scientific questions and so does not speak to the expected scientific issues directly (Miller and Soden 2012). Since Genesis 1 does not present scientific claims, such things as the age of the earth can be left to scientific investigation without needing to demonstrate specific correlation.[2]

This entry in *The Dictionary of Christianity and Science* was written by John Soden, a Bible professor at Lancaster Bible College who earned his PhD at Dallas Theological Seminary. I bring in his credentials because it needs to be clear that we are not reading the words of a progressive politician or a liberal theologian. His definition is the one I have heard over and over at science and faith discussion conferences and in conversations in which I have participated.

The most important observations here are these: (1) concordism refers to the belief that the Bible has scientific elements well before anyone else knew that science; (2) concordism thinks the Bible and science are therefore compatible when the Bible is speaking scientifically; (3) direction matters: some begin with the Bible and interpret science accordingly, while others begin with science and interpret the Bible accordingly.

That last point is vital, and I agree with it. Here's why: *the history of the Christian engagement with science is a history of shifting conclusions of a concordist nature.* There has been so much shifting in this discussion that we are learning we ought to let the Bible say what it says in its ancient Near East context and let science say what it says and not pretend that an ancient Near East text—Genesis 1–11—is speaking scientifically. Many scholars today, including John Walton at Wheaton College, argue that the Bible shows no signs of prescient science! When concordists interpret the Bible in light of science, their interpretations become outdated, outmoded, and wrong when newer discoveries in science emerge. Time and time again Christian Bible readers have to eat crow for their former concordist interpretations of the Bible.

Concordism then teaches us that we ought to avoid thinking of the Bible in scientific terms and instead read it in its context according to the purposes an author of that era would have. If it so happens that something in the Bible accords with science, we ought first to calm ourselves down and realize that it happens at the most general of levels: creation, order, and design and not in details like genomes, quarks, and photosynthesis. What I have learned as a Christian Bible reader is that learning about science affords me the opportunity to expand what the Bible says (God creates; Psalm 19) with the immensity of space and detail and design that the Bible's authors only glimpsed from afar.

Evolutionary Creationism

Let me briefly mention a significant development among evangelical scientists teaching mostly in Christian schools. An increasing number of well-known scholars have their credentials in science, affirm the authority, infallibility, and at times inerrancy of Scripture, and at the same time affirm a theory of evolution that also affirms God as Creator. They are then creationists who believe *God, the God of the Bible revealed definitively in Jesus Christ and whose King and His Kingdom Story is their story, created through evolution.* Hence, they are evolutionary *creationists.* It is inaccurate to call them baldly evolutionists because they believe the one true Creator God created evolutionarily. To return to the mapping of models above, evolutionary creationists fit into the third or fourth model above. The prominent names include Francis Collins, Denis Alexander, Karl Giberson, and John Polkinghorne.

I cowrote a book with one such scientist, Dennis Venema, who did his work in genetics at the University of British Columbia in Vancouver. Next to the University is Regent College, a highly regarded evangelical seminary, and Dennis himself attended or listened to many lectures while studying genetics (and fruit flies!). He now teaches biology at the Christian college down the road from Vancouver called Trinity Western University. A few years back Dennis, having heard me say how much I appreciated his academic article on genome theory, approached me to see if I would be willing to apply with him for a grant from BioLogos to write a book now called *Adam and the Genome: Reading Scripture after Genetic Science*.[3] The pleasure has been all mine because I have been able to learn about genome theory—the mapping of our DNA so it can be compared with the DNA in chimpanzees, gorillas, et al.—and Dennis has answered so many of my festering questions about science. His theological learning has made him a good partner in proposing theories that advance our understanding of what the Bible says about Adam and Eve.

Adam and Eve in the Story

There is a stubborn conviction among many Christians—from conservative evangelicals to Roman Catholics—that messing with the historical Adam jeopardizes the whole of Christian thinking. This is not only a conviction but quite true for many because their system of thought requires a very specific understanding of Adam, and I want now to map that understanding of Adam. Then we will analyze it a bit and ask, true to form in *The Blue Parakeet*, whether this is a tradition that needs to be challenged or one that must be retained.[4]

First, recent studies of Genesis 1–2 conclude that this text in its context presents all of creation as God's temple and summons Adam and Eve, who are sub-rulers under God, to worship this one true God alone. Adam and Eve are also summoned to guard and protect and flourish in God's creation.[5] These scholars conclude that "image of God" is a term used by God for humans in their *vocation* of worship as well as sub-governing, sub-ruling, and flourishing. This makes the best sense when reading Genesis 1–2 in the context of other ancient Near East creation stories. The so-called "Fall," which is not the Bible's own language, occurs because Adam and Eve choose not to worship God by obeying but instead worship themselves by making themselves like God! The result: banished from Eden. The Story of the Bible takes on a completely different set of chapters because Adam and Eve, as is the case with all humans, choose not to worship God but to do their own thing. The Theocracy of God then is divine rule of humans who sometimes do and sometimes do not worship the one true God.

Second, Adam and Eve are called to procreate in order to multiply many other sub-rulers under God who are just like Adam and Eve in equality. They are also called to work the land for provisions as part of their human calling. Inherent to the King and His Kingdom Story then is work or labor or vocation: *Eikons* are co-laborers with one another under God. As co-rulers together under God, they are not to rule over other humans, as we see in the chapter on slavery (chapter 11). Adam and Eve are also called to diminish the curse of Genesis 3 by co-creating, co-nurturing, and co-governing creation. Medicine and healing and systemic justice and peace and reconciliation are also inherent to the King and His Kingdom Story from the very beginning.

Third, perhaps most importantly, Adam and Eve *have a relationship with every other human being because each human being is made as an Eikon of God.* That relationship can be described as archetypal, paradigmatic, representative, literary, physical, genetic, and other such terms. This leads us to the stubborn conviction I mentioned at the beginning of this section. Often any conversation about science and faith, more particularly about Adam-Eve and science, becomes a conversation or a debate (often the latter) about the so-called "historical Adam." I want to map what people tend to mean when they ask, "Do you believe in the *historical* Adam?" (That they never ask, "What do you believe about the historical Adam *and Eve*?" speaks volumes.) Here's what most tend to mean when they say "historical Adam":

1. Two *actual* (and sometimes only two) persons named Adam and Eve existed suddenly as a result of God's "creation" (actual or real Adam and Eve).
2. Those two persons have a *biological* relationship to all human beings that are alive today (biological Adam and Eve).
3. Their DNA is our DNA (genetic Adam and Eve).
4. Those two *sinned*, *died*, and *brought death into the world* (fallen Adam and Eve).
5. Those two *passed on their sin natures* (according to many) to all human beings (sin-nature Adam and Eve).
6. Without their sinning and passing on that sin nature to all human beings, *not all human beings would be in need of salvation.*
7. Therefore, if one denies the *historical* Adam, one denies the gospel of salvation.[6]

This is the more or less official tradition of much of the church, and for that reason alone it deserves both our respect and our attention. However, there are more than a couple weaknesses here. While some may want to dispute how it is that the original Adam and Eve of Genesis "passed on" their sin nature (original sin) to all subsequent humans, there is a larger problem lurking. I want to explain it in light of what was said about concordism. *This theory of the historical Adam, which again omits Eve almost every time it is mentioned, is rooted in concordist theories of science and faith.* No one questioned the possibility of Adam and Eve somehow passing on original sin to their descendants as long as most everyone believed Genesis 1–2 was scientific. That is, as long as everyone believed Adam and Eve were plain and simply the first two human beings alongside no other similar hominins or individuals like them, no one worried about the possibility of passing on a sinful nature. The need to look again at the Bible in its ancient Near East context was not as important because there was a stubborn and untroubled theory at work: Adam and Eve were alone in the garden of Eden with no others around them.

Then came Darwin, but Darwin was at first mostly ignored and only over time did the accumulation of data and facts and hypotheses and theories complicate that stubborn conviction. But when the genome theory came along, demonstrating scientifically and mathematically[7] that the DNA characteristic of humans today could not have come from anything less than a population of humans/individuals around the number of 10,000, then the stubborn conviction became more stubborn than fact. It is not concordist now to say, "Let's go back to Genesis and read it in its context." It is in fact the wisdom of the church to listen to science and to let it open up new questions for us as we return to the Bible to read it in its ancient context.

A conclusion of a number of evangelical scholars, from John Walton to Tremper Longman to J. Richard Middleton and dozens of others, is that *Adam and Eve in Genesis can be read as theologically informative without necessarily thinking they had to be the figure in the historical Adam (and Eve) theory above.* Adam and Eve are humans in a narrative, so they are minimally a literary Adam and Eve; they represent all humans, so they are archetypal, paradigmatic, and representative. But if we push the "historical" Adam in the direction of two and only two solitary humans—and no others before them or like them in existence—then we have made the Bible wrong *because of our demand of a concordist theory.* I don't know how to say this softly: we are courting with making the Bible what it is not in order to protect our theory of what the Bible ought to be. It is true that this theory of Adam and Eve fits into every narrative Bible readers sketch of the Bible's big story, whether it is the main plot (creation, fall, redemption) or, as I prefer to see it, as the redemptive benefits of the main plot (the King and His Kingdom). This theory has what we call "explanatory power." That doesn't make it right, and it in fact skirts on thin ice because it is shaped too much by the concordist theory of science and faith. There's hope for a better way.

This realization (by reading Dennis Venema and other scientists, like RJS who posts regularly at my blog, Jesus Creed at Patheos blogs) led me to investigate Genesis in its historical context, and it led me to investigate Adam ("and Eve" was often dropped) in the Jewish tradition between the Bible and the New Testament's own texts about Adam and Eve. My fourth point is this: *Adam and Eve in the Jewish tradition were very flexible human beings, and each author used Adam and Eve in differing ways because each author saw the literary Adam and Eve as archetypal or representative humans.* They were in many ways not so much particular humans but *Everyone, Every Man and Every Woman.* The most important theme in the Jewish texts was that they were moral archetypes: Adam and Eve were charged by God to be *Eikons*—worshiping God, sub-governing God's creation—and they were given moral capacities to obey or disobey. They disobeyed, and that theme in the literary Adam and Eve becomes the dominant theme in Judaism: *Each of us too is summoned by God to obey, but we can choose to disobey.* The Jewish tradition assumes but does not explain why each human is like Adam and Eve in that each human sins. In the King and His Kingdom Story, then, everyone is in need of redemption (cracked *Eikons* becoming whole *Eikons*).

This all leads me to my fifth point: when the apostle Paul writes Romans 5:12–21, he is both assuming the literary and archetypal Adam and Eve of Genesis but also how that Adam and Eve were interpreted in the Jewish tradition before him and in his own context. Paul's basic understanding of Adam and Eve is that they were moral exemplars who failed, while Jesus is the redeemer because he did not fail. Adam was the First Adam, but Jesus is the Second Adam. In my chapter on Romans 5 in *Adam and the Genome*, I argue that Paul's presentation of Adam is schematic, with Adam being a tragic hero and Jesus a redeemer hero, and in this point *Paul's Adam is not identical to anything we've seen in the Jewish traditions.*[8] Notice these analogies between Adam and Christ:

Adam	Christ
Sin	Obedience
Death	Life
Condemnation	Justification
Union with others	Union with others[9]

Paul's only "explanation" of how Adam and Eve pass on their sinfulness is found in Romans 5:12, and it needs to be read carefully and briefly explained: "Therefore, just as sin entered the world through one man, and death through sin, and in this way death came to all people, because all sinned." Paul pins Adam to the wall for his sin; he pins him again to the wall because his sin unleashed sinfulness in the world. But he also pins each of us because Paul's only explanation is found in these words: "because all sinned." Paul does not say we sinned *in Adam*; nor does he say *Adam's sinfulness was passed on to us; and he doesn't say he passed a sin nature on to each of us by way of procreation.* Perhaps Paul believed each of those claims, and surely the church's Great Tradition more or less believes that. But the Bible does not say that.

Why is this important? Because if we make this "historical Adam" map of the church's tradition inflexible in our faith, then we have the problem of serious tension with science. Does that matter? Yes it does. Why? Because this church tradition happens to be anchored in a concordist reading of the Bible. How so? It believes that only Adam and Eve existed all alone in the garden of Eden; it believes they sinned and their natures got corrupted (sin nature, original sin); and it believes they passed on their sin nature to every descendant through the procreative process. Two problems: not only does science show this to be very, very unlikely, if not impossible, but *no one in the Bible or in the Jewish tradition taught this historical Adam theory as the church tradition teaches it.*

Both the Bible's General Plot—the King and His Kingdom—and the Bible's redemptive benefits story fit into other approaches to understanding what the Bible actually says about Adam and Eve. Jesus is King and he summons all humans into His Kingdom whether or not this historical Adam theory is accurate. But more importantly, the approach to Adam and Eve detailed above—as personally responsible for their sin and we are responsible for our sin ("because all sinned")—is all we need for us to believe the gospel's saving benefits: that Jesus died for our sins and was raised for our justification (Romans 4:25).

NOTES

Chapter 1: The Book and I

1. Of course, I know many scholars have defended our current Christian practice; some of these are ingenious and profound and the like, but the implications we draw from some New Testament texts are not what the earliest Christians drew from them (as far as we know). The early Christians, especially the earliest Jewish Christians, continued to practice Sabbath alongside Sunday worship. For some New Testament references to Sabbath practice, see Acts 16:13; 18:4; 20:7; 1 Corinthians 16:2. Paul tolerated gentile difference (Colossians 2:16), but Sabbath was not abandoned probably until the time of Constantine.

2. William D. Mounce, *Pastoral Epistles*, Word Biblical Commentary (Dallas: Word, 2000), 289.

Chapter 2: The Birds and I

1. I swiped this from this website: www-personal.umich.edu/~bbowman/birds/humor/birdrif6.html.

2. Tokunboh Adeyemo, ed., *Africa Bible Commentary* (Grand Rapids: Zondervan, 2006).

3. C. C. Kroeger, M. J. Evans, and E. K. Elliott, eds., *The IVP Women's Bible Commentary* (Downers Grove, IL: InterVarsity Press, 2002).

4. Christopher Smith, *The Bible Made Impossible: Why Biblicism Is Not a Truly Evangelical Reading of Scripture* (Grand Rapids: Brazos, 2011),

provides a multitude of examples illustrating this problem. Smith's solution to this "every reader for themselves" was to turn to the Roman Catholic tradition, illustrating the point of this paragraph.

5. T. Oden, *The Rebirth of Orthodoxy* (San Francisco: HarperSanFrancisco, 2003); J. I. Packer and T. Oden, *One Faith: The Evangelical Consensus* (Downers Grove, IL: InterVarsity Press, 2004); see also C. Colson, *The Faith* (Grand Rapids: Zondervan, 2008).

6. There are two series of commentaries under way designed to do just this for Bible readers: *The Ancient Christian Commentary on Scripture* from InterVarsity Press and *The Church's Bible* from Eerdmans. Of course, there are oodles of options here, but one can use the *Ante-Nicene Fathers* and *Nicene and Post-Nicene Fathers* from Eerdmans, and then read Augustine and Aquinas and Luther and Calvin and Wesley and various others up to the modern day. One cannot read each of these for each sitting with the Bible, but it is our ongoing exposure to the past that creates in us a serious respect.

Chapter 3: Inkblots and Puzzles

1. Edith Humphrey, *Ecstasy and Intimacy* (Grand Rapids: Eerdmans, 2006), 41.

2. A pastor friend of mine, John Frye, wrote a novel explaining this very thing. It is called *Out of Print* (Grand Rapids: Credo House, 2007).

3. In my text in Appendix 2, there are no right answers; the score correlates similarities between how we view Jesus and how we view ourselves. For the studies, see L. J. Francis and J. Astley, "The Quest for the Psychological Jesus: Influences of Personality on Images of Jesus," *Journal of Psychology and Christianity* 16 (1997): 247–59; J. Astley and L. J. Francis, "A Level Gospel Study and Adolescents' Images of Jesus," in L. J. Francis, W. K. Kay, and W. S. Campbell, *Research in Religious Education* (Herefordshire, England: Gracewing, 1996), 239–47. Available online at: http://books.google.com/books?hl=en&id=n4Pm b9ik3GgC&dq=research+in+religious+education+leslie+j+francis& printsec=frontcover&source=web&ots=CvRMG4mvpX&sig=bhado HLZcAHuZtdtFCt0ev27sCc#PPP2,M1.

4. Mark Twain, *The Bible according to Mark Twain*, ed. H. G. Baetzhold and J. B. McCullough (New York: Simon & Schuster [Touchstone], 1996), 139.

5. Eugene Peterson, *Eat This Book: A Conversation in the Art of Spiritual Reading* (Grand Rapids: Baker, 2006), 66.

Chapter 4: It's a Story with Power!

1. Robert Webber, *The Divine Embrace* (Grand Rapids: Baker Academic, 2007), 128.

2. John Goldingay, *Old Testament Theology*, vol. 1, *Israel's Gospel* (Downers Grove, IL: InterVarsity Press, 2003), 31.

3. Abraham Joshua Heschel, *Moral Grandeur and Spiritual Audacity*, ed. S. Heschel (New York: Farrar, Straus, & Giroux, 1996), 12–13 (emphasis original).

4. See Alister McGrath, *Christianity's Dangerous Idea* (New York: HarperOne, 2007).

5. For Tyndale, I have relied on David Daniell, *William Tyndale: A Biography* (New Haven: Yale University Press, 1994). Quotations and allusions are from pp. 1, 141, 148, 182, 279, 319, 381, 383.

6. Goldingay, *Old Testament Theology*, 1:24.

Chapter 5: The Plot of the Wiki-Stories

1. It is impossible to know how many "authors" are involved in the composing of the thirty-nine Old Testament books. Since it is likely that one author wrote more than one book (say 1–2 Samuel and 1–2 Kings and 1–2 Chronicles), I have simply said there are at least thirty authors.

2. Andy Crouch, *Culture Making: Recovering Our Creative Calling* (Downers Grove, IL: InterVarsity Press, 2013).

3. I am summarizing the work I have done in *The King Jesus Gospel: The Original Good News Revisited*, rev. ed. (Grand Rapids: Zondervan, 2016), 152–58; *Kingdom Conspiracy: Returning to the Radical Mission of the Local Church* (Grand Rapids: Brazos, 2014), 21–42.

4. Irenaeus, *On the Apostolic Preaching*, trans. J. Behr (Crestwood, NY: St. Vladimir's Seminary Press, 1997).

5. In a section below I will discuss the Genesis, Adam and Eve, and Christian evolutionary theories.

6. The Hebrew word translated "image" is *tselem* and the one translated "likeness" is *demut*. The word *tselem* was translated into Greek as *Eikon*, and because Jesus is the Perfect *Eikon* in the New Testament and because the expression "image of God" has endured constant battles over its precise meanings, I have been using *Eikon* instead of "image of God."

7. Mark Twain, *The Autobiography of Mark Twain*, ed. C. Neider (New York: HarperCollins, 1990), 277.

8. For more than a hundred years, too many have divorced "kingdom" from Israel and from church. To keep those connected, I wrote *Kingdom Conspiracy*.

Chapter 7: God Speaks, We Listen

1. Dave Isay, *Listening Is an Act of Love* (New York: Penguin, 2007). I've not read this book.

2. Alan Jacobs, *A Theology of Reading: The Hermeneutics of Love* (Boulder, CO: Westview, 2001).

3. Ibid., 13.

4. Klyne Snodgrass, "Reading to Hear: A Hermeneutics of Hearing," *Horizons in Biblical Theology* 24 (2002): 1–32.

Chapter 8: The Boring Chapter (on Missional Listening)

1. Scholars think he began this work late in the fourth century and finished in AD 427.

2. This is the title of Gordon Fee and Douglas Stuart's book, *How to Read the Bible for All Its Worth* (Grand Rapids: Zondervan, 2003).

3. Augustine, *On Christian Doctrine*, trans. and intro. by D. W. Robertson Jr. (Upper Saddle River, NJ: Prentice Hall, 1997), 30–31. Later in this work Augustine defines "charity" as "the motion of the soul toward the enjoyment of God for His own sake, and the enjoyment of one's self and one's neighbor for the sake of God" (88).

4. P. H. Towner, *The Letters to Timothy and Titus*, New International Commentary on the New Testament (Grand Rapids: Eerdmans, 2006), 581.

5. See Scot McKnight, *Open to the Spirit: God in Us, God with Us, God Transforming Us* (Colorado Springs: WaterBrook, 2018), ch. 4.

6. This translation seeks to show the chiasm of 2 Timothy 3:16. There are four elements. The first and the fourth are together, and the second and third are together. Thus:

   A Inform (*didaskalia*)

      B Rebuke (*elegmon*)

      B' Restore (*epanorthosis*)

   A' Instruct (*paideia in dikaiosune*)

7. The TNIV has a note after "so that all God's people" that reads, "Or *that the servant of God*." The Greek text, in a more literal rendering, reads "so that the *man of God* may be ..." Rendering this "all God's people," which I think is correct, recognizes that Paul's comments were intended to apply to more than just Timothy but also to Timothy's churches—both males and females, both laity and clergy.

Chapter 9: The Year of Living Jesus-ly

1. A. J. Jacobs, *The Year of Living Biblically: One Man's Humble Quest to Follow the Bible as Literally as Possible* (New York: Simon and Schuster, 2007).

2. Ibid., 4.

3. Ibid., 6–7.

4. Ibid., 8.

5. Ibid., 328.

6. See my piece online: www.christianvisionproject.com/2008/03/the _8_marks_of_a_robust_gospel.html. The paper copy can be found at *Christianity Today* (March 2008), 36–39.

Chapter 10: Finding the Pattern of Discernment

1. For an excellent study, see David Instone-Brewer, *Divorce and Remarriage in the Bible: The Social and Literary Context* (Grand Rapids: Eerdmans, 2002); see also his online piece at www.christianity today.com/ct/2007/october/20.26.html.

2. For commentary on this passage, see Scot McKnight, *The Sermon*

on the Mount, Story of God Bible Commentary (Grand Rapids: Zondervan, 2013), 94–109.

3. There is serious dispute if this "exception" was granted by Jesus explicitly or if Matthew, knowing what Jesus meant, clarified it later. I consider the exception clause to be accurate for what Jesus meant.

4. See Scot McKnight, *It Takes a Church to Baptize: What the Bible Says about Infant Baptism* (Grand Rapids: Brazos, 2018).

5. See Appendix 7.

6. Many manuscripts do not include this text, but most experts think it records an actual event in Jesus's life.

7. Gordon Fee, *The First Epistle to the Corinthians* (Grand Rapids: Eerdmans, 1987), 423.

Chapter 11: Slaves in the King and His Kingdom Redemption Story

1. I am grateful to my Northern Seminary colleague Claude Marriotini for sharing with me a manuscript he is working on about slavery in the Old Testament. I made use of some of his work in what follows.

2. In this section I draw from Scot McKnight, *The Letter to Philemon*, New International Commentary on the New Testament (Grand Rapids: Eerdmans, 2017).

3. The New Testament scholar is N. T. Wright. See his *The Kingdom New Testament* (New York: HarperOne, 2011), 440–41.

Chapter 12: Atonement in the King and His Kingdom Redemption Story

1. For discussions, Scot McKnight, *A Community Called Atonement* (Nashville: Abingdon, 2007); Scot McKnight, *Jesus and His Death: Historiography, the Historical Jesus, and Atonement Theory* (Waco, TX: Baylor University Press, 2005); N. T. Wright, *The Day the Revolution Began: Reconsidering the Meaning of Jesus's Crucifixion* (San Francisco: HarperOne, 2016). For a more general survey, Henri A. G. Blocher, "Atonement," in *Dictionary for Theological Interpretation of the Bible*, ed. Kevin J. Vanhoozer (Grand Rapids: Baker Academic,

2005), 72–76. I draw in this chapter from my *A Community Called Atonement*, 110–14.

2. For a good study, see John Goldingay, "Your Iniquities Have Made a Separation," in *Atonement Today*, ed. J. Goldingay (London: SPCK, 1995), 39–53.

3. Ibid., 53.

Chapter 13: Justice in the King and His Kingdom Redemption Story

1. E. T. Sankowski, "Justice," in *The Oxford Companion to Philosophy*, 2nd ed., ed. T. Honderich (New York: Oxford University Press, 2005), 463–64. I am grateful to an email exchange with Ben Davis for helping me to clarify my thoughts in this section.

2. For full discussion, see C. J. H. Wright, *Old Testament Ethics for the People of God* (Downers Grove, IL: InterVarsity Press, 2004), 23–99.

3. Ibid., 254.

4. I discuss love in *A Fellowship of Differents: Showing the World God's Design for Life Together* (Grand Rapids: Zondervan, 2014), 51–81.

5. Connecting love with justice has been an intellectual pursuit of Nicholas Wolterstorff, *Justice in Love* (Grand Rapds: Eerdmans, 2011), though I think he falls short of the Bible's fuller perspective in defining love as "care." But he is surely right in connecting love to justice: love that isn't just isn't love and justice that isn't love isn't justice.

Part 5: Women in Church Ministries Today

1. Perhaps the most significant innovation in the history of Christian theology is the addition of the *filioque* clause to the Nicene Creed. The original Nicene Creed of 325 AD had I believe . . . "in the Holy Spirit." In 381, that same Article read "I believe in the Holy Spirit *the Lord and Giver of life, who proceedeth from the Father, who with the Father and the Son together is worshiped and glorified, who spake by the prophets*." From the sixth century on, however, "who proceedeth from the Father" read "who proceedeth from the Father and the Son." "And the Son" in Latin is *filioque*. This became the official Creed in 1014 AD. The churches

of the Western world (Catholics, Protestants) have accepted this as the Creed while the churches of the East (Orthodoxy) have not.

2. For a series of informed, judicious, and long blog posts, posts that deserve to become a book, see those of an Anglican professor of theology, William G. Witt: http://willgwitt.org/theology/a-new-page-a-guide-to-my-essays-on-womens-ordination/.

3. Scot McKnight, *Galatians*, NIV Application Commentary (Grand Rapids: Zondervan, 1995), 201–11; Scot McKnight, *1 Peter*, NIV Application Commentary (Grand Rapids: Zondervan, 1996), 180–98.

Chapter 14: The Bible and Women

1. This text is normally cited as Tosefta Berakot 7.18, but my edition of the Tosefta has it at Berakot 6.18. I use J. Neusner, *The Tosefta*, 2 vols. (Peabody, MA: Hendrickson, 2002).

2. This saying, with variants, can be found in Diogenes Laertius, *Vitae Philosophorum* 1.33; Plutarch, *Marius* 46.1; Lactantius, *Divine Institutes* 3.19.17.

3. See *Dictionary of the Old Testament: Pentateuch*, ed. T. Desmond Alexander and D. W. Baker (Downers Grove, IL: InterVarsity Press, 2003), 897–904; *Dictionary of the Old Testament: Historical Books*, ed. B. T. Arnold and H. G. M. Williamson (Downers Grove, IL: InterVarsity Press, 2005), 989–99.

4. *Dictionary of the New Testament Background*, ed. C. A. Evans and S. E. Porter (Downers Grove, IL: InterVarsity Press, 2000), 1276–80.

5. See *Dictionary of Jesus and the Gospels*, ed. J. B. Green, S. McKnight, and I. H. Marshall (Downers Grove, IL: InterVarsity Press, 1992), 880–87; I quote from p. 880.

6. Josephus, *Against Apion* 2.201.

7. A brief sketch of this can be found in Sarah Sumner, *Men and Women in the Church* (Downers Grove, IL: InterVarsity Press, 2003), 58–69.

8. A small sampling, even if not representing the more negative side, can be found in Mark J. Edwards, *Ancient Christian Commentary on Scripture*, vol. 8: *Galatians, Ephesians, Philippians* (Downers Grove, IL: InterVarsity Press, 1999), 183–90.

9. See Ruth A. Tucker and Walter Liefeld, *Daughters of the Church* (Grand Rapids: Zondervan, 1987).

10. The best sketch of this I have seen is William Webb, *Slaves, Women and Homosexuals: Exploring the Hermeneutics of Cultural Analysis* (Downers Grove, IL: InterVarsity Press, 2001), 22–29, upon which I have relied in this section.

11. I don't like the term "egalitarianism" because it smacks too much of an Enlightenment sense of rights and justice and less of the biblical sense of mutuality designed in creation and reestablished in new creation. I believe there is something real in femininity and masculinity that distinguishes women from men, though I cannot define what that might be. I believe "mutuality" encourages a profound unity, equality, and distinctiveness better than the term "egalitarian." The term "egalitarian" conveys a battle while the term "mutuality" conveys partnership, companionship, and unity.

12. See Edwards, *Galatians, Ephesians, Philippians*, 190 (quoting Chrysostom).

Chapter 15: What Did Women Do in the Old Testament

1. For my study of what the Bible says about Mary, see *The Real Mary: Why Protestant Christians Can Embrace the Mother of Jesus* (Brewster, MA: Paraclete, 2016).

2. I am deeply aware of the amount and depth of scholarship on the many passages I will mention in what follows, but in this context it is not remotely possible to enter into the many debates. I recommend the following books for your own personal study: R. W. Pierce and R. M. Groothuis, eds., *Discovering Biblical Equality: Complementarity without Hierarchy* (Downers Grove, IL: InterVarsity Press, 2005); A. Mickelsen, ed., *Women, Authority and the Bible* (Downers Grove, IL: InterVarsity Press, 1986); B. Clouse and R. G. Clouse, eds., *Women in Ministry: Four Views* (Downers Grove, IL: InterVarsity Press, 1989); James R. Beck, ed., *Two Views on Women in Ministry*, rev. ed. (Grand Rapids: Zondervan, 2005).

In addition to those more general surveys, I also recommend Craig S. Keener, *Paul, Women, and Wives: Marriage and Women's Ministry in the Letters of Paul* (Grand Rapids: Baker Academic, 2004); S. Sumner, *Men and Women in the Church* (Downers Grove, IL: InterVarsity Press, 2003); J. Stackhouse, *Finally Feminist: A Pragmatic Christian Understanding of Gender* (Grand Rapids: Baker, 2005); R. T. France, *Women in the Church's Ministry: A Test Case for Biblical Interpretation* (Grand Rapids: Eerdmans, 1995); B. Witherington III, *Women in the Ministry of Jesus* (Cambridge: Cambridge University Press, 1987) and *Women in the Earliest Churches* (Cambridge: Cambridge University Press, 1991); Lynn Cohick, *Women in the World of the Earliest Christians: Illuminating Ancient Ways of Life* (Grand Rapids: Baker Academic, 2009); Lynn H. Cohick and Amy Brown Hughes, *Christian Women in the Patristic World: Their Influence, Authority, and Legacy in the Second through Fifth Centuries* (Grand Rapids: Baker Academic, 2017).

3. While some think the "fall" is an unbiblical category and not even taught in this passage, I believe "fall" remains a useful category. Something happened in Eden that impacts other humans and also describes the way of humans.

4. I follow here the interpretation of two leading Old Testament scholars: see Bill Arnold, *Genesis*, New Cambridge Bible Commentary (New York: Cambridge University Press, 2009), 69–71; Tremper Longman III, *Genesis*, The Story of God Bible Commentary (Grand Rapids: Zondervan, 2016), 67. Some today think "desire" is not a desire to dominate but simply a romantic desire (as in Song of Songs 7:10); but as Arnold and Longman show, the more immediate parallel to this verb "desire" is a desire to control in Genesis 4:7.

5. From Peter J. Leithart, *1 and 2 Kings* (Grand Rapids: Brazos, 2006), 267.

Chapter 16: What Did Women Do in the New Testament?

1. See my *The Real Mary* (Brewster, MA: Paraclete, 2016).

2. For the sake of completeness, I do not see the same influence in the book of Jude, which tradition claims was written by another son of Mary.

3. For a fuller discussion of Junia, see Appendix 6.

4. An exhaustive study by a specialist in textual criticism is E. J. Epp, *Junia: The First Woman Apostle* (Minneapolis: Fortress, 2005); for a brief discussion, Lynn Cohick, *Women in the World of Earliest Christianity* (Grand Rapids: Baker Academic, 2006), 214–17.

5. Epp, *Junia*, 32.

6. Other "co-workers" (or "fellow workers") can be found in Romans 16:9, 21; 1 Corinthians 3:9; 2 Corinthians 8:23; Philippians 2:25; 4:2–3; 1 Thessalonians 3:2; Philemon 1, 24.

7. See 1 Corinthians 3:5–9: "What, after all, is Apollos? And what is Paul? Only servants, through whom you came to believe—as the Lord has assigned to each his task. I planted the seed, Apollos watered it, but God has been making it grow. So neither the one who plants nor the one who waters is anything, but only God, who makes things grow. The one who plants and the one who waters have one purpose, and they will each be rewarded according to their own labor. For we are co-workers in God's service; you are God's field, God's building."

8. Douglas J. Moo, *The Epistle to the Romans*, New International Commentary on the New Testament (Grand Rapids: Eerdmans, 1996), 914.

9. An imaginative approach to Romans can be found in Reta Halteman Finger, *Roman House Churches for Today* (Grand Rapids: Eerdmans, 2007).

10. Robert Jewett, *Romans*, Hermeneia (Minneapolis: Fortress, 2007), 947–48.

11. The technical discussion for what I state here can be found in G. H. R. Horsley, *New Documents Illustrating Early Christianity* (Macquarie, Australia: Macquarie University Press, 1987), 4:239–44.

Chapter 17: Silencing the Blue Parakeet (1)

1. For a more technical defense of this, see Susan Foh, "What Is the Woman's Desire?" *Westminster Theological Journal* 37 (1974–75): 376–83; but see also the excellent study of Richard S. Hess, "Equality with and without Innocence: Genesis 1–3," in *Discovering Biblical Equality: Complementarity without Hierarchy*, ed. R. W. Pierce and R. M. Groothuis (Downers Grove, IL: InterVarsity Press, 2005), 79–95.

2. See Appendix 3 for a special problem with these verses.

3. C. S. Keener, "Learning in the Assemblies: 1 Corinthians 14:34–35," in *Discovering Biblical Equality*, 161–71.

4. Ibid., 171.

5. Ibid.

6. There are basically two views of this passage and, in fact, of women in ministry; one sides with the Restorationist and Roman Catholic views of how we read the Bible and the other sides with the reformed and always reforming view. The former is often called "complementarian" and the latter "egalitarian," though simple labels mask both the seriousness of the views as well as nuances within and between such views. The term "complementarian" fudges the reality; this view is really a "hierarchical" view, for the focus is on male leadership and female subordination. I am with the reformed and always reforming view, and while I can be labeled an "egalitarian," I prefer to use other terms for my view of women in ministry. Two technical studies of this passage, the first from the complementarian side and the second from the egalitarian side, are W. D. Mounce, *Pastoral Epistles*, Word Biblical Commentary (Nashville: Nelson, 2000), 94–149, including eight dense pages of bibliography; and Towner, *Letters to Timothy and Titus*, 190–239.

Chapter 18: Silencing the Blue Parakeet (2)

1. B. P. Reardon, *Collected Ancient Greek Novels*, 2nd ed. (Berkeley: University of California Press, 2008), 125.

2. Juvenal and Perseus, *Satires*, trans. G. G. Ramsay, LCL (Cambridge: Harvard University Press, 1961), 6.434–44 (p. 119). The English text is also available online at http://en.wikisource.org/wiki/Satire_6.

3. On this, see especially B. W. Winter, *Roman Wives, Roman Widows: The Appearance of New Women and the Pauline Communities* (Grand Rapids: Eerdmans, 2003). Phil Towner, in his excellent commentary on the Pastoral Epistles, has sifted through recent studies on the context at Ephesus and brings them all to bear upon this passage in his extensive, excellent analysis; see *Letters to Timothy and Titus*, 190–239.

4. See the discussion in Winter, *Roman Wives, Roman Widows*, 39–58.

5. Towner, *Letters to Timothy and Titus*, 239.

Appendix 1: A Discernment Quiz

1. Originally in *Leadership Journal*.

Appendix 2: Images of Jesus

1. North England Institute for Christian Education.

Appendix 3: 1 Corinthians 14:34–35

1. See Gordon Fee, *The First Epistle to the Corinthians* (Grand Rapids: Eerdmans, 1987), 699–708; Fee expanded his arguments in his book *God's Empowering Presence* (Peabody, MA: Hendrickson, 1994), 272–81. These issues are complex and few have taken Fee on at the level of his expertise.

2. P. B. Payne, "Vaticanus Distigme-obelos Symbols Marking Added Text, Including 1 Corinthians 14.34–5," *New Testament Studies* 63 (2017): 604–25.

3. I believe Fee got this right, but many of my readers will not agree with Fee, so I have pursued this argument in a different direction.

Appendix 4: Petronius on the New Roman Woman

1. I use the online edition of Petronius, *Satyricon*, found at www.igibud .com/petron/satyr/satyr.txt. Another translation of this Latin text can be found at Petronius, *Satyricon* (Cambridge, MA: Harvard University Press, 1987), section 67.

Appendix 5: Juvenal on First-Century Women

1. Juvenal and Perseus, *Satires*, trans. G. G. Ramsay, LCL (Cambridge: Harvard University Press, 1961), 6.434–44 (p. 119). The English text is also available online at http://en.wikisource.org/wiki/Satire_6.

Appendix 6: Junia Is Not Alone

1. E. J. Epp, *Junia: The First Woman Apostle* (Minneapolis: Fortress Press, 2005).

2. He makes this point because some have said "Junias" (a supposed man's name) is a contraction of Junianus (clearly a man's name).

There is no evidence for such a contraction, and it goes against other examples of contraction.

3. See *Mounce's Complete Expository Dictionary of Old and New Testament Words* (Grand Rapids: Zondervan, 2006), 26–27.

4. The use of the term "prophetess" is problematic to me: it tends to diminish the meaning of "prophet" into a female kind of thing instead of the robust sense of "prophet." I prefer that we speak of a woman prophet as a prophet and not a "prophet-ess."

5. See pages 228–29.

6. See pages 229–35.

7. See page 235–36.

8. See pages 238–40.

9. See pages 243–46 regarding Priscilla and Phoebe.

10. R. H. Finger, *Roman House Churches for Today: A Practical Guide for Small Groups* (Grand Rapids: Eerdmans, 2007).

11. Epp, *Junia*, 38.

12. See also R. R. Schulz, "Twentieth-Century Corruption of Scripture," *Expository Times* 119.6 (2008).

13. B. J. Brooten, "'Junia … Outstanding among the Apostles' (Romans 16:7)," in *Women Priests: A Catholic Commentary on the Vatican Declaration*, ed. L. Swidler and A. Swidler (New York: Paulist, 1977), 142.

14. Epp, *Junia*, 57, italics added.

15. Ibid., 32 (*In ep. ad Romanos* 31.2).

16. K. I. Stjerna, *Women and the Reformation* (Malden, MA: Blackwell, 2009), 133–47; M. Dentière and M. B. McKinley, *Epistle to Marguerite de Navarre and Preface to a Sermon by John Calvin* (Chicago: University of Chicago Press, 2004). I quote from Stjerna, pages 135, 136, 142, 146; from Dentière-McKinley, page 5.

17. C. E. White, *The Beauty of Holiness: Phoebe Palmer as Theologian, Revivalist, Feminist, and Humanitarian* (Grand Rapids: Francis Asbury Press, 1986).

18. L. C. Warner, *Saving Women: Retrieving Evangelistic Theology and Practice* (Waco, TX: Baylor University Press, 2007), 224, 233–34, 250–51.

Appendix 7: Genesis and Science

1. A good sketch can be found in G. Rau, *Mapping the Origins Debate: Six Models of the Beginning of Everything* (Downers Grove, IL: IVP Academic, 2012).

2. John Soden, "Concordism," in *Dictionary of Christianity and Science*, eds. P. Copan, T. Longman III, C. L. Reese, M. G. Strauss (Grand Rapids: Zondervan, 2017), 104–5.

3. Dennis Venema, Scot McKnight, *Adam and the Genome: Reading Scripture after Genetic Science* (Grand Rapids: Brazos, 2017).

4. I sketch these ideas more at length in Venema and McKnight, *Adam and the Genome*, 111–91. Our view is noticeably non-concordist in that there is no attempt to show that the Bible is prescient in its presentation of what some have taken to be scientific.

5. I recommend the following very limited selection: John H. Walton, *Genesis 1 as Ancient Cosmology* (Winona Lake, IN: Eisenbrauns, 2011); John H. Walton, *The Lost World of Genesis One: Ancient Cosmology and the Origins Debate* (Downers Grove, IL: InterVarsity Press, 2009); John H. Walton, *The Lost World of Adam and Eve: Genesis 2–3 and the Human Origins Debate* (Downers Grove, IL: IVP Academic, 2015); J. Richard Middleton, *The Liberating Image: The* Imago Dei *in Genesis 1* (Grand Rapids: Brazos, 2005); Peter Enns, *The Evolution of Adam: What the Bible Does and Doesn't Say about Human Origins* (Grand Rapids: Brazos, 2012); Edward J. Larson, *Evolution: The Remarkable History of a Scientific Theory* (New York: Modern Library, 2006).

6. A slightly edited form from Venema and McKnight, *Adam and the Genome*, 107–8.

7. Again, see Dennis Venema's sections in Venema and McKnight, *Adam and the Genome*.

8. Venema and McKnight, *Adam and the Genome*, 181. That much of what Paul says about Adam is not found in the Old Testament has been emphasized by Enns, *The Evolution of Adam*, 82–88.

9. Venema and McKnight, *Adam and the Genome*, 181.

The King Jesus Gospel

The Original Good News
Revisited

Scot McKnight

Contemporary evangelicals have built
a "salvation culture" but not a "gospel
culture." Evangelicals have reduced the
gospel to the message of personal salva-
tion. This book makes a plea for us to recover the old gospel as
that which is still new and still fresh. The book stands on four arguments: that the gospel is defined by the apostles in 1 Corinthians
15 as the completion of the story of Israel in the saving story of
Jesus; that the gospel is found in the four Gospels; that the gospel
was preached by Jesus; and that the sermons in the book of Acts
are the best example of gospeling in the New Testament. *The King
Jesus Gospel* ends with practical suggestions about evangelism
and about building a gospel culture.

Available in stores and online!

From the Publisher

GREAT STUDIES

ARE EVEN BETTER WHEN THEY'RE SHARED!

Help others find this study:

- Post a review at your favorite online bookseller.

- Post a picture on a social media account and share why you enjoyed it.

- Send a note to a friend who would also love it—or, better yet, go through it with them.

Thanks for helping others grow their faith!

Do you ever wonder, "Why doesn't God answer my prayers?" Do you wish you could see the evidence that prayer changes lives? Are you tired of playing it safe with your faith? In *Dangerous Prayers*, *New York Times* bestselling author Craig Groeschel helps you unlock your greatest potential and tackle your greatest fears by praying stronger, more passionate prayers that lead you into a deeper faith.

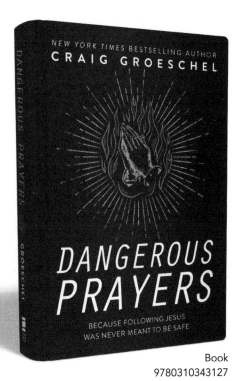

Prayer moves the heart of God—but some prayers move him more than others. He wants more for us than a tepid faith and half-hearted routines at the dinner table. He's called you to a life of courage, not comfort.

This book will show you how to pray the prayers that search your soul, break your habits, and send you to pursue the calling God has for you. But be warned: if you're fine with settling for what's easy, or you're OK with staying on the sidelines, this book isn't for you. You'll be challenged. You'll be tested. You'll be moved to take a long, hard look at your heart.

But you'll be inspired, too.

Book
9780310343127

You'll be inspired to pray boldly. To pray powerfully. To pray with fire. You'll see how you can trade ineffective prayers and lukewarm faith for raw, daring prayers that will push you to new levels of passion and fulfillment. You'll discover the secret to overcome fears of loss, rejection, failure, and the unknown and welcome the blessings God has for you on the other side.

You'll gain the courage it takes to pray dangerous prayers.

Available now at your favorite bookstore.

CRAIG GROES

WITH DUDLEY DELFFS

LEAD LIKE IT MATTERS

WORKBOOK

7 Leadership Principles for a Church That Lasts

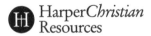

HarperChristian
Resources

Lead Like It Matters Workbook
© 2022 by Craig Groeschel

Requests for information should be addressed to:
HarperChristian Resources, 3900 Sparks Dr. SE, Grand Rapids, Michigan 49546

ISBN 978-0-310-15121-0 (softcover)
ISBN 978-0-310-15135-7 (ebook)

HarperChristian Resources titles may be purchased in bulk for church, business, fundraising, or ministry use. For information, please e-mail ResourceSpecialist@ChurchSource.com.

Published in association with Winters & King, Inc.

First Printing August 2022 / Printed in the United States of America

Contents

Introduction

Some ministries have *it*. Some don't.

Most churches want *it*. Few have it.

When a church has *it*, everyone knows it. When one doesn't—well, everyone knows that too.

The same is true with pastors and leaders. Some have *it*. Some don't. It is obvious when someone has *it* and when someone doesn't.

It is always unique. It is always powerful. It is always life-changing.

So . . . what is *it*?

My answer is . . . I don't know. Really, I don't.

It is hard to define because you can't see it. But here's what I do know: If you've ever been involved in a ministry that had *it*, you had this sense you were part of something special. Although you probably couldn't describe *it*, you still knew it when you saw it. It was an indescribable work of God that could not be explained or contained.

If you've never seen *it* up close, ask around and see if you can find it. Just listen to what people around you are saying. I promise, if a ministry or church near you gets *it*, people will be talking about it. When a ministry has *it*, there's electricity in the air; the ground seems to rumble. Everyone becomes aware of it. You'll see it on social media. People will talk about it at the office. Your friends will tell you they heard about it from their friends.

Because of the buzz, people flock to check out churches that have *it*. Not only do they kick the tires, but many of them also join. Not only do they join, but many also get obsessed with the ministry and throw their whole hearts and lives into it. They seem to intuitively grasp whatever *it* is. They can't get enough of it.

Here is something else I know: while *it* is always and only a gift from God, I believe that he makes *it* available to anyone who wants it. I believe that he wants to give *it* to you and your ministry. In whatever capacity you serve, you can learn to lead like *it* matters.

In this workbook, we will dive into the concepts that I present in the *Lead Like It Matters* book. Here's the game plan. In part 1, we'll talk about what *it* is and why we need to lead like it matters. In part 2, we'll explore seven leadership principles for building a church, ministry, or organization that lasts. In part 3, we'll discuss three important realms of leadership that every church or ministry leader must master to lead like *it* matters and maximize their God-given potential.

If you believe God wants to use you in his church and as his church, this study is for you. As you read on, do so prayerfully. If possible, don't go through this material alone. Invite friends from your small group, staff, or church leadership team to join you. Finally, be sure to keep an open mind, be alert to God's prompting, and believe by faith that he will hear the cries of your heart and move freely and powerfully through your church and ministry.

NOTE

This workbook is a biblical approach to practical leadership. For your convenience, in the following pages, you will find significant portions from the book *Lead Like It Matters*. The segments from the book are provided for you in this workbook so that you don't have to flip back and forth between the workbook and the book. In the following pages, you will also find additional biblical application to support the leadership content, to enable you to lead a church that lasts, and discussion questions to cover with your team.

PART 1

WHAT IS *IT*?

When God gives it to you,
it is unmistakable.

Depending on your church background, you likely think some things are necessary to have a great church worship experience. Whatever you think you need, though, we didn't have that when we started Life.Church.

We didn't have a nice building. We didn't have our own offices. We didn't have a church phone number (unless you count my home phone number). We didn't have a paid staff. We didn't have a logo. We didn't have a website. We didn't serve Starbucks. We didn't have an organ. We didn't have a choir with robes or a rock band with guys wearing skinny jeans and sporting lots of hair product. We didn't have candles to spark the mood or a laser light show that pierced through the smoke from the fog machines. We didn't have hymnals or sermon series with titles copied from the most popular TV shows.

What did we have? We had a few people, but those few people were off-the-charts excited about Jesus. We had enough Bibles to go around. And we had *it*.

At the time, I didn't call it *it*.

But we were definitely full of *it*.

Even though we didn't know what *it* was, we knew it was from God. And it was special.

Whatever *it* was, everyone felt it. They talked about it. New people came and experienced it. The church grew. And grew. And grew. Lives were changed by the dozens. Then by the hundreds. Then by the thousands. Twenty-five years later, we are known as the largest attended church in the history of North America.

God's Word Has *It*

You can find *it* in all types of churches. It is in traditional churches, contemporary churches, charismatic churches, seeker-sensitive churches, and emergent churches. You can find it in rural communities, in suburbs, in big cities, and in underground churches in countries where it's illegal to meet for corporate worship.

Even though you can find *it* in all of those places, you can also go to thousands of these same types of churches that don't have it.

But when God gives *it* to you, it is unmistakable.

And when a ministry has *it*, most things the leaders try seem to work.

When a ministry has *it*, the staff knows they're part of something much bigger than themselves. They are important players participating in a divine mission, an unstoppable force, flowing with contagious passion. They show up early for almost everything. They often stay late. They rarely fight. When they do disagree, they grow through their differences, usually quickly.

When a church has *it*, creativity flows. Everyone comes up with ideas, and those ideas just seem to change lives.

On the other hand, when a ministry doesn't have *it*, most of what they try doesn't work. A ministry that doesn't have *it* simply follows the same formula they used the year before and the year before that. People are bored, uninspired, and complacent.

When a church doesn't have *it*, the staff is simply doing a job, drawing a paycheck, passing time. They're territorial. Jealous. Dissatisfied. Discontented. Even bitter.

When a church doesn't have *it*, few people seem to even notice. They don't seem to realize that no one new is showing up. It's certainly not a cause for alarm. Mostly they're just committed to and comfortable with the status quo.

When a church does have *it*, everyone knows it. They can feel it, though they would have trouble describing it. Everyone recognizes it, but no one knows precisely what it is.

It's a lot like the first-century church you read about in the book of Acts. They unquestionably had *it*. Look for *it* in this description of the early church and then answer the questions that follow.

> [42] They devoted themselves to the apostles' teaching and to fellowship, to the breaking of bread and to prayer. [43] Everyone was filled with awe at the many wonders and signs performed by the apostles. [44] All the believers were together and had everything in common. [45] They sold property and possessions to give to anyone who had need. [46] Every day they continued to meet together in the temple courts. They broke bread in their homes and ate together with glad and sincere hearts, [47] praising God and enjoying the favor of all the people. And the Lord added to their number daily those who were being saved.
>
> **—Acts 2:42–47**

■ Based on this passage, what are some key elements necessary for a church to have *it*? How have you experienced these elements in your church today?

■ Knowing that the early church contained both Jews and Gentiles, both free people and slaves, both men and women (see Galatians 3:28), what does it means that "all the believers were together and had everything in common"?

■ In what ways did the attitudes of believers have an impact on the early church? In your experience, what has the greatest influence on the attitudes of church members?

■ Why do you think the early church attracted others who came to know the Lord? How did the early church reflect the qualities and characteristics of Jesus?

They Got *It*

You can lead like *it* matters, but you can't create it. How might leaders try to do that? Someone might visit a growing church and observe outward signs of success—videos, buildings, fancy kids' rooms, a certain style of music, and so on. These well-meaning guests mistakenly think, *That's why they have it. If we had all that, we'd have it too.*

They couldn't be more wrong.

The first-century church in Jerusalem clearly had *it*. Yet they didn't have anything extravagant. No historic cathedrals. No professionally produced video roll-ins to the latest four-part sermon series. No climbing walls in the youth wing or LED wall in the auditorium.

So, *it* can't possibly be stained-glass windows, hand-carved cherubs, custom silk tapestries, gold-inlaid hymnals, thousand-pipe organs, marble floors,

mile-high steeples, hand-painted ceilings, mahogany pews, giant cast-iron bells, and a three-piece, thousand-dollar suit. *It* doesn't stick any better to a young, hip pastor with tattoos and overpriced kicks than it does to an older, stately gentleman in a robe.

Nor is *it* spotlights and lasers, video production, satellite dishes, fog machines, shiny gauze backdrops, four-color glossy brochures, creative billboards, loud "contemporary" music, free donuts, coffee shops, hip bookstores, break dancing or acrobatics, sermon series based on movies, or a retro-modern matching chair and table onstage. It is not being on television, streaming on YouTube, speaking at conferences, having your own leadership podcast, or doing Instagram Live with the hottest celebrities.

What is *it* and how do you get it? I don't know. But God does. And I think he would tell you it's not one thing; it's the right combination of some essential ingredients. You can develop it from the recipe he's handed down, generation to generation, from those first Christians we read about in the book of Acts.

[31] After they prayed, the place where they were meeting was shaken. And they were all filled with the Holy Spirit and spoke the word of God boldly.

[32] All the believers were one in heart and mind. No one claimed that any of their possessions was their own, but they shared everything they had. [33] With great power the apostles continued to testify to the resurrection of the Lord Jesus. And God's grace was so powerfully at work in them all [34] that there were no needy persons among them. For from time to time those who owned land or houses sold them, brought the money from the sales [35] and put it at the apostles' feet, and it was distributed to anyone who had need.

—Acts 4:31–35

- What stands out to you in this description of the early church? Why?

- What *it*-qualities, both for a leader and a church, emerge from this passage? How have you seen these qualities manifest in churches where you've served?

- How did the Holy Spirit empower and facilitate *it* in the believers of the early church? What's the Spirit's role as you pursue leading like it matters?

- When have you experienced God's grace "powerfully at work" in you and your ministry? What did you learn about *it* from that experience?

Factoring *It* In

Part of what makes it *it* is that it defies categorization. It won't reduce to a memorable slogan or catchy formula. It is far too special for that.

That's why we have to embrace the fact that God makes *it* happen. It is from him. It is by him. It is for his glory. We can't create it. We can't reproduce it. We can't manufacture it.

It is not a model. It is not a style. It is not the result of a program. You can't purchase it or assemble it. It can't be copied.

Not everyone will get *it*. It can't be learned in a classroom. Yet even though it can't be taught, it *can* be caught.

As you begin considering what *it* is and where it comes from, remember:

- Beautiful buildings, cool environments, and the right technology aren't necessary to have *it*.
- A person surrendered fully to Christ gets *it*.
- Once a person has *it*, he can't keep it to himself.
- The good news: if you don't have *it*, you can get it.
- The bad news: if you have *it*, you can lose it.
- *It* is not a model, system, or result of programs.
- You cannot purchase *it*. It can't be copied.
- Not everyone will get *it*.
- *It* cannot be learned. Even though it can't be taught, it can be caught.
- *It* happens when we allow God to grow certain vital characteristics in us and in the ministries we lead.

_____

- Have you ever been part of a ministry or organization that had *it?* What were some of the qualities that you experienced and appreciated?

- Do you agree or disagree that *it* can be found in all types of churches? Why? What's the basis for your answer?

- Sometimes you can identify *it* by what it isn't. What comes to mind when you consider describing what *it* isn't?

- When have you tried to add or subtract something in your ministry in order to get *it?* What were your results?

Putting *It* into Action

You may feel challenged, frustrated, confused, and overwhelmed as you begin experiencing *it* and putting *it* into action in your ministry. And you may also feel excited, intrigued, exhilarated, and connected to God and others like never before. As you prepare to examine the various elements contributing to *it* in Part 2 of this workbook, think about how you would define *it* based on your own experience. Use the questions below to help you consider what you already know about *it* and where you're already seeing God using it in your life and work.

■ Based on your observations and experiences, as well as what you see in God's Word, how would you define *it* in a sentence or two? How do you think members of your team would define it?

■ What are the strongest areas in your church or organization, the places where you see *it* making an impact? What areas are struggling and lacking in *it*?

■ How do the seven key ingredients listed below work together to reflect Christ and advance God's kingdom? While you will examine each one in more detail in Part 2, write down your initial thoughts about how each ingredient contributes to *it* based on your experience and observations.

Vision:

Divine Focus:

Unmistakable Camaraderie:

Innovative Minds:

Willingness to Fall Short:

Hearts Focused Outward:

Kingdom-Mindedness:

■ Finally, based on what we've covered so far, what stands out most to you? What's required for you to lead like it matters? Contact a close, trusted friend or colleague and share your answers to these two questions.

PART 2

WHAT CONTRIBUTES TO *IT*?

Vision

Without a God-given vision, our ministries
will never get **it** *or keep* **it**.

Not every church can achieve *it* the same way. They'd be foolish to try. Not every church will have a charismatic preacher or a well-known worship pastor. Not every church can afford a nice building. Not every church can bus in hundreds of kids to their youth ministry or host a large vacation Bible school. Not every church can have sermon clips go viral or have thousands of downloads on YouTube.

No two churches achieve *it* the same way. But I've found that churches that have *it* do have some consistent qualities. The first of these qualities is vision.

If you want to lead like it matters, vision is essential. And not just having a vision, but casting it, sharing it, bringing it to life, and updating it as God leads. Churches and ministries that have *it* always have a clear vision. The people know, understand, believe, and live out the vision. The vision guides, motivates, energizes, and compels them. Large numbers of people passionately move in the same direction. They know it's not simply the leader's vision—it's God's vision for them as his people. In other words, it's a shared vision.

The Bible couldn't be clearer on the necessity of this key ingredient: "Where there is no vision, the people perish" (Proverbs 29:18 KJV). Without direction, people drift. Without a goal, motivation wanes. Without a mission, ministries fade. Youth groups lose their life. Once-vibrant churches slowly die. We need a clear and compelling vision that is constantly and enthusiastically cast.

People in a visionless church are often busy doing activities without any clear idea of how they relate or fulfill a larger purpose. They're moving in place without going toward a destination. Without a compelling vision, people quickly wear themselves out from all the activities and busyness. Those who frequently serve burn out. Staff members grow frustrated. Boards, elders, deacons, and leaders often disagree and split into factions. The ministry may have tons of activity, but there's little spiritual movement. Without alignment between the vision and the movement, they crash.

Vision matters to God and to those who serve him: "And the Lord answered me and said, Write the vision and engrave it so plainly upon tablets that everyone who passes may [be able to] read [it easily and quickly] as he hastens by" (Habakkuk 2:2 AMPC). Other translations say this vision is supposed to be carried by a "runner" or a "herald," and it should be so clear, displayed so prominently, that people can see it and read it at a glance.

With a known and implemented vision, you have clarity, focus, and direction. A white-hot vision inspires generosity, motivates selflessness, and releases an unstoppable passion to honor God and serve people. A vision empowers a church to have *it.*

Leaders who want vision seek God, find a divine burden, examine their resources and context, and present a Spirit-breathed, God-sized vision! As a leader, this is your role. This certainly doesn't mean that you won't listen to people, seeking their wisdom and input. But ultimately, the vision comes from the leader's time of hearing from God.

Don't assume you're not responsible for casting a God-given vision because

you're not in a formal leadership role. When we follow Christ, we are all leaders. Because, at its core, what is leadership? Leadership is influence. Whether or not you have a title, your role, gifts, and contribution always matter in God's church. You always have influence—so use it!

As God gives you clarity, you'll want to work hard to communicate this vision. A powerful vision is memorable, portable, and motivational. If people can't remember your vision, your church will never have *it*. If your vision isn't concise and easy to grasp and implement, people will not buy in and feel part of it. If your vision doesn't stir people and move them to action, your vision is too small. Your vision must be something that burns in your heart but is too big for you to do on your own. If you could do it, you wouldn't need God.

If you want to lead like it matters, then never underestimate vision.

God's Word Has *It*

When a leader and a church share a vision, everyone knows it. They can feel it, though they might have trouble describing it. Everyone recognizes *it*, but no one knows precisely what it is. We see *it* clearly in the first-century church described in the book of Acts. Peter, a follower of Jesus not particularly known to be a dynamic leader—in fact, just the opposite—managed to share Christ's vision for what this community of believers could be. Shortly after receiving the Holy Spirit at Pentecost (see Acts 2:1–4), these followers of Jesus began to speak through the power of the Spirit—yet each could understand one another in their own native language. They were so amazed and bewildered by this experience that others around them began to assume they were drunk on wine (see verse 13).

Peter seized the opportunity to preach, and not only did his words convey the essence of the gospel of Jesus Christ to a largely Jewish crowd, but his sermon also ignited a vision of who Jesus was and consequently who they were as

his followers. Read through the following excerpt from Peter's sermon and then answer the questions that follow.

> [29] "Fellow Israelites, I can tell you confidently that the patriarch David died and was buried, and his tomb is here to this day. [30] But he was a prophet and knew that God had promised him on oath that he would place one of his descendants on his throne. [31] Seeing what was to come, he spoke of the resurrection of the Messiah, that he was not abandoned to the realm of the dead, nor did his body see decay. [32] God has raised this Jesus to life, and we are all witnesses of it. [33] Exalted to the right hand of God, he has received from the Father the promised Holy Spirit and has poured out what you now see and hear. [34] For David did not ascend to heaven, and yet he said,

> "'The Lord said to my Lord:
>> "Sit at my right hand
> [35] until I make your enemies
>> a footstool for your feet."'

> [36] "Therefore let all Israel be assured of this: God has made this Jesus, whom you crucified, both Lord and Messiah."

> [37] When the people heard this, they were cut to the heart and said to Peter and the other apostles, "Brothers, what shall we do?"

> [38] Peter replied, "Repent and be baptized, every one of you, in the name of Jesus Christ for the forgiveness of your sins. And you will receive the gift of the Holy Spirit. [39] The promise is for you and your children and for all who are far off—for all whom the Lord our God will call."

> [40] With many other words he warned them; and he pleaded with them, "Save yourselves from this corrupt generation." [41] Those who accepted his

message were baptized, and about three thousand were added to their number that day.

⁴² They devoted themselves to the apostles' teaching and to fellowship, to the breaking of bread and to prayer. ⁴³ Everyone was filled with awe at the many wonders and signs performed by the apostles. ⁴⁴ All the believers were together and had everything in common. ⁴⁵ They sold property and possessions to give to anyone who had need. ⁴⁶ Every day they continued to meet together in the temple courts. They broke bread in their homes and ate together with glad and sincere hearts, ⁴⁷ praising God and enjoying the favor of all the people. And the Lord added to their number daily those who were being saved.

—Acts 2:29–47

■ How did Peter help his listeners, many of whom were likely resistant to accepting Jesus as the Messiah, accept Christ and his sacrifice on the cross? In other words, how did Peter share a new vision of how they saw Jesus?

■ Why do you think Peter mentioned David's tomb before transitioning to Christ's resurrection? Why did Peter quote David from one of the Psalms (110:1)?

■ What impact did Peter's sermon have on those listening? Why did they ask, "What shall we do?" (Acts 2:37)?

■ What evidence is provided at the end of this passage that this church had *it*? How did they put their vision of Christ into action?

———————————

They Got *It*

The seven ingredients that reflect *it* don't just emerge from contemporary leaders and churches—we find plenty of examples throughout the Bible. While numerous people in Scripture demonstrate vision, one in particular reveals how crucial it is to get everyone on board to see the vision realized. Nehemiah, part of the exiled remnant of Jewish people still in Babylon, served as cupbearer to King Artaxerxes, a role of honor reflecting Nehemiah's integrity. Although he wasn't a priest, prophet, or scribe, Nehemiah used his influence to initiate change and follow through.

After two groups of Jews had returned to Israel, word apparently got back to those remaining in Babylon about what they found. Basically, their homeland was in ruins. The walls around Jerusalem had fallen, leaving the city vulnerable to thieves and vandals. When Nehemiah heard the news, he mourned the loss, but he also trusted God to carry out Jerusalem's restoration. Read the following passage describing Nehemiah's vision quest, and then answer the questions that follow.

¹In the month of Nisan in the twentieth year of King Artaxerxes, when wine was brought for him, I took the wine and gave it to the king. I had not been sad in his presence before, ²so the king asked me, "Why does your face look so sad when you are not ill? This can be nothing but sadness of heart."

I was very much afraid, ³but I said to the king, "May the king live forever! Why should my face not look sad when the city where my ancestors are buried lies in ruins, and its gates have been destroyed by fire?"

⁴The king said to me, "What is it you want?"

Then I prayed to the God of heaven, ⁵and I answered the king, "If it pleases the king and if your servant has found favor in his sight, let him send me to the city in Judah where my ancestors are buried so that I can rebuild it."

⁶Then the king, with the queen sitting beside him, asked me, "How long will your journey take, and when will you get back?" It pleased the king to send me; so I set a time.

⁷I also said to him, "If it pleases the king, may I have letters to the governors of Trans-Euphrates, so that they will provide me safe-conduct until I arrive in Judah? ⁸And may I have a letter to Asaph, keeper of the royal park, so he will give me timber to make beams for the gates of the citadel by the temple and for the city wall and for the residence I will occupy?" And because the gracious hand of my God was on me, the king granted my requests. ⁹So I went to the governors of Trans-Euphrates and gave them the king's letters. The king had also sent army officers and cavalry with me.

¹⁰When Sanballat the Horonite and Tobiah the Ammonite official heard about this, they were very much disturbed that someone had come to promote the welfare of the Israelites.

¹¹I went to Jerusalem, and after staying there three days ¹²I set out during the night with a few others. I had not told anyone what my God had put in my heart to do for Jerusalem. There were no mounts with me except the one I was riding on.

¹³ By night I went out through the Valley Gate toward the Jackal Well and the Dung Gate, examining the walls of Jerusalem, which had been broken down, and its gates, which had been destroyed by fire. ¹⁴ Then I moved on toward the Fountain Gate and the King's Pool, but there was not enough room for my mount to get through; ¹⁵ so I went up the valley by night, examining the wall. Finally, I turned back and reentered through the Valley Gate. ¹⁶ The officials did not know where I had gone or what I was doing, because as yet I had said nothing to the Jews or the priests or nobles or officials or any others who would be doing the work.

¹⁷ Then I said to them, "You see the trouble we are in: Jerusalem lies in ruins, and its gates have been burned with fire. Come, let us rebuild the wall of Jerusalem, and we will no longer be in disgrace." ¹⁸ I also told them about the gracious hand of my God on me and what the king had said to me.

They replied, "Let us start rebuilding." So they began this good work.

—Nehemiah 2:1–18

■ What's striking about the fact that the king asked Nehemiah, his cupbearer, why he was sad? What does their exchange reveal about the kind of relationship they had?

■ What are the main pieces required to fulfill Nehemiah's vision of a restored Jerusalem? How does he go about getting others to help him make these pieces fall into place?

■ What obstacles did Nehemiah face in the pursuit of fulfilling his vision? How did he handle them?

■ How does Nehemiah rely on God rather than his own abilities to execute his vision for rebuilding Jerusalem? What difference does this make in how he interacts with those around him?

Factoring *It* In

Though people may drift toward comfort and complacency, they don't really like it. Deep down, they desire more—a lot more. Everyone craves a cause worth fighting for. We want to feel like our lives are significant and have purpose. We love to be part of something bigger than ourselves, something making a real, even an eternal, difference. As leaders, it's our role to seek God, see the vision, communicate it in a compelling way, and invite people to give their lives for the greatest cause on earth—the cause of Christ.

When it comes to vision, remember:

- Without a vision, the people will never get *it* and keep *it*.
- Without a compelling vision, staff and volunteers get frustrated, disagree, and burn out.

- *It* doesn't show up on its own. *It* follows big vision.
- The vision must be memorable, portable, and motivational.
- You can't overcommunicate vision!
- People give sacrificially toward, tolerate inconveniences for, and love to share a compelling vision.

Now spend a few minutes considering your leadership tendencies as they relate to vision. Be as openhanded and clear-eyed as possible when considering the role vision has played in the ways you lead. Use these questions to help you clarify and improve your God-given vision and how you implement it.

———————————————

■ What's one area of your ministry that's currently struggling because of lack of vision? How can you tell this area needs a clearer, sharper vision? Commit to praying about the vision God wants you to share so that this area really has *it.*

■ As concisely and accurately as possible, write down your current vision statement for ministry:

■ Now evaluate your vision statement in regard to the three criteria below. For each one, give yourself a score between 1 to 10, with 1 being "needs help" and 10 being "just like Jesus."

Memorable: _____

Portable: _____

Motivational: _____

■ Think through how you can sharpen your vision statement to raise your score for each of these criteria. How can you seek God and cast a clear vision that others can embrace and execute?

Putting *It* into Action

Ministries that have *it* are filled with people who understand and believe in the vision. Without it, you will have people who like the ministry but don't understand—or care—where it's going. Generally, people fall into three levels of vision buy-in. Some believe in the vision enough to benefit from it. These are often people who attend church with a consumer mindset, expecting only to receive something or benefit from the ministry. They want to know there's a vision but don't feel personally compelled to invest in it.

Others believe in it enough to contribute comfortably to it. They have likely shifted from the casual first level to a place where they want to contribute if it's not inconvenient or too costly. These individuals like being part of the cause as long as it fits in with the rest of their lives.

Ideally, more and more people believe in the vision enough to give their lives to it. They understand it and get it. They want to serve a cause greater than themselves. They love Jesus and consider themselves merely stewards of all the resources—time, money, energy, relationships—in their lives. They don't look for what church can do for them but know they *are* the church. They're all in and totally get it.

With these three groups in mind, think about the people who participate in your church, ministry, or organization. Then answer the questions below and consider what your responses reveal about how you can increase buy-in for the vision God has given you.

■ Approximately what percentage of participants fall into each group?

Level 1: _____ %
Level 2: _____ %
Level 3: _____ %

■ How do you imagine the people in each group grasp your ministry's vision? How many of them would be able to express this vision?

Now spend a few moments praying about your relationships with these people. Ask God to show you how to communicate, connect, and care about them just as much as he does. Then choose one individual from each category and reach out to them this week. Let them know you're refining and clarifying your vision for ministry and would like their input.

PRINCIPLE #2

Divine Focus

To be great at a few things and experience **it**,
you'll have to say no to many things.

The second ingredient in churches and organizations that have *it* may seem obvious: *divine focus.* After all, if Jesus is the hope of the world—and he is—then the church, as the body of Christ, exists to serve others as his hands and feet, showing them the love of God in action. As his church, we are chosen and called by God to be light in the darkness and to give hope to those in despair. We are God's conduits of grace to a world of people who need him. Which is why *it* matters!

The problem with having a divine focus is that, filtered through you, your team, and those in your care, that focus tends to sprawl. Divine focus through human filters can become an ever-increasing list of new methods, new ministries, and misplaced resources. Because doing more requires allocating more—more time and money, more staff and volunteers, more resources and energy.

Most ministries that have *it*, however, tend to be focused on a limited set of targets. They do a few things as if all eternity hinged on their results, and they do these things with godly excellence. They clearly see the vision and drive toward it

with laser-guided precision. Those who have *it* know what they are called to do. Perhaps just as important (maybe even more so), they also know what they are *not* called to do. Their vision is characterized by three things.

Specificity. Selectivity. Exclusivity.

Of course, focused ministries don't necessarily see immediate and overwhelming results. It often takes time, patience, discipline, and endurance. Then gradually they begin to realize that God is doing something special in their midst—they have *it.*

These churches remain relentlessly passionate about a few important things. They choose to deliberately ignore the rest. Their zeal and effectiveness attract the right leaders. The right leaders use their gifts and give their lives to make a difference. And God blesses them and their endeavors with *it*—his mysteriously awesome presence and power.

Unfortunately, when a ministry is faithful and one day wakes up and has *it,* they can be blinded by their success. Instead of seeing with the crystal clear vision that helped attract *it,* they find their vision begins to become blurred. Instead of staying focused on the main thing, the leaders become distracted by doing more and more. Sadly, the very thing that God blessed—strategic obedience to his specific calling—is one of the first things successful ministries unknowingly abandon.

The process of diluting divine focus usually happens subtly or covertly. Someone has a good idea that gets accepted and implemented—but the problem is that it's not a *God* idea. Someone's good idea sounded logical, reasonable, and feasible at the time, the natural progression of your ministry's growth. But it pulled focus away from God and what your ministry is called to do.

Rather than doing lots of things halfway, divine focus requires directing energy and resources at your God-given target with laser intensity. Because doing the wrong new things, things that usurp what God calls you to do, is dangerous. Focus tends to let *it* breathe. Lack of focus generally suffocates *it.*

To be great at a few things and experience *it,* you'll have to say no to many things. Instead of thinking about what you want to add to your ministry to-do

list, maybe you should pray about what to add to your ministry to-*don't* list. Some call it planned abandonment—planning what things you *won't* do, that others do, in order to do best what God called you to do.

Most people think you achieve more by doing more. As counterintuitive as it sounds, you actually achieve a greater impact by doing less. If you say "yes" to too many different things, you lose focus and effectiveness. That's why you strategically and ruthlessly must say no. You don't grow by saying yes to everything. You grow by saying no.

Those who have *it* stick with what brings it. When you know you're doing a great work, do your best not to get distracted. If you have *it*, guard it. Don't distort it by doing the wrong things. When you increase your focus, you decrease your options. Good things are not necessarily God things.

Focus on what God has uniquely called and equipped you and your church to do. And then do it with excellence for his glory and his kingdom.

God's Word Has *It*

In order to rely on a divine focus, you must rely on the Divine. Your ability to infuse your leadership with *it*—the amazing power and presence of God's Spirit—depends on the quality of your personal relationship with God. Your example should inspire and motivate those you lead and serve to make their personal relationship with him their priority as well. Your ministry team must be plugged into the same power source in order to keep your focus on God and what he's calling you to do.

The best example of this kind of unified focus comes from the earthly ministry of Jesus. He didn't choose the most educated, most religious, or most successful people for his team—Jesus chose people willing to give him their all. Christ expects the same from us today. Just as he relied on his heavenly Father, so must we. Through our relationship with Jesus, we have access to God's presence, power, and purpose for our lives.

Regardless of your role or title, your leadership depends on your willingness to rely on him. As Jesus explains in the following passage, everything you do is based on your relationship to God. In order to bear fruit in your ministry, you rely on him. Read through his explanation and underline any words or phrases that jump out at you. Then answer the questions that follow.

[1] "I am the true vine, and my Father is the gardener. [2] He cuts off every branch in me that bears no fruit, while every branch that does bear fruit he prunes so that it will be even more fruitful. [3] You are already clean because of the word I have spoken to you. [4] Remain in me, as I also remain in you. No branch can bear fruit by itself; it must remain in the vine. Neither can you bear fruit unless you remain in me.

[5] "I am the vine; you are the branches. If you remain in me and I in you, you will bear much fruit; apart from me you can do nothing. [6] If you do not remain in me, you are like a branch that is thrown away and withers; such branches are picked up, thrown into the fire and burned. [7] If you remain in me and my words remain in you, ask whatever you wish, and it will be done for you. [8] This is to my Father's glory, that you bear much fruit, showing yourselves to be my disciples."

—John 15:1–8

■ What words and phrases did you underline above? Why do they resonate with you right now?

■ When have you and your ministry been especially fruitful by relying on God and remaining in him? How did your divine focus allow God to work through you to produce spiritual fruit?

■ Now think of a time when you and your team did not rely on God, resulting in withering and pruning results. How did you lose focus in this attempt? What did you learn from this experience about staying focused on what God calls you to do?

■ What are some withering vines that are choking out the fruit of your primary focus? In other words, what activities, efforts, and expenditures are diluting the impact of your divine focus?

They Got *It*

Imagine that you were hosting Jesus at your house for dinner. Naturally, you would want your home to be clean and tidy, the food to be delicious, and the atmosphere to be warm and welcoming. But those details don't happen by accident—they require planning, preparation, and execution. So if you were going to have Jesus come and dine with you, there would be a lot to do, right?

Perhaps that's what a woman named Martha was thinking in anticipation of Jesus visiting the home she shared with her sister, Mary. It's hard to fault her desire for everything to go smoothly in order to enjoy a wonderful meal. And then to have to do it alone while her sister just sat and listened to their guest—she must have felt angry and frustrated. Yet when Martha asks Jesus to intervene, his response reframes her focus—as well as ours.

Read through their exchange and then answer the questions that follow.

[38] As Jesus and his disciples were on their way, he came to a village where a woman named Martha opened her home to him. [39] She had a sister called Mary, who sat at the Lord's feet listening to what he said. [40] But Martha was distracted by all the preparations that had to be made. She came to him and asked, "Lord, don't you care that my sister has left me to do the work by myself? Tell her to help me!"

[41] "Martha, Martha," the Lord answered, "you are worried and upset about many things, [42] but few things are needed—or indeed only one. Mary has chosen what is better, and it will not be taken away from her."

—Luke 10:38–42

- When have you experienced a situation in which you let your preparations distract you from the divine focus at the heart of your efforts? How did you feel at the time?

- Why did Jesus acknowledge the way Martha felt—"You are worried and upset about many things"—before redirecting her focus back to the one essential thing?

- What tasks, responsibilities, and activities are currently pulling you, like Martha, away from the one thing that will not be taken from you? What needs to be cut, shortened, or dropped from your schedule?

- How do you usually handle the Marthas on your team? How can you gently and compassionately, just like Jesus, remind them not to be distracted by that which is not essential?

Factoring *It* In

To have *it*, you'll have to choose not to do everything. Those who attempt to do everything always lose *it*. An Italian proverb says, "Often he who does too much does too little." Too many ministries are doing too little by doing too much. Is yours one of them?

When it comes to divine focus, remember:

- Those who do it all tend to lose *it*.
- The clearer your vision becomes, the easier it is to guard what God calls you to do.
- Instead of saying "and," maybe you need to say "or."
- To be great at a few things and experience *it*, you'll have to say no to many things.
- Innovation requires saying no to a thousand things.
- When focus increases, options decrease.
- Those who have *it* stick with what brings it.
- When you know you're doing a great work, do your best not to get distracted.

With these *it*-factors in mind, spend a few minutes reflecting and praying on how to sharpen and tighten your divine focus. Use the following questions to assist in your reflection and assessment.

■ When have you most recently realized you were doing too much and spreading efforts and resources too thin? What did you do once you realized your focus was blurring?

■ How many things have you turned down and said no to in the past month? The past week? How many things should you have turned down recently in order to maintain your primary divine focus?

■ Do you agree that "innovation means saying no to a thousand things"? Why or why not?

■ What are you presently doing that is outside the focus God has called you to fulfill? What must go as soon as possible?

Putting *It* into Action

Spend a few moments in prayer and ask God to guide you back to the heart of your divine focus. Then think about where you are currently in your ministry. Look carefully at the people God has put around you, the resources you have available to you, and the people who are within reach of your ministry, and then answer this question: *What can we be the best in the world at?*

■ Good things are often the enemy of great things. As you narrow in on what great thing you can do, on what God has uniquely equipped and empowered you to do, what good things should you let go?

■ As most churches grow and develop, they usually continue adding more and more (and more) ministries to their organization. Remember, human sprawl is the enemy of divine focus. So now may be a great time to "prune your vines" and return to doing what only your church can do. With this in mind, if you could remove one part of your ministry today, what would it be?

■ What essential ministries are necessary to fulfilling your vision and maintaining focus? If you could do only a few things for the greatest ministry return, what things you would do?

_____

PRINCIPLE #3

Unmistakable Camaraderie

*As **it** goes with the leaders, so **it** goes
with the whole organization.*

Ministries that have *it* enjoy it together. They have an unmistakable camaraderie. Anyone close to them can see it. They can feel it. Affinity, community, sincerity, family. Christianity at its best. The people love being together. And when they are, when the people interact, *it* is electric.

Simply put, the team with *it* love each other. Not only do they minister together; they do life together. What they have is more than friendship. It's something that God gives—a partnership of people with deep love committed to a single mission. You're more than friends. You're a team.

For the church to have *it*, the staff (or volunteers) will likely have it first. As it goes with the leaders, so it goes with the whole organization. To have *it* everywhere, it has to start somewhere. It must begin with your team. As the leader of your team, it begins with you!

You can't fake this kind of bond. Not every ministry team has *it*. Most don't. And its absence is as obvious as its presence in a team.

All too often, people accept and foster independence and self-sufficiency. Not

only are they independent, but they're also afraid to open up and be honest with who they are, what they think, and what they feel. With as much relational pain as they endure, especially those who have served in ministry and leadership roles, it's no wonder they're gun-shy.

They're paralyzed with fear, certain that if they let someone in, they'll get hurt—again. As long as you're afraid of intimacy and spiritual partnership, however, you likely won't experience *it*. To have *it*, you have to share it with each other. Just as there's no *I* in *team*, there's no *it* in *independence.*

To be a strong team with *it*, every staff member and volunteer must understand the mission of the organization. This is where vision and camaraderie overlap and enhance each other. Everyone gives respect and credit to one another.

Great teams have real fun together and provide heartfelt, edifying ministry to each other. Fun doesn't require expensive retreats and the latest team-building exercises. Fun is most often a serendipitous by-product of fulfilling a mission with people you love.

Teams with genuine camaraderie are willing to be relationally vulnerable with one another. Teams without camaraderie tend to cover up. Those without *it* can be two-faced. Those with *it* are true-faced. There is no substitute for being transparent and real. People would rather follow a leader who is always real than one who is always right. Others may be impressed with your strengths, but they'll connect with you when you reveal your weaknesses.

Many ministries have victories. But too many wins go by without celebrations. Teams with *it* look for excuses to celebrate. Anniversaries. Completion of significant projects. Ministry launches. Personal victories. Even funny mistakes, missteps, or embarrassing moments can be fun to commemorate.

Teams that have *it* are like family. Part of being family is fighting. Teams that have *it* know how to mix it up good and still be friends. They maintain their identity as a team, loyal to the end. Part of having *it* is knowing that as a group we can have it out and still be friends. Any successful organization knows how to work

through conflict. Teams without *it* avoid conflict. Teams with *it* understand that conflict is sometimes necessary to have *it*.

God told Adam that it isn't good to be alone. Solomon said two are better than one. Jesus even said that God is present when two or three gather in his name. Those who have *it* experience it best together.

The apostle Paul says, "You are citizens along with all of God's holy people. You are members of *God's family*. Together, we are his house, built on the foundation of the apostles and the prophets. And the cornerstone is Christ Jesus himself. We are carefully *joined together* in him, becoming a holy temple for the Lord" (Ephesians 2:19–21 NLT, emphasis added).

God wants us to be active members of his family.

We are to be joined together.

God's Word Has *It*

When we lead, serve, and grow together, we each have our unique contributions that work in harmony with everyone else's gifts. Paul famously compared the body of Christ to the human body. The body needs all of the parts functioning together.

A mouth or hand or foot or eye lying on the ground by itself is not just an independent body part—it's useless detached from all the other parts of the whole. Outside of the body, seeking to work on its own, a body part will cease to function.

And it's the same in the church. That's why an independent ministry mindset kills *it*. *It* needs others with *it* to flourish. Read through Paul's descriptive explanation below, and then answer the questions that follow.

> [12] Just as a body, though one, has many parts, but all its many parts form one body, so it is with Christ. [13] For we were all baptized by one Spirit so as to form one body—whether Jews or Gentiles, slave or free—and we

were all given the one Spirit to drink. [14] Even so the body is not made up of one part but of many.

[15] Now if the foot should say, "Because I am not a hand, I do not belong to the body," it would not for that reason stop being part of the body. [16] And if the ear should say, "Because I am not an eye, I do not belong to the body," it would not for that reason stop being part of the body. [17] If the whole body were an eye, where would the sense of hearing be? If the whole body were an ear, where would the sense of smell be? [18] But in fact God has placed the parts in the body, every one of them, just as he wanted them to be. [19] If they were all one part, where would the body be? [20] As it is, there are many parts, but one body.

[21] The eye cannot say to the hand, "I don't need you!" And the head cannot say to the feet, "I don't need you!" [22] On the contrary, those parts of the body that seem to be weaker are indispensable, [23] and the parts that we think are less honorable we treat with special honor. And the parts that are unpresentable are treated with special modesty, [24] while our presentable parts need no special treatment. But God has put the body together, giving greater honor to the parts that lacked it, [25] so that there should be no division in the body, but that its parts should have equal concern for each other. [26] If one part suffers, every part suffers with it; if one part is honored, every part rejoices with it.

[27] Now you are the body of Christ, and each one of you is a part of it. [28] And God has placed in the church first of all apostles, second prophets, third teachers, then miracles, then gifts of healing, of helping, of guidance, and of different kinds of tongues. [29] Are all apostles? Are all prophets? Are all teachers? Do all work miracles? [30] Do all have gifts of healing? Do all speak in tongues? Do all interpret? [31] Now eagerly desire the greater gifts.

—1 Corinthians 12:12–31

- The early church to whom Paul addressed this passage was composed of people from various backgrounds, both Jews and Gentiles, rich and poor, merchant and beggar, slave and free. What are the various kinds of people making up your church or organization? List them below using whatever descriptors or demographics come to mind.

- According to Paul here, what happens when one body part tries to detach itself from the rest of the body? When have you experienced a similar issue with your team?

- Based on how Paul explains his metaphor, what happens when one body part envies another and tries to perform its function? How have you seen this occur in your ministry?

PART 2: WHAT CONTRIBUTES TO *IT?*

■ With your own ministry team in mind, write down each person (or department/group, depending on the size of your team) and how they serve the body.

Person or group:
How they serve the body:

Person or group:
How they serve the body:

Person or group:
How they serve the body:

Person or group:
How they serve the body:

Person or group:

How they serve the body:

They Got *It*

When you think about the intimacy of a ministry group, the bond experienced by Jesus with his disciples is beyond compare. By choosing to pour himself into these twelve men, Christ exemplified how to do ministry—by starting with a core team who gets it. The dozen people hand-picked by the Son of God to accompany him during his time of public ministry had no special training or prior experience. They left behind their former jobs and responsibilities and went all in.

Not only did the disciples recognize the promised Messiah and see him in action, but they also experienced firsthand his love, compassion, strength, honesty, and devotion to them. Nowhere is this more evident than when their Master humbled himself to perform a personal service to each of them. Read through John's account of this special gift, and then answer the questions below.

[1] It was just before the Passover Festival. Jesus knew that the hour had come for him to leave this world and go to the Father. Having loved his own who were in the world, he loved them to the end.

[2] The evening meal was in progress, and the devil had already prompted Judas, the son of Simon Iscariot, to betray Jesus. [3] Jesus knew that the Father had put all things under his power, and that he had come from God and was returning to God; [4] so he got up from the meal, took off his outer

clothing, and wrapped a towel around his waist. [5] After that, he poured water into a basin and began to wash his disciples' feet, drying them with the towel that was wrapped around him.

[6] He came to Simon Peter, who said to him, "Lord, are you going to wash my feet?"

[7] Jesus replied, "You do not realize now what I am doing, but later you will understand."

[8] "No," said Peter, "you shall never wash my feet."

Jesus answered, "Unless I wash you, you have no part with me."

[9] "Then, Lord," Simon Peter replied, "not just my feet but my hands and my head as well!"

[10] Jesus answered, "Those who have had a bath need only to wash their feet; their whole body is clean. And you are clean, though not every one of you." [11] For he knew who was going to betray him, and that was why he said not every one was clean.

[12] When he had finished washing their feet, he put on his clothes and returned to his place. "Do you understand what I have done for you?" he asked them. [13] "You call me 'Teacher' and 'Lord,' and rightly so, for that is what I am. [14] Now that I, your Lord and Teacher, have washed your feet, you also should wash one another's feet. [15] I have set you an example that you should do as I have done for you. [16] Very truly I tell you, no servant is greater than his master, nor is a messenger greater than the one who sent him. [17] Now that you know these things, you will be blessed if you do them.

—John 13:1–17

■ Why did Jesus choose to perform such a humbling act of service right before his death? What is the significance of his timing?

■ You don't necessarily need to have washed their feet, but when was the last time you served your team members in an equally humble and sacrificial way?

■ What does it mean that "no servant is greater than his master"? How does your leadership style reflect the servanthood of Christ?

■ What are some bonding and camaraderie-building activities you can initiate with your ministry team this week? How can anything you do together draw your team closer together?

Factoring *It* In

Friendships matter. Studies reveal just how important friendships at work are to *it*. Happier people make better team members. They not only enjoy being together—they look forward to those times. Laughter seasons their gatherings, and mutual respect and sincere caring flavor every interaction. They're comfortable enough to know and accept one another—and love one another—in virtually every setting. This includes in each other's homes.

The importance of relationships isn't simply the conclusion of studies made by workplace experts. Jesus told his followers, "By this everyone will know that you are my disciples, if you love one another" (John 13:35). The people you lead need to see that you don't just believe this as an abstract theological tenet—they need to feel it as you interact with them day in and day out.

When it comes to camaraderie, remember:

- People on teams that have *it* enjoy it together.
- As long as you're afraid of intimacy and spiritual partnership, you likely won't experience *it*.
- God is calling us to more than just a personal relationship with Jesus. He wants us to experience a *shared* relationship with him.
- Those who don't have *it* compete with one another. Those with *it* complete one another.
- We need to take time to celebrate our wins together.
- To have *it*, you have to share it with each other. *It* dies when it is alone.
- Leaders with *it* understand the big picture, have fun, get vulnerable, celebrate the wins, and fight behind closed doors.

- As you look over this list of *it*-factors for camaraderie, which ones stand out to you as areas for improvement on your team? Which ones do you already practice regularly?

- What do you and your team do to have fun together? When was the last time you made fun a priority in a meeting, gathering, or fellowship time?

- How do you celebrate your ministry's wins as a team? What's a win you can celebrate together in the next week?

- How would you describe the way your team usually handles internal conflicts? What needs to change in order to disagree with one another while maintaining team loyalty and cohesion?

Putting *It* into Action

Relationships require constant, deliberate investment. It's great when everyone likes one another and seems to get along. It's even better when they enjoy and respect each other in pursuit of shared ministry goals. But even the best teams require work and intentional development if they are to remain healthy, grow with the ministry, and experience the power of God's presence in their efforts.

Camaraderie can also seem like something that's beyond one person's control—and it is. But whatever your role as a leader may be, others are watching you and learning by your example. Whatever you really think and feel and believe about them comes through, no matter how hard you may try to disguise or sugarcoat your attitudes about them. So perhaps the place to start is with a basic inventory to assess your team's health. You should complete this kind of assessment along with everyone on your team. It doesn't have to be a formal questionnaire or expensive testing service. It does, however, need to be open, honest, candid, and constructive.

Use the following questions to get you started and then decide how to invite your team members to weigh in. Spend some time in prayer both as their leader and then together as a team.

■ On a scale of 1 to 10, with 1 being "very independent" and 10 being "totally interdependent," how would you rate your team today? What factors come to mind that influence the score you're giving?

■ What are three specific ways you regularly, daily even, cultivate camaraderie on your team?

1.

2.

3.

■ How would the people served by your team describe the way you function together? Write down your response below and then text, call, or email three trusted individuals from your congregation or constituency and ask for their honest feedback.

■ What are the greatest obstacles to your team growing closer and experiencing more of *it* in order to be more effective in ministry? What obstacles have you already overcome in order to grow stronger? What obstacles need to be addressed before they grow into bigger problems?

_____

Innovative Minds

If you are ready for change, you are ready for growth.

I f what your church or ministry is doing now is effective and changing lives, enjoy it while it lasts. Because what's working now won't work in the future. While the message we preach must never change, how we communicate it must change as the world changes.

This reality may sound discouraging, but it's true. If you don't change, you won't last. If you don't adapt how you share the gospel, your effectiveness will likely lessen over time because the world is changing too fast. You only have to think back on the ways church has been done over the past few decades to realize that it evolves as our culture changes. Again, the truth of the gospel and God's Word never changes—but how you present the message needs to fit the people you serve.

Paul experienced this necessity while in Rome. He realized that the way he preached in Ephesus or Corinth wasn't necessarily the way he should preach to reach the Romans. So he looked for a way to connect with his audience and found it. Paul saw an opportunity to innovate his presentation and went for it: "So Paul, standing before the council, addressed them as follows: 'Men of Athens, I notice

that you are very religious in every way, for as I was walking along I saw your many shrines. And one of your altars had this inscription on it: "To an Unknown God." This God, whom you worship without knowing, is the one I'm telling you about'" (Acts 17:22–23 NLT).

In case you think you're not innovative, just consider what it really means. Innovation is different from creativity. Creativity is thinking up new ideas. People with new ideas are not necessarily innovators. People who *carry out* new ideas are innovators. It's easy to come up with all kinds of new ideas and talk about them at every meeting. But trying them out, seeing what works and learning from what doesn't work—that's the way creative solutions come to life.

Innovation cannot be ignored if you want to grow. Accepting this mindset changes how you see problems. When you think about it, every innovation is really a solution to a problem. Too often, teams work hard to prevent problems or come up with easy-but-temporary solutions. But problems aren't things to be feared; they're opportunities to embrace. In fact, many great innovations are solutions to a problem people did not even know they had.

If you're facing a problem in your ministry today, try to think of it as an opportunity for innovation. You might have lost a key staff member, can't find the right facility, or struggle to stream online. What if you reframed this problem into a chance to try something new? What if you told yourself this is not just a problem to solve, but an opportunity to seize?

Rather than recognizing the potential for innovation within each problem, it's easier to stall and blame lack of resources, circumstances beyond your control, and decisions by other people. But what if your limitations could inspire your creativity to achieve your goal another way? God might even guide you to see something you normally would have missed if you had the "obvious solution" or abundant resources.

Whenever you're tempted to whine about what you don't have, remember that God has given you everything you need to do everything he wants you to do. Peter

wrote, "Everything that goes into a life of pleasing God has been miraculously given to us by getting to know, personally and intimately, the One who invited us to God" (2 Peter 1:3 MSG). If you don't have something you *think* you need, maybe it's because God wants you to see something you've never seen. Those with *it* recognize that God brings *it*. *It* is not found in the things the eye can see.

Innovation is more about mindset than money. If you believe you can't, you can't. If you believe you can find a way, you probably will. If you think you lack what you need to do what you need to do, you won't do what you need to do even if you have what you need.

Having more is not always better. It can be worse. Why? More people can slow things down. More time can make you lazy. More money can train you to buy solutions rather than create them. When you look at the business world, you see this reality. Most innovative companies are startups that don't have much or mature organizations that enforce artificial restraints to push innovation. So try thinking about innovation as a good thing. Toward that goal, use this concise formula:

$$\text{Problem to Solve} + \text{Limited Resources} + \text{Increasing Passion} = \text{Exponential Innovation}$$

Your greatest ministry innovation could come from your greatest limitation—*if* you have a sincere passion to reach and care for people. When you ask God for eyes to see, you may see what has always been there but you have never noticed before. Have you ever bought a car, and then as you drove it around noticed dozens of other people driving the same car? They were all around you last week; you just didn't have the mindset to see them. Limitations and passion have a way of changing our minds and our eyes.

What obstacles are you facing? Ask God for breakthrough thinking.

Don't think about small changes.

Think radically.
Think out of the box.
And then destroy the box!

God's Word Has *It*

When you don't have what you think you need, you often overlook what you actually do have. Many times our own assumptions and expectations get in the way of using the resources God has given us. Instead of focusing on what we lack, we must learn to innovate with what we have.

We see a great example of this in Acts 3. Peter and John were traveling to their afternoon temple prayer meeting when they saw a man being carried to his begging post. He had been crippled his whole life. The beggar apparently recognized Peter and held out his cup, hoping to get some change to buy food.

Which is when God began using Peter's limitations—what Peter *didn't* have—to guide him into giving the man much more than his next meal. If Peter had given money, it might have been easy to smile politely, drop some coins, and keep going to his destination. Because he did not have what the man *wanted*, however, Peter was able to give the man what he *needed*. Read through their encounter below and the answer the questions that follow.

[1] One day Peter and John were going up to the temple at the time of prayer—at three in the afternoon. [2] Now a man who was lame from birth was being carried to the temple gate called Beautiful, where he was put every day to beg from those going into the temple courts. [3] When he saw Peter and John about to enter, he asked them for money. [4] Peter looked straight at him, as did John. Then Peter said, "Look at us!" [5] So the man gave them his attention, expecting to get something from them.

[6] Then Peter said, "Silver or gold I do not have, but what I do have I

give you. In the name of Jesus Christ of Nazareth, walk." [7] Taking him by the right hand, he helped him up, and instantly the man's feet and ankles became strong. [8] He jumped to his feet and began to walk. Then he went with them into the temple courts, walking and jumping, and praising God. [9] When all the people saw him walking and praising God, [10] they recognized him as the same man who used to sit begging at the temple gate called Beautiful, and they were filled with wonder and amazement at what had happened to him.

—Acts 3:1–10

■ Notice that instead of dodging the lame man's attention, Peter said, "Look at us!" Why did Peter embrace this opportunity when he knew he didn't have what the man expected?

■ How often are you inclined to give your team as well as those you serve what you think they expect rather than what you know they need? How often does pleasing others interfere with your ability to innovate?

- When have you experienced God rewarding your willingness to innovate? How did your attitude shift as you realized he had provided you with everything you really needed?

- What's a current limitation that has frustrated your team's ability to move forward in ministry? How might God be guiding you to go forward in a new direction?

They Got *It*

The old adage about necessity being the mother of invention holds true in ministry as well. So often, when you're determined to find a way forward, you will. The trick is surrendering your usual ways of seeing and doing things. By clearing space for your imagination to work, you open up new possibilities that aren't normal or expected but may, in fact, be better. When you surrender your will to God's will, you discover that he has already provided a way where you once thought it was impossible.

We see this kind of inspired innovation in a dramatic encounter Jesus had with a paralyzed man. As his reputation for healing began to spread, Jesus found that many people sought his help in order to be free of the physical limitations,

illnesses, and diseases that held them. Sometimes, however, other obstacles prevented them from the opportunity to experience the Great Physician's healing touch. And in the case of the encounter below, such occasions allowed innovation to shine brightest. Read through the following scene and then answer the questions that follow.

[17] One day Jesus was teaching, and Pharisees and teachers of the law were sitting there. They had come from every village of Galilee and from Judea and Jerusalem. And the power of the Lord was with Jesus to heal the sick. [18] Some men came carrying a paralyzed man on a mat and tried to take him into the house to lay him before Jesus. [19] When they could not find a way to do this because of the crowd, they went up on the roof and lowered him on his mat through the tiles into the middle of the crowd, right in front of Jesus.

[20] When Jesus saw their faith, he said, "Friend, your sins are forgiven."

[21] The Pharisees and the teachers of the law began thinking to themselves, "Who is this fellow who speaks blasphemy? Who can forgive sins but God alone?"

[22] Jesus knew what they were thinking and asked, "Why are you thinking these things in your hearts? [23] Which is easier: to say, 'Your sins are forgiven,' or to say, 'Get up and walk'? [24] But I want you to know that the Son of Man has authority on earth to forgive sins." So he said to the paralyzed man, "I tell you, get up, take your mat and go home." [25] Immediately he stood up in front of them, took what he had been lying on and went home praising God. [26] Everyone was amazed and gave praise to God. They were filled with awe and said, "We have seen remarkable things today."

—Luke 5:17–26

_____

■ The paralyzed man's friends had brought him too far not to meet Jesus, so they found a way where there wasn't one—by turning a roof into a door! When have you been forced to find another way forward because an unexpected obstacle blocked your usual path?

■ Like Peter and John with the lame man they encountered (Acts 3), how did Jesus use this opportunity to give the paralyzed man more than he hoped to receive?

■ Why does Jesus ask the onlookers which is easier, to heal a paralyzed man or to forgive his sins? What point was Christ making in the moment?

■ When has your team innovated a solution only to discover it required even more innovation than you first realized? How does an innovative mindset allow you to experience more of God's power?

_____

Factoring *It* In

Many leaders make excuses for not trying something new. It's easy to maintain status quo by claiming you don't have creative people or enough resources to fulfill a ministry objective. Eventually, though, God often turns our excuses into opportunities to strengthen our faith. Like all the other ingredients required to get *it* and keep it, innovation requires regular practice. Learning to see problems, obstacles, and limitations as opportunities is foundational to innovative solutions.

Remember, when it comes to innovation:

- Leaders with *it* do more than just think of new ideas; they actually do the new ideas.
- Innovation is more about mindset than money.
- God often guides by what he *doesn't* provide.
- Problems are opportunities in disguise.
- A Problem to Solve + Increasing Passion + Limited Resources = Exponential Innovation
- You have everything you need to do what God wants you to do.
- Innovative leaders do anything short of sin to reach the lost.
- "All it takes is one idea to solve an impossible problem" (Robert Schuller).
- Innovation is awesome, but don't put your faith in it. Keep your faith in Christ.

■ What are the current limitations you and your team face? How has God guided you by what he hasn't provided?

PART 2: WHAT CONTRIBUTES TO *IT?*

- What are three problems, blocked goals, or seemingly impossible dreams that your team could tackle right now through innovation?

Problem #1

Problem #2

Problem #3

- When was the last time you and your team attempted something that didn't work out as planned? What can you learn to do differently from this experience?

- What experiences, conversations, and events have shaped your ability to innovate? Consider those that have had a negative, inhibitive impact as well as those that resulted in a positive, can-do attitude.

Negative Experiences   Positive Experiences

Putting *It* into Action

As you can see, innovation is a mindset more than a method. Your willingness to remain open and creative when problems occur, as they always do, often determines your ability to innovate successfully. In many cases innovation is underutilized in ministry. Some people always focus only on what they've seen and experienced before. Others are limited by criticism and embarrassment from past failures. A few simply allow their fear of failure to restrain their imagination.

In order to lead like it matters, however, your team must welcome innovation as essential to the ministry God has called you to do. Remember, he has already given you everything you need. He wouldn't guide you to minister the way you're called if he hadn't already equipped and empowered you. What God hasn't provided often reveals how to proceed as much as what he does provide.

Spend a few minutes in prayer and ask the Holy Spirit to free your thinking and to inspire your imagination. Then answer the following questions before implementing what used to seem impossible.

_____

- If you knew you couldn't fail, what would you want your team to attempt? Why? What's been holding you back from even trying so far?

- What off-the-wall idea or crazy notion has been simmering inside you? Is there something new God is calling you to do that may seem strange or uncomfortable at first but ultimately change lives and advance his kingdom?

- Based on your responses to the two previous questions, identify one obstacle, problem, or limitation currently holding back your ministry. As concisely and accurately as possible, write it below:

■ Now, set your phone or another timer for five minutes and get ready to brainstorm. Turn off the practical, critical, logical voices inside that usually edit, censor, and prevent you from suggesting solutions. Rule nothing out because everything has potential. Nothing is silly, impossible, or a stupid idea. Okay, get ready, get set, and go!

———————————————

Now that you've brainstormed, look over your ideas. Choose three of them to share with your team this week. Use this same exercise with them in order to brainstorm even more potential innovations. Spend some time praying as a team before choosing one of these innovations to implement.

PRINCIPLE #5

Willingness to Fall Short

No one enjoys failing, but when those with **it**
fail, they think in terms of failing forward.

Faith in a big God will lead you to take some big risks.

But risks are, well, *risky*. You could fail. Fall flat on your face. Embarrass yourself and the team or even the whole church. But here's the thing: *You cannot play it safe and please God!*

The fifth leadership principle for a church that has *it* and lasts is a willingness to fall short. If you look at any church that has *it*, you will see a church that's failed after many faith-filled attempts. Most of them have failed *often*. These churches are generally led by aggressive, do-what-it-takes, thick-skinned people who are willing to make mistakes. They know that without faith it is impossible to please God. They understand that faith often requires risk.

In contrast, the ministries without *it* are usually the ones playing it safe, doing only what is sure to succeed. They retreat in fear, never having the faith to walk into something new and unknown. As counterintuitive as it sounds, failing can often help a ministry experience *it*. Being overly cautious can kill *it*. On the surface, these ideas don't seem to make sense. But they're true.

Aggressive leaders with *it* are often dreaming, experimenting, and testing the limits. They don't know what can't be done and are willing to try things others think impossible. Because they know they are more than conquerors through him who loves us, these passionate spiritual entrepreneurs take risks. They are not always successful, failing often. But when they do fail, they tend to rebound quickly. Temporary failures are often followed by lasting success. They try, fail, learn, adjust, and try again.

After a series of accidental learning experiences, these hard-hitting leaders often stumble onto innovative ministry ideas they never would have discovered without taking a big risk. They take risks not only because they may succeed, but also because when they fail, they *fail forward.*

In the church world, it's easy to stay where you enjoy the greatest success. You think, *Why take unnecessary risks when this is working so well?* But here's the thing: *Ministry is inherently risky!* You'll likely make some mistakes, fail, and struggle. That's scary, so most stick with what they know. They stay in their comfort zone, where they feel like they know what to do, what to expect, and how to keep *it.*

Only, playing it safe usually leads to losing *it.*

To keep *it,* you will have to go through some failures—probably a lot of them. Disheartened by setbacks and frustrated by failures, you understandably may pull back and resist risking much. You may even begin avoiding risks altogether. Instead, you slide back into a place of mastery, where you feel validated and safe. Only, when you stop risking, you stop growing. And when you stop growing, you lose *it.*

Because the leaders with *it* push through the failures. They know setbacks can be setups for better things to come. They study their failures and learn from them. No one enjoys failing, but when those with *it* fail, they think in terms of failing forward.

Those who have *it* usually grow to understand: *Failure is a necessary part of success.* While great leaders are generally innovative, they are also often scared.

But that doesn't stop them. They know the path to your greatest potential is often straight through your greatest fear. Those who swing hard will strike out often. But they will also knock some out of the park.

As you seek God and he ignites *it* in your heart, let him lead you to the edge of safety, comfort, and mastery. Let him lead you out of your comfort zone and into something that stretches your faith. Something that causes you to rely on him more than ever. Maybe he already has. If God hasn't yet, he will soon. And when that happens, the enemy will see an opportunity to activate fear.

Why? Because one of the devil's greatest tools is fear.

But once you fear something and push through it, you realize you can do what's required despite feeling afraid. You discover that God is there with you no matter what happens. You don't have to let fear paralyze you from moving forward.

The same is true with failure. Once you fail and realize that failing is not the end of the world, you're not as afraid to fail again. You learn something to apply to your next innovation. You realize how God is equipping you for something new. You glimpse where he wants to lead you next.

If you don't have *it*, maybe you need to try something new—and fail at it. Because if you're not failing, then you're not dreaming. When you're not dreaming, you stop learning and growing. God has given you the gift of the freedom to fail forward.

Those who have *it* fail often.

God's Word Has *It*

If you're waiting for your venture to have guaranteed success, you will probably be waiting for the rest of your life. Sometimes the fruit of your steps of faith is measured not so much by what God does *through* you as by what God does *in* you. Sometimes he may want you to risk more in order to trust him more.

God may also want you to risk—even if you fail—in order to cultivate the

abilities, gifts, and talents that he has placed in you. Because the greater failure is never to have risked at all. At least, that conclusion emerges from a familiar parable that Jesus shared with his followers. In this parable a master, just before going away, entrusts his wealth to his three servants. When he returns, his response to what they did with what he had entrusted to them is very revealing.

Read through this parable below and then answer the questions that follow.

[14] "Again, it will be like a man going on a journey, who called his servants and entrusted his wealth to them. [15] To one he gave five bags of gold, to another two bags, and to another one bag, each according to his ability. Then he went on his journey. [16] The man who had received five bags of gold went at once and put his money to work and gained five bags more. [17] So also, the one with two bags of gold gained two more. [18] But the man who had received one bag went off, dug a hole in the ground and hid his master's money.

[19] "After a long time the master of those servants returned and settled accounts with them. [20] The man who had received five bags of gold brought the other five. 'Master,' he said, 'you entrusted me with five bags of gold. See, I have gained five more.'

[21] "His master replied, 'Well done, good and faithful servant! You have been faithful with a few things; I will put you in charge of many things. Come and share your master's happiness!'

[22] "The man with two bags of gold also came. 'Master,' he said, 'you entrusted me with two bags of gold; see, I have gained two more.'

[23] "His master replied, 'Well done, good and faithful servant! You have been faithful with a few things; I will put you in charge of many things. Come and share your master's happiness!'

[24] "Then the man who had received one bag of gold came. 'Master,' he

said, 'I knew that you are a hard man, harvesting where you have not sown and gathering where you have not scattered seed. [25] So I was afraid and went out and hid your gold in the ground. See, here is what belongs to you.'

[26] "His master replied, 'You wicked, lazy servant! So you knew that I harvest where I have not sown and gather where I have not scattered seed? [27] Well then, you should have put my money on deposit with the bankers, so that when I returned I would have received it back with interest.

[28] "'So take the bag of gold from him and give it to the one who has ten bags. [29] For whoever has will be given more, and they will have an abundance. Whoever does not have, even what they have will be taken from them. [30] And throw that worthless servant outside, into the darkness, where there will be weeping and gnashing of teeth.'"

—Matthew 25:14–30

- Based on this parable, how does the master define what it means for his servants to be "faithful"? Is this how you usually define faithful?

- What fear prevents the third servant from investing his master's wealth? What does his master's response reveal about God's expectations for what he's entrusted to you?

- When has fear prevented you from taking a risk you believed God wanted you to take? What were you afraid might happen, your worst-case scenario, if you took this risk?

- When have you taken a risk you know was worth taking only to see it fail? Looking back, how has God used this experience to help you fail forward?

They Got *It*

Perhaps there's no better case study in the Bible for failing forward than Peter. Time and time again, his education consisted of trying, failing, learning, adjusting, and then trying again. One minute he's brandishing a blade at a soldier during Jesus' arrest in Gethsemane, and then only a few hours later, Peter denies even knowing who Jesus is—not once but three times, just as Christ had warned Peter at the disciples' final meal together.

But Peter's devotion to Jesus was constant despite his failings. And his "failing forward" most likely contributed to God's decision to choose Peter as the guest speaker on the day of Pentecost. Can you imagine anyone preaching with more passion than the guy who was forgiven after denying Jesus three different times?

Peter failed often. He learned from his failures. Then he told people to repent

of their sins and call on Jesus, and he led three thousand people to Christ and helped birth the church. Peter failed often. But he still had *it*.

One incident illustrates Peter's willingness to risk and demonstrates both his reward and the subsequent failure of allowing his fears to sink his courage. When you lead on the edge, you learn to face your fears and conquer them, only to have new ones emerge. You learn that the illusion of security evaporates with your last accomplishment. But like Peter, you'll recognize you're safer when you're out of the boat and *with Jesus* than if your fears keep you in the boat.

Read through this memorable scene below and imagine you're in Peter's place. Use the questions that follow to help you think through how God is calling you to step out of the boat.

²² Immediately Jesus made the disciples get into the boat and go on ahead of him to the other side, while he dismissed the crowd. ²³ After he had dismissed them, he went up on a mountainside by himself to pray. Later that night, he was there alone, ²⁴ and the boat was already a considerable distance from land, buffeted by the waves because the wind was against it.

²⁵ Shortly before dawn Jesus went out to them, walking on the lake. ²⁶ When the disciples saw him walking on the lake, they were terrified. "It's a ghost," they said, and cried out in fear.

²⁷ But Jesus immediately said to them: "Take courage! It is I. Don't be afraid."

²⁸ "Lord, if it's you," Peter replied, "tell me to come to you on the water."

²⁹ "Come," he said.

Then Peter got down out of the boat, walked on the water and came toward Jesus. ³⁰ But when he saw the wind, he was afraid and, beginning to sink, cried out, "Lord, save me!"

[31] Immediately Jesus reached out his hand and caught him. "You of little faith," he said, "why did you doubt?"

[32] And when they climbed into the boat, the wind died down. [33] Then those who were in the boat worshiped him, saying, "Truly you are the Son of God."

—Matthew 14:22–33

- The disciples became frightened because they didn't immediately recognize Jesus. When have you been afraid because you couldn't tell if God was calling you to take a risk?

- When have you risked big and experienced the thrill of walking on water? What happened after the thrill wore off?

- When have you taken your eyes away from Jesus and lost sight of your goal? What did you learn from this experience?

■ What risks are you sensing God wants you to take as you step out of the boat of safety? What gives you courage to overcome your fears as you do what you have never done before?

Factoring *It* In

There's no way around it.

You will have to continue to take risks to get *it* and keep it. That means you have to make a choice. For most leaders, their greatest fear is often failure. But their greatest pain is regret. That is why you will have to make some conscious, faith-filled choices. You can avoid risks, minimize the downside, and continue to play it safe. But if you choose this path, you also give up the upside and you will never know what might have been if you had developed the faith to try. Even if you've never taken many risks—especially if you've never taken many risks—it may be time to go for it.

Because, simply put, in order to continue to have *it*, you will have to face your fears or you will likely end up with regrets.

So get out of the boat. Face your fears. Fail. Learn. Adjust. Try again.

And watch God do more than you can imagine!

Remember, when it comes to falling short:

- Failure is not an option. It is a *necessity*.
- If you're not failing, you've stopped dreaming. You'll eventually stop learning and you will stop growing. Those who have *it* fail often.

- It is impossible to please God without faith, which means we have to risk.
- Sometimes the fruit of your steps of faith is measured not so much by what God does through you as by what God does in you.
- Failure is often the tuition for success (adapted from Walter Brunell).
- Debrief after you fail so it becomes a learning experience.
- If you're breathing, God's not finished with you.
- If you've failed, you have learned something others haven't and are in the perfect position to try again and succeed.
- Great leaders learn the art of failing forward.
- The pain of regret is often greater than the pain of failure. So get out of the boat.

■ What do you consider your biggest failure in ministry, something you attempted that resulted in disappointing results? What did you take away from this experience—to risk more next time, or to avoid risk when possible?

■ What's your biggest regret regarding a risk you didn't take but now wish you had? How has your perspective changed since that time when you chose not to risk?

■ What's been your greatest leap of faith since you started in this ministry? In other words, when have you stepped out in faith way beyond your own ability and comfort and trusted God for the results?

■ Other than Jesus, whose example in the Bible gives you strength, courage, and determination to overcome your fears? Do you relate to Peter, with his many ups and downs? Or identify more with someone like Paul, who had a dramatic before-and-after encounter with Christ?

Putting *It* into Action

In Jesus' parable of the servants' investments (Matthew 25; Luke 19), those who risked saw an increase and received their master's favor. The one who played it safe lost it all. The point of the parable seems to be that in order to grow—your resources, your abilities, your ministry—you must risk. Otherwise, when you choose not to risk, you bury yourself and your future. Simply put, "Risk your life and get more than you ever dreamed of. Play it safe and end up holding the bag" (Luke 19:26 MSG).

Remember, when you take a step of faith, the fear of failure might creep up on you, as it does with most people. *What if this doesn't work? What will people think?*

What if this bombs? But so what? If you believe God is calling you to do something, then feel the fear and do it anyway.

Let God turn the fear into faith. Instead of becoming a hesitant leader, ask God to make you bold and aggressive. Ask him to help you lead like it matters!

———————————————————

■ What dream have you buried because you were afraid of failing? What burden has God given you that you've put aside? Pray and ask God if it's time to dig it up, pull it out, and risk big.

■ Out of the following risks, which ones have you taken, regardless of the outcome? Place a check mark next to all that apply.

___ Add a new location

___ An additional mission

___ A new community outreach

___ A nontraditional service

___ An online ministry

___ Additional technology (an app, streaming, etc.)

___ Hiring more staff

___ Hiring someone who seems unqualified or inexperienced on paper

___ Unconventional marketing or promotional tactics

___ Shutting down a struggling ministry

___ Reallocating resources

___ Something else

■ Now which of these risks would you like to try? Which seem like risks God is calling you to take? Go back through the list and place a star next to all these items.

■ Go back and read your answer to the following questions in "Putting *It* into Action" from Session 4. Now, reconsidering the risk involved and how God is leading you after Session 5, how would you answer it?

■ "If you knew you couldn't fail, what would you want your team to attempt? Why? What's been holding you back from even trying so far?"

_____

PRINCIPLE #6

Hearts Focused Outward

Do whatever it takes to make your ministry a place
that welcomes those who don't know Christ.

If your ministry doesn't have *it* and you want it, then shifting to an outward, evangelistic focus is essential. Examine a church that leads like it matters, and you'll find a virtual obsession with reaching those who don't know Christ. They don't add to their mission. Helping people find new life *is* their mission. A passion to share Christ consumes them in a beautiful way.

Churches without *it* can be so tight, so bonded, so close—to each other—that they unintentionally overlook those they don't know. They are welcoming, warm, and hospitable—to their own. But if you are from the outside or your clothes look different or you have tattoos, you might be ignored or even shunned.

Ministries with *it*, however, remember that Jesus came for outsiders. He came for those who were lost. Broken. Hurting. Disenfranchised. Alone. Overlooked. Poor. Jesus came for those whom religion rejected.

Many churches unknowingly focus inwardly, forgetting those who need Jesus the most. These churches are like a hospital that no longer accepts patients. Or a soup kitchen that no longer feeds hungry people. Those without it are often filled

with very sincere, Bible-believing Christians. Unfortunately, they're simply more concerned about themselves than about people who are not yet Christians and don't yet believe the Bible. They love the comfort of their Christian bubble so much they're not willing to follow Jesus as he tries to lead them to become friends with sinners so they can seek and save the lost.

But loving people—all people—is not optional. Loving others is *essential*. The Bible is clear: If you love God, you should love people. If you do not love people, you do not love God. "Anyone who loves is a child of God and knows God. But anyone who does not love does not know God, for God is love. . . . If we don't love people we can see, how can we love God, whom we cannot see?" (1 John 4:7–8, 20 NLT).

We're quite comfortable loving those who are like us, but we're also called to love those who aren't like us, and we are especially called to love those who are far from God.

But honestly, many so-called Christians don't. You don't have to look far to find churches full of people who are insulating themselves from the world, hunkering down, avoiding popular movies and secular music. These inward-looking religious types keep their distance from anyone who drinks beer, cusses after a bad golf swing, smokes anything, has a tattoo, listens to rap music, or wears jeans with holes in them. They judge people who voted differently. They criticize rock stars. They stay away from those with a different color of skin. They stare disapprovingly at purple hair and mohawks. They're afraid of bars, rock concerts, and some social media sites.

Too many believers are avoiding "that kind" of person.

Somehow, they've forgotten Jesus came for that kind of person.

Churches that have *it* care for each other *and* for people who are far from God. Churches and ministries without *it* care more about the sheep inside the fold than the goats outside of the church. But think for a moment. What caused the good shepherd to leave the ninety-nine to pursue the one that was lost? Love. What

made the father stand on the front porch, waiting, hoping, and praying that his lost son would return home? Love.

What drove our heavenly Father from heaven to earth? There's no doubt about his motivation: "For God so *loved* the world that he gave his one and only Son, that whoever believes in him shall not perish but have eternal life" (John 3:16, emphasis added). What empowered Jesus to suffer mercilessly, to shed his innocent blood, and to willingly offer his life? Love made him do it.

If you are a leader of your ministry or organization, you need to recognize that, for better or for worse, it reflects you. If you don't care about those far from God, the people you lead are not likely to care either.

You may not even realize the message you're sending to those outside the church. Many churches unintentionally turn their backs on those who need Jesus most. We focus inward. We do our Bible studies. We listen to our favorite Christian music. We watch our Christian shows. We speak our Christian jargon. To those outside our bubble, the message seems clear: You don't belong here.

Churches that have *it* are filled with people who sincerely desire to reach the lost. They won't let any excuses stop them.

Love overcomes the obstacles.

God's Word Has *It*

Struggling to love others, especially those who appear different from us, is nothing new. In fact, when confronted by an expert in the law, Jesus made it clear that loving our neighbors as ourselves is second only to loving God with our entire being. The lawyer followed up with another question, perhaps hoping for a loophole. But then Jesus shared a parable that left little room to dodge loving all people—even those who aren't like us.

Read through the passage below and underline any words or phrases that jump out at you. Then answer the questions that follow.

²⁵ On one occasion an expert in the law stood up to test Jesus. "Teacher," he asked, "what must I do to inherit eternal life?"

²⁶ "What is written in the Law?" he replied. "How do you read it?"

²⁷ He answered, "'Love the Lord your God with all your heart and with all your soul and with all your strength and with all your mind'; and, 'Love your neighbor as yourself.'"

²⁸ "You have answered correctly," Jesus replied. "Do this and you will live."

²⁹ But he wanted to justify himself, so he asked Jesus, "And who is my neighbor?"

³⁰ In reply Jesus said: "A man was going down from Jerusalem to Jericho, when he was attacked by robbers. They stripped him of his clothes, beat him and went away, leaving him half dead. ³¹ A priest happened to be going down the same road, and when he saw the man, he passed by on the other side. ³² So too, a Levite, when he came to the place and saw him, passed by on the other side. ³³ But a Samaritan, as he traveled, came where the man was; and when he saw him, he took pity on him. ³⁴ He went to him and bandaged his wounds, pouring on oil and wine. Then he put the man on his own donkey, brought him to an inn and took care of him. ³⁵ The next day he took out two denarii and gave them to the innkeeper. 'Look after him,' he said, 'and when I return, I will reimburse you for any extra expense you may have.'

³⁶ "Which of these three do you think was a neighbor to the man who fell into the hands of robbers?"

³⁷ The expert in the law replied, "The one who had mercy on him."

Jesus told him, "Go and do likewise."

—Luke 10:25–37

- Notice we're told the lawyer's motive—"He wanted to justify himself"—for asking Jesus who should be considered his neighbor. What are some ways that we justify ourselves for not loving others who are outside the church?

- How have you handled people on your team or in your church who tend to be like the lawyer in this parable, wanting to nail down who they should love? How have you handled your own biases toward others?

- When Jesus asked the expert on law who had been a neighbor to the robbery victim, he answered, "The one who had mercy on him." What does it mean for you and your ministry to have mercy on those who are outsiders?

■ What are some ways your church currently seeks to love and serve those who don't know Jesus? What are some new ways you can go about showing God's love to those outside your congregation?

They Got *It*

Most Christians don't wake up one day and decide, "I really don't care about the lost anymore." Instead, this kind of attitude creeps in over time. After being a Christian for a few years, you may not have a ton in common with non-Christians, so it's tough to develop quality relationships. That's why you have to be deliberate about never losing sight of the lost. If you're struggling with this tendency, ask God to break your heart for those without Christ.

Before long, God will send you someone—maybe many someones—whom you will grow to care about. Your love for them will increase. When that happens, you get *it*, and *it's* almost impossible to turn off. Your passion to pray grows. You start looking for opportunities to shift conversations toward spiritual things. You become ever aware that you are representing Christ. When you have *it*, people tend to want it. Your passion for Jesus and his mission becomes contagious.

As you seek out those who don't know the Lord, be prepared to confront your own biases and prejudices. Our human tendency to draw conclusions about one another is a natural result of social interactions. But sometimes we focus on the ways others are different from us rather than how we are all the same. Remember, God looks at the heart while we tend to look at the outside of a person.

The apostle Paul experienced this kind of rocky reception from the Christian community right after he became a believer, when he was still known as Saul. Read through the following passage and then answer the questions that follow.

> [19] Saul spent several days with the disciples in Damascus. [20] At once he began to preach in the synagogues that Jesus is the Son of God. [21] All those who heard him were astonished and asked, "Isn't he the man who raised havoc in Jerusalem among those who call on this name? And hasn't he come here to take them as prisoners to the chief priests?" [22] Yet Saul grew more and more powerful and baffled the Jews living in Damascus by proving that Jesus is the Messiah.
>
> [23] After many days had gone by, there was a conspiracy among the Jews to kill him, [24] but Saul learned of their plan. Day and night they kept close watch on the city gates in order to kill him. [25] But his followers took him by night and lowered him in a basket through an opening in the wall.
>
> [26] When he came to Jerusalem, he tried to join the disciples, but they were all afraid of him, not believing that he really was a disciple. [27] But Barnabas took him and brought him to the apostles. He told them how Saul on his journey had seen the Lord and that the Lord had spoken to him, and how in Damascus he had preached fearlessly in the name of Jesus. [28] So Saul stayed with them and moved about freely in Jerusalem, speaking boldly in the name of the Lord. [29] He talked and debated with the Hellenistic Jews, but they tried to kill him. [30] When the believers learned of this, they took him down to Caesarea and sent him off to Tarsus.

—Acts 9:19–30

■ How had Saul/Paul's previous actions and reputation biased other believers against him? What was required for them to accept him into their community?

■ Notice that when Paul tried to join the other followers of Jesus, they were afraid of him. How does fear often keep us from pursuing others who are different from us? What are we usually afraid of?

■ What do you think Barnabas saw in Paul that caused him to trust Paul's story and welcome him into the group? What do you look for in others in order to continue pursuing them with God's love?

■ How has God used your past experiences before becoming a Christian to relate to nonbelievers? What common interests and experiences help you connect with those outside your ministry?

Factoring *It* In

To see people come to Christ in your ministry, you'll need to have those who don't know him present. This may seem obvious, but you'd be surprised how often it's overlooked. If people far from God aren't coming to your church, you'll want to identify why. Some reasons could include:

- Your church members don't have relationships with the lost.
- Your people are too embarrassed to bring their friends to your church.
- Your building, your services, or the people in your church are subtly communicating "stay away."

Consider how to do whatever it takes to make your ministry a place that welcomes those who don't know Christ.

Another reason your pursuit of those who need Jesus may be struggling is how the gospel is presented. Some churches preach a message that might be straight from the Bible and what some would call "deep," but they make the assumption that everyone listening is already a Christian. They teach the believer and forget that so many of their listeners have not yet crossed the line of faith. Others are simply "How to have a better life" type of messages. That may be helpful, but don't

expect people to be saved. If messages contain more self-help than gospel, people will not hear or embrace the good news.

When Jesus came to earth, he was full of both *grace* and *truth* (see John 1:14). Therefore, we should consider how to welcome people with our comfortable environment and friendliness *and* confront them *lovingly* with truth. If someone doesn't see themselves as a sinner, they will never see their need for a Savior.

Finally, you need real faith. If you don't *really* believe in the power of Christ to change a life, people will know it. The opposite is true as well. If you believe with every fiber in your being that Christ can and will instantly transform a life through the power of his grace, people will sense it, feel it, and will often come to believe it as well.

When you consider the role of evangelism in your ministry, remember:

- When we love deeply, love makes us do things we wouldn't otherwise do.
- To have *it*, we have to care about those who are far from God. Many people don't.
- We need to recognize that our friends desperately need Jesus.
- When our churches look inward instead of outward, we're basically saying to nonbelievers, "We don't care if you go to hell."
- Outreach is a team event, and we each have a part to play.
- Be careful not to blame yourself if someone rejects Christ. If you do, you might be tempted to take credit when someone accepts him.
- Love overcomes any obstacle. We need to be willing to do whatever it takes to reach people who are far from God.
- We need to have the faith to clearly share the gospel story and expect people to respond.

- What's the main way your church pursues those who don't know Jesus? How well has this worked based on the number of those who become new believers?

- When was the last time you've had a lost person in your home? How many meaningful conversations did you have with non-Christians this week?

- When was the last time you talked about your faith with someone far from God? Who are the lost individuals weighing on your heart?

- Who are the nonbelievers you prayed for today? How often does your team hold a prayer meeting just to focus on praying for reaching the lost?

Putting *It* into Action

A great evangelistic ministry should offer both grace and truth, both comfort and confrontation. Most churches tend to tilt toward one more than the other. They either have great facilities, amazing worship, warm welcomes, and tasty snacks or they focus more on outreaches, missions, and cold-call evangelism. In order to get *it*, you usually have to find a way to include both.

If you can make your environment comfortable for the person externally and confrontational and convicting for them internally, they often see their need and invite Jesus into their lives. From there, it's about relationships and how they can learn, grow, and share the same message of grace with other people they know who need it just as much as they did.

Toward this goal of striking a balance between comfort and confrontation, think through the way your ministry does things. Use the following questions to help your assessment as you consider how you might need to improve one or both in order to reach more people with the good news of Jesus Christ.

■ On a scale of 1 to 10, with 1 being "not comfortable at all" and 10 being "as comfortable as possible," how do you think nonbelieving visitors would rate your church? Why?

- Now consider the same thing except focused on "confrontation." On a scale of 1 to 10, how clearly would outsiders visiting your church hear that they need Jesus?

- What is the current evangelistic temperature of your church—warmer or colder toward the lost? Are you willing to lose some people from your church to reach those without Christ?

- Is your church focused more outward or inward? What needs to change right away in order to engage with more people who need Jesus? Commit to make one improvement today in how your church balances comfort with confrontation.

———————————————

PRINCIPLE #7

Kingdom-Mindedness

*If you're looking to find more of **it** in your ministry,*
maybe you should look for more ways to give
*whatever part of **it** you have to others.*

Leaders and ministries that have *it* work together for a cause bigger than anything their respective churches are doing. They know that Christ is at the center of all we do no matter who's doing it. They share a vision for advancing the kingdom of heaven here on earth. Being kingdom-minded is the seventh and final *it*-ingredient for leaders to cultivate.

Simply put, being kingdom-minded means focusing more on God's kingdom than your little corner of it. Rather than being competitive, possessive, and territorial, a kingdom-minded ministry is generous, openhanded, and collaborative.

A kingdom-minded ministry is one whose leaders care more about what God is doing everywhere than what God is doing right here. Kingdom-minded leaders know it's not just about their own ministry. A kingdom-minded ministry is generous and eager to partner with others to get more done for the glory of God.

It's hard to have *it* without desiring for other ministries to succeed. When you

have *it*, you know that it doesn't belong to you. *It* belongs to God. He gives it. And since it is his and not yours, you're grateful to have it and willing to share it.

On the other hand, the more possessive and competitive we are, the more divided we become. But ministry is not a competition. It's not a reality TV show in which you're about to be voted off, sent home, or told you can't serve. Remember, the ways you minister are part of something bigger God is doing, not only in your own church, but throughout your area, your region, your country, and your world.

Which is another way of saying it's not about your numbers, whether they be attendance, dollars, or whatever you're counting. *It* is not about *your* student ministry, *your* children's ministry, *your* YouTube presence, *your* church app, *your* new logo or website. And *it* is certainly not about your name. *It* is about Jesus. There's no other name under heaven by which we can be saved and so no other name that *really* matters. *It's* all about him.

We say our church or ministry is not about us. But for many of us, "us" is all we can talk or think about. Not only is our kingdom not of this world, but to build our own is surely one of the grossest sins. But what if we prayed, *God, make me more generous. Expand my heart for others. Make me truly a kingdom-minded leader.*

As pastors and Christian leaders, we should be thrilled when other ministries succeed. You may think you are, but have you noticed how much easier it is to be pumped for those who are growing in *another* town? *Yeah, God! I'm thrilled their ministry in that other state is growing!* But if they're in *my* town, it's easy to feel threatened or competitive. *What? The church down the street is doing well? They must be preaching a feel-good message.*

That attitude is wrong.

It's not only wrong—it's dangerous.

God usually won't let a ministry keep *it* for long if they won't give it away. Keeping it to yourself is a sure way to kill it. Ministries that don't have much of *it* often work hard to guard what little of it they do have. What's funny about *it* is the

more you try to hoard it, the less of it you tend to have. The more you're willing to give it away, the more of it God seems to give.

Think what believers could do if we all partnered together. Instead of being jealous, territorial, or easily threatened, what if we became extravagantly generous with our resources, ideas, and ministries?

Be generous with *it*! Find a church that could benefit from what you're doing and adopt them. Whatever you can do, do it. As church leaders, we should continually ask, "What do we have that could benefit the kingdom?" God has given you something valuable, and he doesn't want you burying it—he wants you investing it for his kingdom.

Whenever God blesses your ministry, find a way to partner with others. Ask yourself what you can give away. Whatever he gives you, share it.

God's Word Has *It*

Despite our human tendency to want to possess, own, and compete, God's Word urges us to surrender, share, and give generously. The world around us says to be self-sufficient, independent, and at the front of the pack. But the Bible says to depend on God, serve one another, and that the last shall be first. So remember to focus on the truth of what God says the church should be rather than what everyone around you might want it to be.

Because when we lose focus on sharing the gospel and being the hands and feet of Jesus, it's easy for a church to become human-based instead of God-based. Some churches feel like elite country clubs where only certain people are welcomed and accepted. Others feel more like a rec center, filled with activities and events but without a cohesive focus on Jesus. Some churches seem more like school and a kids' center while others are more like group counseling at a therapist's office.

As you seek to be a more kingdom-minded leader, it's essential to remain

grounded in God's Word—otherwise, your church can easily drift and morph into something it's not supposed to be. With this goal in mind, read through the familiar passage below and consider how it can help you clarify and sharpen your ministry's kingdom focus.

¹ If I speak in the tongues of men or of angels, but do not have love, I am only a resounding gong or a clanging cymbal. ² If I have the gift of prophecy and can fathom all mysteries and all knowledge, and if I have a faith that can move mountains, but do not have love, I am nothing. ³ If I give all I possess to the poor and give over my body to hardship that I may boast, but do not have love, I gain nothing.

⁴ Love is patient, love is kind. It does not envy, it does not boast, it is not proud. ⁵ It does not dishonor others, it is not self-seeking, it is not easily angered, it keeps no record of wrongs. ⁶ Love does not delight in evil but rejoices with the truth. ⁷ It always protects, always trusts, always hopes, always perseveres.

⁸ Love never fails. But where there are prophecies, they will cease; where there are tongues, they will be stilled; where there is knowledge, it will pass away. ⁹ For we know in part and we prophesy in part, ¹⁰ but when completeness comes, what is in part disappears. ¹¹ When I was a child, I talked like a child, I thought like a child, I reasoned like a child. When I became a man, I put the ways of childhood behind me. ¹² For now we see only a reflection as in a mirror; then we shall see face to face. Now I know in part; then I shall know fully, even as I am fully known.

¹³ And now these three remain: faith, hope and love. But the greatest of these is love.

—1 Corinthians 13:1–13

- This passage often gets applied to couples, wedding vows, and relationships, but Paul was actually addressing the early church in the city of Corinth. With this in mind, make a brief list of all the qualities a kingdom-based church should include according to Paul.

- How does being anchored by love keep your church from losing sight of God's kingdom?

- When have you seen your ministry style become competitive, possessive, or territorial? What impact did it have on your team and those you serve?

- How have you seen putting God's kingdom first improve your church's ability to fulfill its mission as the body of Christ?

They Got *It*

A self-centered and competitive ministry generally loses *it*. A kingdom-minded ministry seems to attract it. As you become more generous, God will likely increase your impact and reach. As your influence expands, you will likely attract stronger leaders, pastors, and creative ministers. You'll reach more people for Christ and meet the needs of more in your community.

The more of *it* we give away, the more of *it* God gives back. Isn't that exactly what Jesus promised in Luke 6:38? "Give, and it will be given to you. A good measure, pressed down, shaken together and running over, will be poured into your lap. For with the measure you use, it will be measured to you."

Holding on to what God wants us to give away never ends well. When we try to keep what God has given us for ourselves, we almost always lose it. If we try to profit from what God wants us to give away, the results can be disastrous. We get caught in the greed trap, and we're never satisfied. One new building leads to a second one, one new ministry calls for the next, and numbers and dollar amounts are never high enough.

This tendency was a problem in the early church as seen in the passage below. The consequences of this particular couple's sin resulted in death, and they provide a sober warning that holding back what belongs to God for the use of his church can be very dangerous and destroy your ministry.

[1] Now a man named Ananias, together with his wife Sapphira, also sold a piece of property. [2] With his wife's full knowledge he kept back part of the money for himself, but brought the rest and put it at the apostles' feet.

[3] Then Peter said, "Ananias, how is it that Satan has so filled your heart that you have lied to the Holy Spirit and have kept for yourself some of the money you received for the land? [4] Didn't it belong to you before it was

sold? And after it was sold, wasn't the money at your disposal? What made you think of doing such a thing? You have not lied just to human beings but to God."

[5] When Ananias heard this, he fell down and died. And great fear seized all who heard what had happened. [6] Then some young men came forward, wrapped up his body, and carried him out and buried him.

[7] About three hours later his wife came in, not knowing what had happened. [8] Peter asked her, "Tell me, is this the price you and Ananias got for the land?"

"Yes," she said, "that is the price."

[9] Peter said to her, "How could you conspire to test the Spirit of the Lord? Listen! The feet of the men who buried your husband are at the door, and they will carry you out also."

[10] At that moment she fell down at his feet and died. Then the young men came in and, finding her dead, carried her out and buried her beside her husband.

—Acts 5:1–10

■ What resources of your church tend to be guarded or held more tightly than needed? What motivates this kind of holding back?

■ When has your ministry used all of a certain resource and then watched God replenish it and provide more? What did you take away from this experience?

■ Remember the third servant in the parable Jesus told in Matthew 25 (and Luke 19). How is his choice similar to the one made by Ananias and Sapphira? Why were the consequences of their actions so severe in both cases?

■ From your experience, how does your example of generosity influence your team's decisions about using resources?

Factoring *It* In

If you choose to share *it*, the impact for God's kingdom can be amazing. By having a generous attitude and sharing resources, you automatically help other pastors and leaders do better jobs in ministry. You recognize that you're all working together, so you contribute as much as you can to the kingdom team.

You also develop kingdom partnerships that produce results that your ministry could never achieve on its own. You network and make friends, build bridges, and share best practices—all for the benefit of God's people and the advancement of his kingdom.

By modeling godly stewardship, you extend the use of your resources and materials. For example, if you preach a sermon once, it's used once. If you give it away, it might be used fifty times. If five hundred people attend your church, and you spend five hundred dollars on staff and the use of equipment to make a video, that video's cost is one dollar per person. But if just ten other churches use that same video, and each has 150 members, then you've dramatically reduced the cost to just twenty-five cents per person. Any pastor will tell you that God honors that kind of sensible faithfulness.

Your example of noncompetitive generosity will also encourage others to do the same. As others realize you are for them and not against them, that you're all on God's side together, they begin to let go of their personal agendas and work with you for God's agenda.

When you practice kingdom-mindedness, God will bless your efforts. It might be more creative biblical content and ideas. It could be generous givers or evangelistic leaders. God might send you more people who don't know Christ. The bottom line is that when you give *it*, God gives *it* back to you.

The more you share *it*, the more kingdom unity emerges. The things that divide us become less important. We all share our humanity, our fallenness. When we see others being real about who they are, we are drawn together and more likely to help each other. We also all share a mission, and sharing our resources wars against the "competition" mindset that breaks God's heart.

Only God can see the whole picture. Just as a certain message, a certain song, or a certain turn of phrase can surprise you by catalyzing life change in people, we often don't know what God's trying to do until we take a risk. If we truly believe we are his people, that this is his world, and we trust in him for eternity, what

do we really have to lose? It's time to focus on God's kingdom and let go of our limited perspective.

When you think about being kingdom-minded, remember:

- The more possessive and competitive we are, the more divided we become.
- A kingdom-minded ministry is more about what God is doing everywhere than what God is doing right here.
- If you are kingdom-minded, you will speak well of and promote other churches and ministries.
- A kingdom-minded ministry is generous and hungry to partner with others to get more done for the glory of God.
- When you have *it*, you know that it doesn't belong to you. *It* belongs to God. He gives *it*. Since *it* is his and not yours, you're willing to share it.
- The more you try to keep *it*, the less of it you tend to have. The more you are willing to give *it* away, the more of it God seems to give.
- Kingdom-minded churches ask, "What do we have that we can give away?" and "How can we partner with other ministries to grow God's kingdom?"

■ When has your ministry successfully partnered with another church or ministry for a larger impact that neither could have achieved alone? What prevents you from doing this more often?

- What's one resource your church currently has plenty of but isn't sharing with other churches or ministries? While there may be good reason for this, at least from a human perspective, with whom can you share this resource in your area?

- Name a local church or ministry in your area that you admire for their generosity. How could you team with them to achieve even greater results for God's kingdom?

- When has your church or ministry benefited from the kindness and generosity of other churches? What (or whose) examples have inspired you to be more kingdom-minded?

Putting *It* into Action

It's been said that before we can pray, "Lord, thy kingdom come," we must be willing to pray, "Lord, I let go of my kingdom." In order to get *it* and keep *it*, we must loosen our hold on the resources entrusted to us by giving them away for maximum kingdom impact. Usually, this is a process requiring ongoing daily

decisions to be generous, open, and cooperative. It's easy to retreat inward and try to control your church or ministry, but you must depend on God if you want to do the most with what he's given you.

With this goal in mind, read through the following questions before spending some time in prayer. Ask God to show you ways to further his kingdom right where you are with what you have right now.

———————————————

■ When a new church or a similar ministry starts nearby, do you feel more excited or more threatened? How can you train your mind to be focused on the kingdom rather than focused inward on success and ego validation?

■ Take an honest look: Is your leadership focused more on building your ministry or on building God's kingdom? What can you do as a leader to become more kingdom-minded?

■ What can you do to help other local churches simply through your attitude? How can you promote kingdom unity with your words?

■ Review the following list of resources. Place an X by the ones your ministry is currently sharing or giving away to other churches and ministries. Place an O by the ones that you have available that could be given away. Based on the results, consider which resource you will give away first and who you will give it to.

___ Sermons, including notes, downloads, etc.

___ Nursery supplies and materials

___ Curriculum for children and youth

___ Holiday decorations (Christmas, Easter, etc.)

___ Event materials

___ Outreach ideas

___ People (staff and volunteers)

___ Buildings, offices, spaces

___ Finances

___ Web/blog/internet resources

___ Other tech resources, including people

___ Extra worship leaders

___ Other resources: (specify)

PART 3

WHAT IT MEANS TO GET *IT* BACK AND GUARD IT

*Leaders who have **it** don't just motivate; they inspire.*

You've made it this far.

You know all about the seven ingredients to get *it* and keep it.

You've come a long way on this journey. You've seen how *it*-full ministries have a God-inspired vision and are focused on the things that really matter. You've embraced the truth that with-it people share *it* in a deep and sincere camaraderie. You've seen how ministry innovation has increased because of an increasing passion to share the gospel. You've acknowledged that you won't succeed perfectly at everything and that failing is often a step toward succeeding. You're excited that as God softens your heart to be kingdom-minded and focused outward, he tends to give more of *it*.

Most of all, you've recognized that for your ministry to have *it*, *you* need to have it.

If you don't have *it*, then focus on your relationship with God. That's the epicenter for a ministry that has it. Pray to rekindle the passion, the fire, the purity, the hunger for God. Seek him first above all else. "Love the Lord your God with all your heart and with all your soul and with all your mind and with all your strength" (Mark 12:30).

God's Word Has *It*

Unfortunately, even when you have *it*, you can still lose it if you become comfortable and complacent in your relationship with God. In many ways, comfort is the enemy of faith. Complacency is the poison that pollutes passion. Hebrews 11:6

says, "And without faith it is impossible to please God." Keep in mind how Jesus pleaded with his followers, knowing the time was short, reminding them always to "be on guard! Be alert!" (Mark 13:33).

If you want to get *it* and keep it, then keep asking God to strengthen your faith and stretch you. Being stretched once or twice a year isn't enough. Ask him to stretch you daily so that you have to rely on him constantly. Part of being stretched is believing what God already knows: *You have more in you than you realize. God has put more in you than anyone knows.*

Then pray for God to stretch you some more. Follow his direction and go where his Spirit leads you. In order to keep *it*, you might feel like he's undoing whatever you did to get it. He might direct you to change your leadership style or the way you preach. He might challenge you to go to a developing country and leave behind part of your heart. He might ask you to give like you've never given before. He might lead you to do something your closest friends believe is foolish and impossible. He might introduce you to a new church leader who will rock your comfortable world or maybe to a lost person who desperately needs God.

No matter what it may be, always remain open and let God stretch you.

Toward this goal, read the following passage and answer the questions that follow.

> [4] As you come to him, the living Stone—rejected by humans but chosen by God and precious to him—[5] you also, like living stones, are being built into a spiritual house to be a holy priesthood, offering spiritual sacrifices acceptable to God through Jesus Christ. . . . [9] But you are a chosen people, a royal priesthood, a holy nation, God's special possession, that you may declare the praises of him who called you out of darkness into his wonderful light. [10] Once you were not a people, but now you are the people of God; once you had not received mercy, but now you have received mercy.
>
> **—1 Peter 2:4–5, 9–10**

- What does it mean for you to be part of "a holy priesthood"? What have you sacrificed in order to lead and serve those in your ministry?

- Peter noted that Jesus, as the living Stone, was rejected by humans. How have rejection and criticism affected your ability to experience *it* and keep *it* in your ministry?

- How has God stretched you through the process of completing this workbook? What session or theme has stretched you the most? Why?

- Has God been leading you into taking a risk that would stretch you more? What next step do you need to take in order to step out in faith?

They Got *It*

Without a doubt, Jesus models servant leadership in ways that perfectly illustrate *it*. He never sinned. Never strayed. Never missed the target. Jesus always lived the will of his Father. He was unwaveringly confident in the One who sent him and would never leave him. He was consistent to the core, always and only about "his Father's business." And he bled the mission. He literally bled it on the cross, shedding his innocent blood to cover our sins.

If you want to follow Jesus' example, to find *it* and keep it, then ask God to break your heart wide open. Expose yourself to something that you know will move you. Don't shrink back. Don't fight your emotions. Don't lay another brick atop your self-made wall of protection. Give in to the heart. Feed the hurt. Let *it* grow. Let it bother you. Invite it to overtake you. Feel the pain that others carry. Let the burden of leadership sink into your bones because you care about people so much. Hold on to the passion you have for everyone to know the goodness and grace and love of God.

God loves to give *it* to broken people.

Some of these sessions may have been painful to read. But often where there's pain, there's something that needs healing. So ask God to heal you so that you may have more of it for his purposes. When God begins stirring you, drawing you closer, speaking to you, go deeper and listen carefully.

In addition to the example of Christ, another powerful example to consider is that of Paul. He encountered Jesus in a dramatic way that transformed Saul the persecutor of believers into Paul the apostle of Jesus willing to suffer beatings, arrests, jail cells, and shipwrecks. Read the passage below in which Paul describes serving the church, and then answer the questions that follow.

> [24] Now I rejoice in what I am suffering for you, and I fill up in my flesh what is still lacking in regard to Christ's afflictions, for the sake of his body, which is the church. [25] I have become its servant by the commission God gave

me to present to you the word of God in its fullness—[26] the mystery that has been kept hidden for ages and generations, but is now disclosed to the Lord's people. [27] To them God has chosen to make known among the Gentiles the glorious riches of this mystery, which is Christ in you, the hope of glory.

[28] He is the one we proclaim, admonishing and teaching everyone with all wisdom, so that we may present everyone fully mature in Christ. [29] To this end I strenuously contend with all the energy Christ so powerfully works in me.

—Colossians 1:24–29

- When you think of sacrificial servant leadership, who are the mentors that have modeled this directly in your life? What have you learned from them about getting *it* and keeping it?

- When you reflect on your own leadership, what's one vital area you want God to help you develop? What impact would growth in this area have on your ministry?

- What's currently the greatest struggle in your leadership? Do you tend to battle insecurity or self-absorption more?

■ When was the last time you rejoiced in suffering for your ministry? What is God now calling you to sacrifice?

Factoring *It* In

Even after exploring these seven ingredients, you may feel like *it* remains out of reach. You may see other church leaders who have *it* and long to have the impact they have, build a church like they lead, and reach people others aren't reaching. But it just seems to remain elusive, always on the periphery of your ministry.

That's when you must remember that *it* is always a work of God. Yes, God does it through people. But *it* cannot be packaged, produced with human effort, or purchased for a price. God does it, through people, and God can choose anyone he wants to use for his glory—including you!

When you think about it, almost every pastor's and church leader's goals are basically the same. Goals are good, but goals are *not* the solution. Goals do not determine success—*systems do.* Systems create behaviors. Behaviors become habits. Habits drive outcomes. So, if you want better outcomes, create better systems. Small changes in your systems can create big changes in your outcomes.

As you start intentionally creating the right systems, they become the how that will get you to your what. It might not feel significant at first, but never underestimate what God can do with one small habit. "Do not despise these small beginnings, for the LORD rejoices to see the work begin" (Zechariah 4:10 NLT). Define your goal, implement your system, and watch what God can do.

Remember, the ingredients you just explored in the previous seven sessions aren't *it*.

It is what God does as you put them into practice!

So keep in mind:

- Churches without *it* often think the solution is changing their style—it's not. The issue is not the model; it's a mindset.
- The church must be people focused and Jesus centered. While most Christians would say they are, we need to live it out in our actions and in our teaching.
- We need to have the same patience with people that God has with us.
- We have to help people know they are needed and known.
- *It* is always a work of God. God does it through people, and God can choose anyone he wants to.
- You can position yourself to be a stronger candidate for God to choose.
- Goals do not determine success; systems do.
- Strong systems make good people look great. Weak systems make great people look bad.
- A system is a set of principles or procedures that determine how something is done.
- Healthy systems never happen by accident. Systems create behaviors. Behaviors become habits. Habits drive outcomes.
- Never underestimate how God can start something big through one small habit.
- The ultimate *it* is faithfulness.

- What systems presently exist in your ministry? How well are they meeting the goals they're intended to reach?

- Were most of your ministry's current systems created intentionally or by default and convenience? Are you satisfied with the results they're producing?

- What new system do you need to create to move you toward your goals?

- For that system to come to life, what do you need to do next? Who else needs to do what for this system to work?

Putting *It* into Action

Before moving on from what you've learned in this workbook, consider spending some time with the other leaders and team members in your ministry. You might have *it*, but those you're with might not. God can use you to help them get *it*. So describe what this experience has been like as you've completed each session. Discuss the questions at the end of each chapter. Share your thoughts and frustrations. Brainstorm innovative ideas together and look for ways to share resources with other ministries. Pray together. Take risks together.

Once you do get *it*, never take it for granted. Embrace the power of the Holy Spirit working in you to do more than you can ask or imagine. Read through your responses again and see what stands out now that you see a bigger picture. Ask God to show you your next steps in being the leader he wants you to be. Look for opportunities to take more risks and walk by faith more than ever.

Hold *it* loosely. Remember your Source for it. Give it away.

- What's your biggest takeaway from this workbook experience? What difference will this takeaway have on the way you lead?

- Which of your views and beliefs about church and ministry have changed since you began this workbook? Why?

- Do you usually think more about pleasing God or strategizing how to grow your ministry? Do you truly desire his pleasure more than the approval and recognition of others?

Finally, to help you get *it* and keep it, read through the following prayer, a Franciscan benediction, and make it your own:

> *May God bless you with discomfort at easy answers, half-truths, and superficial relationships, so that you may live deep within your heart.*
>
> *May God bless you with anger at injustice, oppression, and the exploitation of people, so that you may work for justice, freedom, and peace.*
>
> *May God bless you with tears to shed for those who suffer from pain, rejection, and starvation, so that you may reach out your hand to comfort them and to turn their pain into joy.*
>
> *And may God bless you with enough foolishness to believe that you can make a difference in this world, so that you can do what others claim cannot be done.*
>
> *That's it. Amen.*

Leader Guide

This workbook is a companion to *Lead Like It Matters,* and it's designed for both individuals and groups. If you're participating in a group study that has designated you as its leader, thank you for agreeing to serve in this capacity. What you have chosen to do is valuable and will make a great difference in the lives of others.

As the group leader, just think of yourself as the host of a dinner party. Your job is to take care of your guests by managing all the behind-the-scenes details so that when everyone arrives, they can just enjoy time together. Your role is not to answer all the questions or reteach the content—the book, this workbook and the Holy Spirit will do most of that work. Your job is to guide the experience and create an environment where people can process, question, and reflect—not receive more instruction.

Make sure everyone in the group gets a copy of the workbook. This will keep everyone on the same page and help the process run more smoothly. If some group members are unable to purchase the workbook, arrange it so that people can share the resource with other group members. Giving everyone access to all the material will position this study to be as rewarding an experience as possible. Everyone should feel free to write in their workbooks and bring them to group every week.

Setting Up the Group

As the group leader, you'll want to create an environment that encourages sharing and learning. No matter what setting you choose, provide enough comfortable seating for everyone, and if possible, arrange the seats in a semicircle. This will make group interaction and conversation more efficient and natural.

Also, try to get to the meeting site early so you can greet participants as they arrive. Simple refreshments create a welcoming atmosphere and can be a wonderful addition to a group study. Try to take food and pet allergies into account to make your guests as comfortable as possible. You may also want to consider offering childcare to those with children who want to attend. Managing these details up front will make the rest of your group experience flow smoothly and provide a welcoming space in which to engage with the content of *Lead Like It Matters*.

Starting Your Group Time

Once everyone has arrived, it's time to begin the group. Here are some simple tips to make your group time healthy, enjoyable, and effective.

First, consider beginning the meeting with a short prayer, and remind the group members to put their phones on silent. This is a way to make sure you can all be present with one another and with God. Then, give each person one or two minutes to check in before diving into the material. In your first session, participants can introduce themselves and share what they hope to experience in this group study. Beginning with your second session, people may need more time to share their insights from their personal studies and to enjoy getting better acquainted.

As you begin going through the material, invite members to share their experiences and discuss their responses with the group. Usually, you won't answer the discussion questions yourself, but you may need to go first a couple of times

and set an example, answering briefly and with a reasonable amount of transparency. You may also want to help participants debrief and process what they're learning as they complete each session individually ahead of each group meeting. Debriefing something like this is a bit different from responding to questions about the material because the content comes from their real lives. Following are the basic experiences that you want the group to reflect on:

- *What was the best part about this week's individual study?*
- *What was the hardest part?*
- *What did I learn about myself?*
- *What did I learn about God?*

Leading the Discussion Time

Encourage all the group members to participate in the discussion, but make sure they know they don't have to do so. As the discussion progresses, you may want to follow up with comments such as, "Tell me more about that," or, "Why did you answer that way?" This will allow the group participants to deepen their reflections and invite meaningful sharing in a nonthreatening way.

While each session in this workbook includes multiple sections, you do not have to go through each section and cover every question or exercise. Feel free to go with the dynamic in the group and skip around if needed to cover all the material more naturally. You can pick and choose questions based on either the needs of your group or how the conversation is flowing. Also, don't be afraid of silence. Offering a question and allowing up to thirty seconds of silence is okay. It allows people space to think about how they want to respond and also gives them time to do so.

As group leader, you are the boundary keeper for your group. Do not let anyone (yourself included) dominate the group time. Keep an eye out for group

members who might be tempted to "attack" folks they disagree with or try to "fix" those having struggles. These kinds of behaviors can derail a group's momentum, so they need to be steered in a different direction. Model active listening and encourage everyone in your group to do the same. This will make your group time a safe space and create a positive community.

At the end of each group session, encourage the participants to take just a few minutes to review what they've learned and write down one or two key takeaways. This will help them cement the big ideas in their minds as you close the session. Close your time together with prayer as a group.

Remember to have fun. Spending time with others and growing closer to God is a gift to enjoy and embrace. And get ready for God to change your thinking and change your life.

Thank you again for taking the time to lead your group. You are making a difference in the lives of others and having an impact on the kingdom of God.

Also Available
from Craig Groeschel

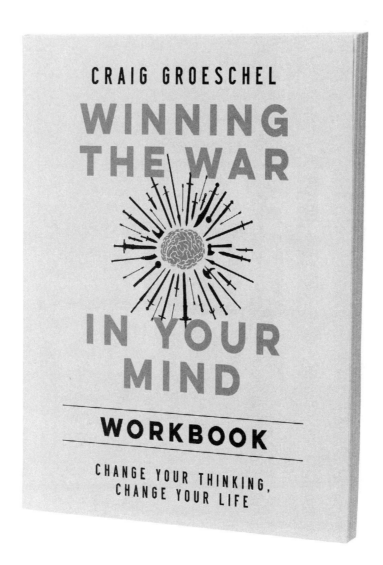

Available wherever books are sold.

Also available from Craig and Amy Groeschel

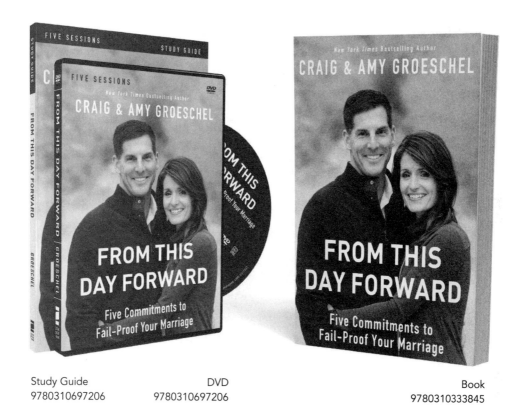

Study Guide
9780310697206

DVD
9780310697206

Book
9780310333845

Is it possible to have a great marriage? Yes, but it is not likely if you treat marriage like everybody else does!

In this five-session video-based small group study and book, *New York Times* bestselling author and pastor Craig Groeschel gives you five commitments to make in order to fail-proof your marriage. You know the stats, and they are horrifying. 50% of marriages don't make it. What other area of your life are you satisfied with 50% odds against you?

Available now at your favorite bookstore,
or streaming video on StudyGateway.com.